THEOLOGY IN THE IRISH PUBLIC SQUARE

Theology
in the Irish
Public Square

Gerry O'Hanlon SJ

the columba press

First edition, 2010, published by
the columba press
55A Spruce Avenue, Stillorgan Industrial Park,
Blackrock, Co Dublin

Cover by Bill Bolger
Origination by The Columba Press
Printed in Ireland by
Colour Books Ltd, Dublin

ISBN 978 1 85607 685-2

Contents

Acknowledgements

1. *The Recession and God: Reading the Signs of the Times:* Extended essay, published as booklet, Dublin, Jesuit Centre for Faith and Justice and Messenger Publications, 2009

2. *How much Equality is needed for Justice?* Previously published in *Working Notes* (56, 2007, pp 24-29)

3. *Crime and Punishment: a Christian Perspective:* Previously published in *Working Notes* (58, 2008, pp 13-17)

4. *Some Christian Perspectives on Health and Sickness:* Previously published in *Working Notes* (60, 2009), pp 14-17)

5. *Europe and the Roman Catholic Church:*Previously published in *The Future of Europe,* Jesuit Centre for Faith and Justice, Dublin, Veritas, 2006, pp 57-72

6. *Asking the Right Questions: Christians, Muslims, Citizens in Ireland:* Previously published in *Working Notes* (54, 2007, pp 8 - 14)

7. *Muslims in the Free Society:* Previously published in *Ecumenics from the Rim, Explorations in Honour of John D'Arcy May,* eds John O'Grady and Peter Scherle, Berlin, LIT, 2007, pp 271-277

8. *Western Muslims and the Future of Islam:* Previously published in *Studies* (97, 2008, pp 421-432)

9. *Religion and Society:* A revised version of an article that appeared in *Studies* (95, Summer 2006, pp 141-152)

10. *Religion and Politics:* A revised version of an address given at a Conference in Zagreb in 2007, later published as an article in *Vjera I politika,* ed Ivan Antunovic S.J., Zagreb 2009, pp 157-173.

11. *The Work for Justice and* Deus Caritas Est: A revised version of an article previously published in *Who Is My Neighbour?,* ed Eoin G. Cassidy, Dublin, Veritas, 2009, pp 119-139

12. *Hope:* Originally given as an address at a Jesuit Conference in Piest'anay, Slovakia, a shortened version of which appeared in *Promotio Justitiae* (97, 2007 / 4, pp 33-41)

13. *A miracle?* Previously published in *The Messenger* (March 2009, pp 15-16)

Grateful acknowledgment is given for permission to use previously published material. My heartfelt thanks also to Director Eoin Carroll and my colleagues in the Jesuit Centre for Faith and Justice, to Lena Jacobs for technical assistance with the manuscript, to Margaret Burns for expert editorial work on many of the articles and in particular to Cathy Molloy for many helpful comments on the whole text. This final version, is, of course, my own responsibility.

Introduction

The exclusion of religion from the public square – and, at the other extreme, religious fundamentalism – hinders an encounter between persons and their collaboration for the progress of humanity. (Pope Benedict XVI, *Caritas in Veritate*, 2009, n 56)

The voice of religion, in particular that of the clerical, Roman Catholic tradition, has often been experienced in Irish public life as authoritarian and harsh. Little wonder then, especially in the context of the significant erosion of authority of the Catholic Church in Ireland due to the child sexual abuse scandals, that there is scant evidence nowadays of nostalgia for those days when religion played a significant role in public discourse. And so, like many other countries in Western Europe in particular, there is a post-modern toleration of religion in the private sphere, but considerable suspicion of any attempt to bring a critique to bear on public life from a religious perspective.

But is this a wise development? Sociologists are abandoning the recently dominant paradigm which equated modernisation with secularisation, and even secularism. The aggressive nature of the New Atheism betrays a certain nervousness about the enduring character of religious belief. Socio-political Islam has forced its agenda into the public forum. Perhaps it is a good moment, at this time of national and global crisis, to re-examine the possibility that a non-fundamentalist religious voice may have significant wisdom to contribute to public discourse.

In what follows, I attempt to outline how this might be so, drawing mainly from the Roman Catholic part of a wider Christian tradition, but indicating resonances with Islam in particular. Part One plunges straight into the matter, offering a religious reflection on particular aspects of life in Ireland and further afield – crime and punishment, health and sickness, Europe, the recession, the debate about equality. With all its good characteristics – in particular the reality of historically low levels of unemployment – the Celtic Tiger era in Ireland was often blind to the kind of social disgrace found in a dysfunctional prison system and a two-tier health system geared more towards affordability than need. In the essay on the recession in particular, I try to show how an analysis that goes beyond the level of natural reason and draws explicitly on the data of faith may offer a wisdom to the body politic that engenders energy, imagination and hope. The chapter on Europe, written before publication of the Ryan and Murphy Reports, offers a perspective on church attitudes to sexuality and power which has, I believe, enduring relevance and implies an agenda to be realised, without which there is little hope of any restoration of the church's own moral credibility. Clearly these watershed Reports will require a deeper analysis and reflection over time, not least with regard to their impact on the role of the Catholic Church in Irish public life.

Part Two discusses the contribution of Islam, in Ireland and further afield. At a popular level many of us are more aware of the less moderate, fundamentalist versions of Islam which have forced themselves on to the public agenda. And yet, without ignoring the difficult issues which need tackling, I hope to show that Islam has done us a service in re-surfacing the question of the intrinsically public nature of religion, and that there is a considerable body of moderate Islamic opinion about which we do well to inform ourselves and with which we do well to dialogue.

Part Three attempts to establish the more theoretical foundations for the earlier applied approaches, including the distinction between church and state, and yet the rich resources which church teaching and theology offer for an understanding of humanity and both state and wider society. At one level this teaching is offered to all people of intelligence and good will: it is based on natural reason, and is accessible to all. But I go on to propose that a truly liberal society is challenged also to be respectful of the distinctively religious level of that teaching, the inspirational and visionary character of its source, due to the respect all true liberals wish to accord the viewpoint of others, no matter how different. Once again it needs to be said that the erosion of the church's own moral authority has, seemingly, made this challenge more difficult, and yet perhaps the voice of a humiliated and, hopefully, more humble church may in time offer a real service of wisdom, truth and love which is more truly evangelical than all the trappings of unaccountable power and superficial glory which so tainted the role of the church in twentieth-century Irish society.

Finally, Part Four is a short and simple illustration of the power of popular devotion – so often ignored in approaches towards political theology – to contribute to public debate.

I have made some slight revisions to these essays, written between 2005 and 2009, but mostly of a style and proof-reading variety. And so the attentive reader will note the occasional anachronistic reference to times when the Celtic Tiger was in full flight, when the full extent of the child sexual abuse scandals had yet to be revealed in the reports generally known as the Ryan and Murphy Reports, when the global and national recession was in its early stages and when the long-awaited social encyclical *Caritas in Veritate* had yet to be published. However, I have deliberately retained these references in order to indicate the fallibility of human commentary and yet, I hope, the enduring quality of the underlying analysis, critique and attempt at reconstruction.

It is my hope that this collection may interest not just Christian believers but also those of other religious traditions, as well as those who have no religious belief as such but who do hope and believe in a better world for us all. It is my firm conviction that we all, believers and non-believers alike, need to work together at this great project, towards which this book is intended as a contribution.

PART ONE:

The Irish Public Square

CHAPTER ONE

The Recession and God:
Reading the Signs of the Times

*'With that kind of talk you may as well close down the whole coun-
try altogether'* – angry public sector worker, in response to reported comment in January 2009 by Turlough O'Sullivan,
Director-General of IBEC (Irish Business and Employers
Confederation), that since 10-20 per cent of private sector
workers had lost their jobs, it would be right that the same
percentage of public workers should lose their jobs as well.

Introduction
We live in worrying times, and the mood is ugly. In Ireland our
financial and economic situation has deteriorated rapidly. Our
economy is in recession, unemployment is rising sharply, there
has been a severe deterioration in the state of our public finances
and we are faced with unpalatable cut-backs in services. The spectre
of mass emigration looms. There is a new caution about spending
and planning for the future. Many of us are still somewhat
bewildered and almost in denial about our plight, but increasingly
one can sense a growing public and private discontent, anger,
anxiety, even fear and desperation. The phenomenon of a vocal
group of elderly people, protesting loudly in a Dublin city-centre
church against medical card cut-backs, was an early, potent symbol of the tsunami-like shock which Ireland is experiencing.

All this is a reflection of what is happening on a larger scale
worldwide. We are learning a new language: the 'credit crunch'
in the USA has resulted in panic on the global financial markets,
widespread economic slow-down and even recession, with civil
unrest in places. As countries battle for their own economic survival, more fundamental global issues such as the UN Millennium Development Goals, including the need for environmental
sustainability, are in danger of being put on the back burner.

What is going on? Often it seems that the complexity and rapidity of our changed situation are baffling even to those we imagined to be the experts – Wall Street insiders, for example, have been heard to admit that they simply did not understand quite what was going on in some of the mystifying, labyrinthine transactions which have characterised the workings of stock markets in recent years.

However, an intelligent and co-ordinated response is urgent and important. Apart from the many millions of ordinary lives that are being adversely affected, history teaches us that economic instability is fertile ground for political totalitarianism. The Great Depression in the late 1920s and 30s undoubtedly contributed to the rise of Hitler and Fascism. How are we to address our current situation in a way that will create the kind of economic stability capable of fostering a just peace?

PART ONE: SIGNS OF THE TIMES

It was somewhat accidental that the group of elderly protesters in Dublin met in a church. And, in truth, even many good Christians might be puzzled that there could be a fruitful connection between their religious faith and the current financial woes of our world. What, after all, does the Blessed Trinity have to do with the likes of fiscal stimulus packages? The more classical form of this query was expressed back in the third century by Tertullian when he asked: 'What has Athens to do with Jerusalem?'

The bishops of the Second Vatican Council (1962-5) would have been in no doubt about the answer. They boldly proclaimed that 'the joys and the hopes, the griefs and the anxieties of the people of this age, especially those who are poor or in any way afflicted, these too are the joys and hopes, the griefs and anxieties of the follower of Christ' (*Gaudium et Spes*, Pastoral Constitution on the Church in the Modern World, n 1).

They went on to express the positive contribution that Christians and the church can make to contemporary issues under the rubric of 'scrutinising the signs of the times' (GS, n 4) and interpreting them in the light of the gospel. Some important principles were articulated to guide this interpretation: in particular, respect for the legitimate autonomy of earthly affairs (including the socio-economic, political and cultural orders – GS, nn 36, 59).

This will mean being attentive to the intelligibility and laws of particular disciplines, even while recognising that these same laws and intelligibility have their source and goal in the mystery that we call God, creator of all that is (GS, n 36). And so, with respect to economic activity, for example, its 'fundamental purpose ... must not be profit or domination ... rather it must be service ... of the whole person ... viewed in terms of their material needs and the demands of their intellectual, moral, spiritual and religious life ... consequently, economic activity is to be carried out by its own methods and laws but within the limits of morality, so that God's plan for humankind can be realised' (GS, n 64). There is, then, respect for the independence of economics, but this is a relative rather than an absolute independence.

This kind of tightrope way of proceeding, by means of which we respect the search for economic intelligibility and yet keep it linked to the bigger picture of human well-being and flourishing, is at the heart of the Christian contribution to our present dilemma.

A second important principle the council asserts is that while Christians look for final solutions to the 'new earth and new heaven' that are post-historical, still 'the expectation of a new earth must not weaken but rather stimulate our concern for cultivating this one' (GS, nn 39, 43). The Christian message will shed light on how this concern may take practical shape. However, Christians must not expect a detailed policy blueprint from this message, but rather must expect that, even among themselves, they may disagree at times on what concrete measures are to be implemented (GS, n 43).

The council is clearly against the kind of sacred / secular dualism which would assert either that economics on its own has all the answers, or that religion should retreat in splendid isolation to the sacristy or should preach from on high without serious dialogue with economics. Instead, under the rubric of 'reading the signs of the times', they are passionately convinced of the positive difference that Christianity can make to all our human dilemmas.

Just now it would seem that our world could do with all the help that it can get. How might we read the signs of our own times through Christian lens, in a way that might aid us to plot our way out of our current crisis with intelligence and hope?

PART TWO: BIBLICAL INSPIRATION – THE CITY UPON THE HILL

In 1630, on board the flagship *Arbella*, off the coast of Massachusetts, John Winthrop addressed his fellow Puritans as follows: 'We shall be as a city upon a hill – the eyes of all people are upon us.' This biblically-inspired notion of being God's chosen people, destined to enter the Promised Land, was shared by Winthrop's co-religionists and co-founders of what we now call the United States of America, the Separatists or Pilgrim Fathers and Mothers. It is a notion which has resonated throughout the history of the United States and finds an echo in the rhetoric of Martin Luther King and President Barack Obama.

It goes back, of course, to the belief of the Israelites, expressed through the Old or Hebrew Testament, that God had called them in a special way and had set up a covenant or agreement with them. This covenant involved God's promise of fidelity to the people, and their commitment to obey God's Law (given principally to Moses in the form of the commandments). It was an agreement which covered every aspect of life, not just some imagined 'holy', in the sense of private, domain.

The covenant was central to the understanding of the group concerning all the major events of its history – its first exodus and sojourn in Palestine (Canaan) in the proto-historical times of Abraham (c. 2000 BC); its first Exile in Egypt and its exodus under Moses (c. 1250); its arrival after the desert experience in the Promised Land of Palestine under Joshua (c. 1200); its rule by Judges and then by Kings; its civil war between North (Israel) and South (Judah); its second Exile in Babylon in 598 and return in 538; its transition from the desert Ark of the Covenant and the Ten Commandments to the establishment of Jerusalem and the Temple as the Royal and Holy City, funded by a taxation system often experienced as oppressive.

It must not be imagined that this group narrative, part myth and part history, reflected a seamless evolution of a society in line with a neat conceptual framework shared by all. Rather it involved huge, disruptive and incomplete transitions from a nomadic to a more settled agricultural, to a mixed urban-rural lifestyle; it involved skirmishes and wars with neigbouring powers like Egypt, Assyria, Babylon, Persia, the Greeks and Romans; it involved assimilation with all these groups and internal divisions about the nature of their own group. It was, in short, as complex and differentiated as the founding narrative and ongoing history of any modern nation-state, not least the founding of our own state in Ireland, emerging from that fraught and complicated, centuries-old relationship with Britain and now trying to chart its way through the troubled waters of today.

The Meaning of the Biblical Narrative
But of course the Hebrew narrative is not simply an historical account, with all the geo-political, socio-economic and cultural factors which such an account would rightly include. It is also, and primarily, an account of faith, redolent of this nation and people's search for meaning.

Central to this account of faith is their belief that God was involved in their history. They understood themselves to have this covenant with God, which involved a commitment on their side to monotheism and to ethical behaviour in all areas of life, in particular to social justice. Such was God's engagement with them in their day-to-day lives (as, for example, in liberating them from their lives of slavery in Egypt) that they came to recognise this God of the covenant as also their Creator.

They were conscious of all the time reneging on their commitment: by turning in idolatry to the Baals on the high places of Canaan, and, as the prophets never tired of admonishing them, by mistreating the poor, the widows and the orphans. Idolatry and morality were closely connected in this understanding: worship of the fertility and nature gods of Canaan involved putting the creature in place of the Creator, it involved becoming a slave of created realities like money, fame, sex, political power and sin of all kinds.

Yet no amount of commandments, of Law, of wise rulers seemed able to prevent this constant turning away from God into immorality, the rejection of the liberation of the God of Exodus and the return to the Exile of sin so characteristic of the narrative. In response there developed a hope for a Messiah, for a Messianic age in which: 'I will make a new covenant with the House of Israel and the House of Judah ... I will put my law within them, and I will write it upon their hearts; and I will be their God, and they shall be my people' (Jer 31:31-34).

And so Second-Isaiah can say towards the end of the exile in Babylon: 'Remember not the former things, nor consider the things of old. Behold I am doing a new thing; now it springs forth, do you not perceive it?' (Is 43:18-19), and again, 'From this time forth I make you hear new things, hidden things which you have not known' (Is 48:6). The Israelites are being advised not to wallow in the past glories of liberation / exodus, but to hope for a new creation, a new redemption, a definitive breakthrough, which they understood to be associated with the Messiah and which would lay less stress on the externalities of Law and more on the inner heart and spirit spoken of by Jeremiah. It is in this context too that the Prophet Joel can say: 'And it shall come to pass afterward, that I will pour out my spirit on all flesh; your sons and your daughters shall prophesy, your old men shall dream dreams, and your young men shall see visions' (Joel 2:28-29).

It is the Christian belief that all this longing for a new covenant, a definitive breakthrough, the pouring out of God's holy spirit are fulfilled and accomplished in the coming of Jesus Christ, his life, death and resurrection, his pouring out of his flesh and blood in the new covenant that is given in the Eucharist and of his Spirit at Pentecost.

And so, just as the Jews constantly went back and forth in memory to events like exodus and exile in order to read the signs of their own times, Luke tells us that the two disciples on the road to Emmaus, downcast because of the death of Jesus and seemingly of their own hopes, were instructed by the apparent stranger who met them on the road about the meaning of the past: 'And beginning with Moses and all the prophets he interpreted to them in all the scriptures the things concerning himself ... and their eyes were opened' (Lk 24:27-31). And the eucharistic re-membering (the term is *anamnesis*, and means the making of the past present in the strongest possible sense) is that new covenant (Lk 22:19; 1 Cor 11:24-26) which unleashes a powerful energy in the world which is like the breath or spirit with which God first created the world, the breath which infuses life into Ezekiel's dry bones, the inspiration of dreamers and visionaries, capable of overcoming all decline and sustaining all progress.

And it became clear, as had already been foreshadowed at least in God's dealing with Israel, that this breakthrough is for all people: the Christian self-understanding involves the notion of the church as the sacrament of salvation for all – not in the sense that all must join the church to be saved, but rather that a central function of the church's visibility is to point to the truth that God wants all people to be saved, the chosen people are now all God's people. The perspective has widened from a partial and limited particularity to that of an inclusive universality.

'Where there is no vision, the people perish' (Proverbs 29:18, *King James version*)
When Martin Luther King cried out 'we have a dream', when Barack Obama proclaimed repeatedly, during his campaign and after his Presidential victory, 'yes we can', they were drawing on this same biblical narrative. It is the narrative tapped into by John Winthrop for his 'city on a hill' speech, and subsequently by such diverse figures as John F. Kennedy, Ronald Reagan, Rudy Giuliani and Sarah Palin.

In our part of the world, we are not so used to this blending of the sacred and the secular: it can offend our notions of church-state separation; it can raise fears of fundamentalism and right-wing political evangelism. And it is true that the disparate range of politicians referred to obviously counsels against any univocal reading of the biblical narrative in its application to current situations.

Yet it would seem that trace-marks of this biblical story still have power to inspire our secular world, even when the source of this inspiration often goes unrecognised or unacknowledged. There is, as theologian James Hanvey has suggested, a kind of 'civic grace' present in the most secular of cultures.[1]

The point of the particular reading of the Bible presented above is precisely to show that this presumed separation or dualism between the so-called sacred and secular is not as obvious as it may appear at first glance. We have come, quite properly, to an understanding of the rightful autonomy of the secular. However, we must nuance this understanding to take account of the biblical claim that ultimately all is in God's hands, a claim which, again, was made so abundantly clear in President Obama's inauguration ceremony and inaugural address. We as believers do well to inquire about what practical purchase this claim may suggest.

Perhaps in what theologian Nicholas Lash calls the 'protocols against idolatry' which the Bible enjoins, and the concomitant pointers to morality and social justice, we may find a helpful tool in reading today's signs of the times. Perhaps above all in the release of that Messianic hope brought about by the Jesus event we can find the energy and vision to tackle our current situation of exile. Perhaps we can find, like the two on the road to Emmaus, that our fear and despair may be turned once again into hope.

PART THREE: CATHOLIC SOCIAL TEACHING

German Chancellor Bismarck once said that you can't run a modern state relying solely on the teaching of the Sermon on the Mount. This brings us back to our earlier remark here about how on earth is one to link the language of the Blessed Trinity with that of fiscal stimulus packages.

In fact, consonant with the desire of Vatican II for a respectful dialogue with secular disciplines, there is a distinguished, sophisticated, if little known, tradition of Christian ethics which focuses precisely on this dialogue. Of particular relevance to our present discussion is the corpus of Catholic Social Teaching (CST). With its help we may adjust and refine the lens of the biblical story so as to provide a sharper reading of today's signs of the times.

1. James Hanvey SJ, *Deus Caritas Est*, The Institute Series, 5, London: Heythrop Institute for Religion, Ethics and Public Life, p 20 (9-40)

At the heart of CST is an anthropology which focuses on the dignity of the human person, with concomitant rights and freedoms, and understood as having an intrinsically social nature. Two important features of this anthropology contrast with what has become almost a conventional orthodoxy of our contemporary world.

First, the human person is more than '*homo economicus*' – *pace* Marx, and, ironically, his contemporary neo-liberal adversaries, the goal of all economic activity is at the service of the *humanum*, of the individual person and of humanity in general, and is not an end in itself. Thus, in the words of Pope John Paul II, there is a priority of labour over capital, and while the economic sphere of life is important, it is so along with other areas (the personal, the cultural, the political and so on) and in service of greater overall human flourishing.

And so a warning shot is fired across the bows of the kind of 'savage capitalism'[2] which, in the phrase of novelist Tom Wolfe, the Masters of the Universe tend to practise. This then affects all of us, putting the making of money at the centre of our lives and imbuing our culture with an acquisitiveness and greed which are infectious and lead all too surely to the kind of Bonfire of the Vanities which we are now experiencing. All this, to return to the biblical story, is idolatry, and its effects lead to an exile of individuals and peoples from the home that they are meant to find in a more balanced anthropology

Secondly, the anthropology at the heart of CST is intrinsically social in a way that values relationships at every level – interpersonal, family, civil society, and state. It values these relationships – and the structures, systems, cultures and treaties which sustain them socially and politically – as both an end in themselves and a means of human flourishing.

In this context it should be noted that the principle of the common good, central to the application of CST to human affairs, is described as 'the sum total of social conditions which allow peo-

---

2. The phrase attributed to Pope John Paul II – cf Clifford Longley, *The Tablet*, 23 August 2008, pp 10-11

ple, either as groups or as individuals, to reach their fulfilment more fully and more easily.[3] I note immediately that, despite deeply-rooted fears of liberal commentators who are suspicious of terms like the common good on the grounds that they may imply some kind of collectivist interpretation, this description holds firmly on to the notion of individual as well as group flourishing, understanding the two as intrinsically linked rather than mutually exclusive.

It should be noted that this description of the common good is both heuristic and multi-layered. By heuristic is meant that, a little like the x in algebra, it functions more as a way to discovering truth than as an already determined content: one has to engage in a search for what constitutes the common good in any given situation, a search which is guided by the description above. Similarly there are very many different layers or horizons within which the notion of the common good operates, including the limited horizon of the socio-political and the absolute horizon of the transcendent-eschatological. Those who accept the limited good involved in the former need not necessarily – but may – also subscribe to the unlimited good of the latter. So, for example, the principle of the common good may well ground the political philosophy of a secular state, without demanding the perfection of the gospels.

It is instructive that ethicist David Hollenbach can write, *apropos* the USA Bishops' 1986 *Letter on the Economy*, that talk of the common good (in line with the dubbing of Catholic social teaching in general as 'our best kept secret') 'was nearly incomprehensible to most of the people the bishops sought to address'.[4] Yet such a notion of the common good may be broadly compatible with the kind of anthropology and political philosophy generated by Socrates, Plato, and Aristotle, not to mention modern systems such as civic republicanism.[5] And one notes that it is entirely con-

---

3. Pontifical Council for Justice and Peace, *Compendium of the Social Doctrine of the Catholic Church*, Dublin: Veritas, 2005, n 164
4. Quoted in John A. Coleman SJ, ed, *Christian Political Ethics*, Princeton and Oxford: Princeton University Press, 2008, p 170
5. cf Iseult Honohan, *Civic Republicanism*, London and New York: Routledge, 2002, ch 5

sonant with the more unlimited horizon and *praxis* of the biblical Jesus, the stress by him on individual flourishing and integrity but always through love of neighbour, the value of community (the people), and all this rooted in the notion of the human as being in the image and likeness of that God who is both One and Three, in the mystery that we call Trinity.

But modernity in general has not been happy with this notion of the intrinsically social nature of the human person. With the 'turn to the subject' in Descartes, followed by Kant's philosophical idealism, and the more empirically based and ultimately politically oriented approaches of Hume, Locke, Mill and Hobbes, there developed in modern times a view of the liberal subject as an individual for whom society was often seen as at best a nuisance, at worst an obstacle.

In this context law becomes a matter of contract, rather than based on deeper notions of the prudential application of the values of truth and justice to a pluralist society. Freedom, highly prized, is reduced to the notion of minimal constraint or coercion, as opposed to the possibility of living the good life. Politics becomes a matter of regulating that 'war of all against all' (Hobbes) or even war by other means (Foucault), in which inherently mutually conflicting forces are regulated for the benefit of the individual – it is no longer the attempt to lay the political foundations for that civilisation of love of which CST speaks, in which individual and social flourishing are co-dependent and which is inclusive of all. It may well be that elements of this managerial culture were evident in some aspects of our own laudable Social Partnership experiment over the last twenty years – one thinks, for example, of some of the excessive pay increases awarded through the benchmarking process, as well as the loss of competitiveness generally in the economy.

The extreme consequence of such a worldview was articulated (in)famously by Margaret Thatcher in her 'there is no such thing as society' remark. And it is this kind of extreme position which is at the heart of the neo-liberal economic paradigm, so influentially proposed by Friedrich von Hayek, in which there is that explicit drive to replace the state by the free market, with a confidence way beyond that of Adam Smith that the 'invisible hand' of the market is best suited to promoting individual human good by means of competition and minimal legal (and no political) regulation.[6]

Catholic Social Teaching rejects this extreme (albeit an extreme which, under the guise of a social Darwinism and economic neo-liberalism, has become a dominant force in today's world). It does so in a way which tries to persuade more moderate liberals that their own values can best be promoted by a more holistic approach.

And so, with liberalism, CST agrees that self-interest is not necessarily a bad thing. The notion of the common good preserves the notion of individual flourishing, as indeed, of course, does the injunction of Jesus 'to love your neighbour as yourself'. There is not, then, in CST some woolly kind of advocacy of a political altruism which, in line with Bismarck's fear about the Sermon on the Mount, would amount to a naïve and unmediated application of biblical stories to the complexities of modern situations.

The argument is rather that the true interest of individuals is best served when the interest of us all is served, when solidarity is practised, and we need to work at ways in which this situation is brought about. We need too to anchor our notions of freedom, law, society and politics in soil that is respectful of a notion of 'the good life' that goes beyond the external observance of rules and regulations but respects the deeper notions of justice, truth, freedom and the virtuous life.

In fact, the temptation to social Darwinism, the survival of the fittest, the abuse of power, is always present. And because this is so, CST is emphatic that the principles of solidarity, the universal destination of goods and the preferential option for the poor, must be an integral part of our understanding of the common good.

Thus, for example, it is never in the interest of individuals, no matter how wealthy they may be, that excessive inequalities exist within societies and between nations, whether these be inequalities of power or of wealth. Apart from these being an offence to

6. cf Angus Sibley, 'The Cult of Capitalism', *Doctrine and Life*, 58, November, 2008, pp 11-20

that natural justice which needs to be satisfied if we are to be happy, they have the effect of increased crime, instability, even war, with concomitant negative economic consequences. Of course, as with the crisis in our environment, some may benefit in the short-term by ignoring such issues. But short-termism is short-sightedness and, as CST argues, we need to work towards a situation of sustainable economic growth, in which inequalities within and between nations are reduced and in which our environment is respected.

To get to this point will demand a more nuanced attitude to the free market: with all its advantages, it still needs appropriate political direction, and there is a role for the notion of a political economy. Otherwise, in the words of John Paul II, there is 'the risk of an "idolatry" of the market'.[7] In addition, as the Pope notes, 'there are collective and qualitative needs that cannot be satisfied by market mechanisms'[8] – one thinks of basic needs such as shelter, housing, health-care, education, transport, welfare provision and so on, some or all of which in particular circumstances may fall outside market provisions. There is indeed wisdom in the maxim that 'the market is a good servant but a very bad master'.[9]

Of particular relevance to our situation of a globalised economy, CST has been speaking for some time about the need for a better form of international, institutional, political governance of the global economy, in which all, and not just the powerful, would have appropriate representation.[10] One is reminded in this respect of the remark of John Palmer, commentator on EU affairs: 'The architecture of global governance has massive gaps in its coverage.'[11]

Secular commentators have begun to take notice of the potentially constructive contribution of CST. One notes, for example, the appreciation of Will Hutton, doyen of British writers on eco-

7. Sibley, op cit, p 15
8. Sibley, op cit, p 15
9. Editorial, *Working Notes*, 59, November, 2008, p 7
10. *Compendium*, op cit, nn 371-2; 440-442
11. John Palmer, 'European Integration', in Jesuit Centre for Faith and Justice, *The Future of Europe*, Dublin: Veritas, 2006, p 136 (130-139)

nomics, for the daring of the Vatican in asking the kind of basic questions that politicians are refusing to ask – questions such as: how can capitalism and its market-driven dynamic be made to serve the good of everyone and not just the wealthy? Writing about a conference which he attended in the Vatican in May 2008, Hutton somewhat bemusedly comments: 'What was I doing standing in the beautiful Vatican gardens at an open-air Mass watching the green parrots swoop overhead? But there are a billion Catholics worldwide, not a trivial force for change if they can be mobilised … we stakeholders, believers in social justice and good work, make common cause with anybody we can find. And I'm delighted the Pope is one of them.'[12]

CST, in expressing the Bible story in a way that is relevant for the public affairs of today, tries to do so in a bi-lingual way that appeals to the inspiration of the Bible as a kind of deep background, but then couches its applied analysis in terms which are accessible to the ordinary canons of human reason.

As we have seen with respect to the biblical inspiration of public affairs in the United States, it is widely acknowledged that CST was extremely influential in shaping the thought of key founders of the EU and thus of the principles which inform it. In our present context it urges us to a more holistic view of the human person, which respects the importance of the economic dimension, but does not allow it to dominate. This anthropological view is integrated into a more positive approach to the notion of society and state, by means of the notion of the common good. In turn, this leads to an appreciation of the real, if limited, value of the free market, the need for appropriate political governance of the market at national and global levels in the interest of greater equality and justice, of the provision of some basic needs, and of the sustainability of our environment. All this is in contrast to a liberal approach which focuses excessively on the individual, and a collectivist approach which sacrifices individual to group interest.

With this kind of sharpening of the lens afforded by the

---

12. *Sunday Observer,* June 1, 2008

Christian story, we are in a better position to look again at our current situation and at possible ways forward. We might note, as we begin to do so, the interesting remark by Pope John Paul II, when commenting on social sin in *Reconciliatio et Paenitentia* (1984), that there is personal sin in taking 'refuge in the supposed impossibility of changing the world' (n 16).

PART FOUR: A CLOSER LOOK AT OUR CURRENT SITUATION

'We have always known that heedless self-interest was bad morals; we know now that it is bad economics.' (Franklin Delano Roosevelt, 2nd Inaugural Address – *Irish Times*, Saturday 8 November 2008, p 13)

What are the main salient features of our present crisis? First, putting it very simply, there has been a breakdown in trust and confidence globally in the financial and economic spheres, resulting from an at least partially dysfunctional financial sector and from the reality that too many of us in the co-called Developed World (governments, banks, companies, private individuals) have been living beyond our means. The primary responsibility for all this rests with those who 'have' in our society (not, emphatically, with the poor) and disastrous consequences have followed, not just for the West, but also for the whole world and for our planet.

This 'living beyond our means' had its most dramatic and consequential manifestation in the sub-prime mortgage lending of banks in the USA. The loss of confidence and trust resulting from the defaulting on these loans led to a crisis in inter-bank lending and that tightening of credit now referred to as the 'credit crunch'. All this was exacerbated by complex and often unregulated dealings on financial markets. These involved hedge-funds, short-selling, securitisation and derivatives, including the bundling or parcelling of high-risk loans, bonds or assets into portfolios which were sold on to investors globally in a less than transparent way. All this was motivated and incentivised by short-term gains. It was driven by the desire to lend more and more in order to acquire profits and bonus payments that had little to do with the delivery of real economic performance. It has led to a massive hemorrhaging of trust and confidence.

It has seemed to the non-specialist outsider that markets have often been behaving in the smoke and mirrors manner of giant gambling casinos, with scant regard for social responsibility. And one doubts that insiders themselves were really on top of what was going on – as one commentator has put it: 'This pace of innovation and complexity simply outstripped the capacity of boards, managements and regulators to manage their institutions and the capacity of regulators to understand and limit the risks of consumers and shareholders.'[13]

This 'heedless self-interest' model of infinite-growth capitalism was replicated in varying degrees worldwide, with distinctive characteristics according to particular local situations. Thus, in Ireland,[14] we developed an excessive reliance on our construction sector, in an economy that was becoming increasingly uncompetitive (we were paying ourselves too much, 'living beyond our means'). Property prices became grossly inflated, and when this 'property bubble' burst our banks became exposed to bad loans, so that questions were being raised not just about their liquidity and capacity to lend, but even about their very solvency. All this was against a background of strong economic growth for well over a decade, with the welcome benefits of record employment levels and a reduction in levels of consistent poverty, but with continuing high rates of relative poverty and the squandering of opportunities to enhance public services, particularly in areas like health, education, social housing and penal reform.

Opposition parties in countries like Ireland, Britain, France and so on, tend to blame their own governments for what has happened. And there may well be at least some merit to their critique. But it is clear too that our situation is of global proportions, not

---

13. Keith Leslie, 'What really caused the crash of 2008?', *The Tablet*, 4 October 2008, p 4
14. cf Oliver Maloney, 'Secularism and the Current Economic Crisis', *The Furrow*, 60, January 2009, for a perceptive commentary on the Irish version of this self-interest model, and its connections with secularism; and The Irish Commission for Justice and Social Affairs (ICJSA), *In the Wake of the Celtic Tiger: Poverty in Contemporary Ireland*, Dublin: Veritas, 2009 for a reflection on the many faces of poverty in Ireland, in the context of the notion of the common good.

least because of the emergence of economic globalisation in the recent decades. The response then will have to be both local and global. What form should it take?

Ways Forward

Let me observe firstly that those of us commenting on this situation from a religious perspective may be tempted to adopt an excessively moralistic and sweeping approach. While there may be some temporary emotional release in fulminating about the idolatry of Golden Calves on the financial High Places of our world, even some gleeful *Schadenfreude* at the bewilderment of economists and politicians at what has happened, the Christian contribution calls for something more serious.

We must indeed acknowledge that our recent past was characterised by some greed, an almost giddy recklessness even (one thinks of our new wealth in Ireland). To some extent we all share responsibility for this, even if one ought to avoid any bland moral equivalence and be clear that the burden of responsibility lies particularly heavily on the shoulders of those with power, our political and economic leaders.

But the recent past was not all bad: it was, for example, wonderful that so many people in Ireland could find work, and that worldwide, particularly in India and China, there were significant reductions in the figures of those who are consistently poor.

We need then, in the language of Canadian philosopher-theologian Bernard Lonergan, to be open not just to moral but also to intellectual conversion. We need to combine our confessions of immorality with the kind of serious attention to data which will yield an understanding capable of retaining what was good in the past and building a new economic system that responds to needs in a more just and sustainable way.

Regulation – and?

It seems that some kind of consensus may be emerging as to how this is to be done. So, there is a new openness, at least in principle, to a less *laissez-faire*, more socially responsible economic paradigm, in which effective, properly targeted regulation and supervision of banks, financial markets and businesses becomes part of the normative culture.

There are still some ideological neo-liberal economists and commentators who may resist this notion, who believe, like Charles Krauthammer[15] that markets should be left unregulated and that it is politics and not economics that is causing market chaos. But really, the extensive bail-out of banks in the USA and elsewhere, and the widespread introduction of Keynesian fiscal stimulus packages at the behest of financial and business interests have shattered this kind of 'small government' neo-orthodoxy unless, as some have noted ironically, this kind of 'socialism' is only for the rich, when they find themselves in need.

It will be important to get the technical details of this regulation right but also to accompany regulation with sanction. In this context I note the approach of Keith Leslie who proposes that the 'cost of failure' (to meet regulatory requirements) be at least as high as the cost of failing to meet profit expectations. So, for example, with regard to the regulatory framework of banks, 'Deeming (mortgage) foreclosures or loss of savings to be *prima-facie* evidence of criminal misconduct by senior management would change behaviour dramatically ... and the regulatory burden could be higher for businesses that operate mis-matched bonus systems that pay out before performance is delivered.'[16]

Similarly, as noted by sociologist Michael Hornsby-Smith,[17] there needs to be a thoroughgoing reform of the bonus culture which invites financial traders to take undue risks. Instead the reward system should be shifted from short-term profits to long-term performance.

There needs as well to be a review of the rules and funding mechanism of pension schemes. It is arguably unwise that these schemes are funded significantly by risky investment in equity markets, involving not just risk to the pension funds themselves but also putting pressure on businesses to opt for the maximis-

15. *Irish Times,* Tuesday 2 December 2008
16. K. Leslie, op cit, *The Tablet,* 4 October 2008, p 4
17. Michael Hornsby-Smith, 'First, protect the weak', *The Tablet,* 20 November 2008, pp 13-14

ation of short-term profits at the expense of more long-term sustainability.

All this talk about rules and regulations points to something deeper. What Keith Leslie and so many others are proposing is more basic than simple regulation. In fact some (C. Jamison)[18] argue that in the past, at least in the financial services industry in Britain, there has been over-regulation but no ethics, a lethal combination. With this in mind, what is required, arguably, is not more, but better regulation, in particular as applied to the so-called 'shadow banking system', involving the likes of specialist investment banks and hedge funds. However, on its own regulation can be sterile and overly-bureaucratic, it can oppose creativity and flexibility, it has a heavy hand which can lead to feelings of oppression and strategies of evasion. What we need instead is a renewed understanding of ethics which does not equate it with simple rule compliance.

Just as the threat of the 'cost of failure' led to the widespread corporate adoption of effective safety and ethical standards over the past twenty years, so too because of our present crisis we have the opportunity to motivate people, by means of a carrot and stick approach, to achieve non-economic values that are more in harmony with the common good and with the notion that the economy is at the service of the human person and not primarily and exclusively for profit. This would involve a culture in which the ethics of virtue is operative,[19] with the ethics of rules and accompanying sanctions as a kind of initial stimulus and fall-back 'long-stop'. In other words, one goes beyond an Pollyannaish, pipe-dream aspiration for virtue by appealing not just to basic human decency, but by insisting that new values and behaviour are necessary and that if they are not implemented there is a 'cost of failure'.

This notion of virtue would include the kind of prudence for which bankers were once proverbial. It would put an onus on all

---

18. Christopher Jamison, 'Might of Metaphysics', *The Tablet*, 15 November 2008, pp 9-10
19. Seamus Murphy SJ, 'The Many Ways of Justice', *Studies in the Spirituality of Jesuits*, 26/2, March 1994; and 'Virtue Ethics and Christian Moral Reflection', *Milltown Studies*, 55, 2005, pp 82-112

of us (not least for the sake of our planet and future generations) to develop a culture of moderation which avoids living beyond our means, akin to the mantra of Gandhi that: 'we need to learn to live more simply, so that others can simply live.' It would involve a commitment to a justice which cannot rest easy with the scandalous inequalities which characterise our national and, above all, global situation.

It would not be the kind of prudish virtue which disallows the values of freedom, initiative, entrepreneurship and due profit. But it would value the kind of integrity at the heart of financial and commercial transactions that leads to that trust and confidence so necessary for an economy to flourish. We are then not talking about merely technical solutions and a return to 'business as usual': we are speaking about the opportunity given us by this present collapse to reframe the debate more radically.

We are talking, in particular, about the need to consider 'how realistic it is to return to the previous model of consumption-led and debt-fuelled growth'[20] – the need, in other words, to consider seriously the limits of growth, to begin the search for sustainable models of growth. This more radical approach is singularly absent from most political and financial commentary over this period: the focus on regulation alone is insufficient, and while there may be a need for fiscal stimulus packages in the short term, we also need to query the operative assumption seemingly underlying these measures that a return to the recent past is desirable.

It will be a real challenge to conceptualise and implement this more radical approach. After all, the model we have become accustomed to of consumption-led and debt-fuelled growth did produce almost full employment in many places, allowing for more inclusive participation in society. Any turn to moderation and restraint needs to take account of the value of an economy which functions sustainably for the good of all.

In this context of a search for a more radical approach, it is interesting to note the observation about the role of ideas made by John Maynard Keynes, the British economist and policymaker who theorised the way out of the 1930s depression. In 1936 he

20. Paul Gillespie, *Irish Times*, Saturday, 11 January 2009

wrote: 'The ideas of economists and political philosophers, both when they are right and when they are wrong, are more powerful than is commonly understood. Practical men, who believe themselves to be quite exempt from any intellectual influences, are usually the slaves of some defunct economist … soon or late, it is ideas, not vested interests, which are dangerous for good or evil.'[21]

At its deepest, this more radical approach involves a seismic cultural shift (Lonergan's notion of conversion) from the dominant individualistic, utilitarian and managerial ethos of neo-liberalism to the more inclusive ethos of the common good. But neo-liberalism was always an extreme version of the kind of liberalism worldwide that rejoices in human rights and that in countries like Britain has been to the fore in operating the welfare state. Now, with the present sword of Damocles hanging over us due to our global economic meltdown, as well as the legally coercive measure suggested above, it may well be that many of us, liberals and non-liberals alike, would turn with some relief to a more humane model of economic development, respectful of our natural environment.

Roy Keane and a Humane Model of Economic Development
I remember being struck, some years ago now, when Roy Keane, still playing football then in the Premiership with Manchester United, negotiated his contract for something like 75,000 pounds sterling a week. At one level it seemed right to say: 'Good on you, Roy.' At another level it seemed at best simply daft, at worst obscene.

More significantly, one could say the same, and a lot more, about the remuneration of the chief executives of banks and other businesses, often amounting to several millions a year, not to mention the profits of property developers.

Are we not uneasy with the brand of capitalism which allows, even encourages, the kind of egregious inequalities which we see evident in the contrast between the salaries of chief executives and those of the worker on the floor or in the office – not to men-

---

21. quoted by Paul Gillespie, *Irish Times*, Saturday, 11 January 2009

tion the myriad other extreme inequalities of the system, from which the professions (one thinks in particular of the legal and medical) are not immune?

Even for the rampant hedonist it would seem that the sums of money involved in this make little sense: at a certain point what individual can use this kind of money, does it become simply a matter of making money for its own sake or, perhaps more likely, an envy or power-trip by means of which 'keeping up with the Jones', 'having more possessions than the other guy' becomes the driver of economic activity?

We need to search for economic models which are less prone to such aberrations. Trade Unionist David Begg[22] observes that there are at least four different socially democratic models of capitalism in Europe: the Rhineland, the Anglo-Saxon, the Mediterranean and the Nordic. He notes that the Scandinavians in particular have combined healthy growth, low unemployment, rising productivity and large export surpluses with some of the lowest levels of inequality in the world.

In a 2004 study on economic equality a group of UCD academics (John Baker, Kathleen Lynch, Sara Cantillon and Judy Walsh) note that while the Nordic countries achieve one of the most equal income distributions within the OECD by means of progressive taxation and extensive social welfare programmes, Japan has taken a different route.[23] With its brand of 'corporate welfarism' public policy has been directed at closing two gaps – 'the gap between high and low wages in different firms and industries, and the gap between economic growth and wage growth, i.e. between national economic prosperity and individual well-being'.[24] In this scenario public policy 'promotes equity in terms of wages and working conditions both within firms and between

22. David Begg, 'The Future of the European Union', in Jesuit Centre for Faith and Justice, *The Future of Europe*, Dublin: Veritas, 2006, pp 73-82; and 'Solidarity and Freedom: Defending the Rights and Dignity of Work in a Global Economy', Eoin G. Cassidy, ed, *The Common Good in an Unequal World*, Dublin: Veritas, 2007, pp 129-146
23. John Baker, Kathleen Lynch, Sara Cantillon and Judy Walsh, *Equality*, London: Palgrave Macmillan, 2004
24. op cit, p 90

larger firms and their smaller counterparts across industries. The primary mechanism employed in relation to equity in the wage structure is the flattening of payment scales within and across firms so that the variation in pre-tax income is relatively low.'[25] Of course the Japanese economy has had its own problems over an extended period now: it would be interesting to discover if any of these problems have to do with this 'corporate welfarism' and the drive to reduce inequality.

With the discrediting of the neo-liberal model of economic development, we have an opportunity not just to tinker with the system but to reframe the debate in a way that allows notions like justice and equity to assume their proper place. Clearly in terms of technical solutions there can be no one-size-fits-all approach. Different countries start from different starting places, with histories and contexts that need to be respected. But perhaps we can get some illumination from countries and economic models that have tried seriously to address these issues. We have a new opportunity, given us by our present crisis, to think big and to go beyond management-speak in our search for that 'sustainable prosperity for all', the holy grail of political economy.[26] We need to do this in an innovative but carefully rigorous way: if one extreme is simply to tinker, another is to adopt a populist anti-market approach that simply increases poverty and unemployment, and replaces old vested interests with newer ones.

Global Dimension
Part of the consensus that is emerging is that any solution must involve an international, global dimension. What this means is not simply economic co-operation, but also the notion of political economy, the need to have effective global political institutions which can exercise wise stewardship over the workings of free markets. It makes sense that it is too difficult to control a global crisis with instruments that are limited to national jurisdictions, and the judgement of Cambridge academic Sir Nicholas Boyle is

---

25. op cit, pp 90-91
26. Clifford Longley, 'An acceptable face for capitalism', *The Tablet*, 23 August 2008, p 10

gaining wider acceptance: 'The world community, of which we are all part, is now paying the penalty for its failure to match economic globalisation with political globalisation.'[27]

At some level this is beginning to be remedied. The G7 / 8 meetings of world leaders have been recently expanded to G20, taking in most of the world's major economies, including Brazil, India, China, Saudi Arabia and South Africa. There is talk of a Bretton Woods mark 2 to refashion the global financial architecture, with increased regulatory powers proposed for the IMF and more funding for it and the World Bank.

It is heartening that these moves are afoot, and that there is some prospect of a more inclusive global economic oversight. One does not underestimate the enormous challenges that this involves, not least the effective coming together of so many countries with such different histories, interests, and structures of government and economics. The 'new thing' of Deutero-Isaiah comes to mind, the dreams and vision of Joel, the hope that now these dreams may be realised in the New Covenant with all humankind sealed by the life and death of Jesus and trumpeted forth in the 'we have a dream' and the 'yes we can' speeches of Martin Luther King and Barack Obama; and the reminder from John Paul II that it is sinful 'to take refuge in the supposed impossibility of changing the world'.

We are at an early stage of this formal conversation between world leaders about what needs to be done. I would note two concerns.

First, however difficult this may be, it would seem necessary that the institutional reform to be proposed should not limit itself to the economic and financial spheres only. We have surely learned that while economics are important, they are so as a subset of overall human flourishing. We must not repeat the mistakes already made and think that a more efficient global economy is sufficient. We need to institutionalise the reality of a global political economy, with inclusive participation. This is particularly important to counteract the natural tendency for the strong and powerful to dominate and oppress the weak. Indeed, at both

---

27. Nicholas Boyle, 'A tax to save the world', *The Tablet*, 25 October 2008, p 6

national and international levels, it should be a concern of governments that the policies they adopt to lead us out of our present
crisis should do as much as possible to avoid the people who are
poor having to bear the brunt of the pain – not least because it is
not they who have caused this crisis.

Whether this global institutional reform can be carried out by
means of the United Nations or through the creation of a different
body is a matter for debate. However, it seems abundantly clear
that this kind of reform is needed. It would be a considerable
achievement of political innovation, evidence of a much needed
'global imagination' (Nicholas Boyle), to create democratically
accountable international institutions of this kind. Kant, in his
1795 essay *Perpetual Peace*,[28] called for the establishment of a
world civil society, a call reiterated in our day by Christian political ethicist Max Stackhouse.[29] The call for effective global political
institutions is even more ambitious but, ironically, perhaps it is at
a time of crisis that this kind of innovation has the best chance of
success.

Secondly, once again to avoid a simple return to a 'business as
usual' model, we need to take serious steps to address the issues
of the Millennium Development Goals, including the notion of
sustainable growth in the context of the environmental crisis. Of
course this presupposes a return to economic stability. But it is
simply unacceptable, for example, and a scandal crying out to
heaven, that, thanks to the scientific and technological gains of
modernity, we are in a position to feed the entire world, and yet so
many fellow human beings continue to suffer and even die of
hunger.

One way of addressing these issues is to introduce the so-
called Tobin tax, as suggested by Nicholas Boyle and Paul
Gillespie.[30] The late James Tobin, a Nobel laureate in economics,
proposed in the 1970s that there should be a worldwide tax on in-

---

28. Quoted by Paul Gillespie, *Irish Times*, Saturday, 13 December 2008
29. Max Stackhouse, 'Christianity and the Prospects for a New Global
Order', in John A. Coleman SJ, ed, *Christian Political Ethics*, op cit, pp 155-169
30. cf N. Boyle, *The Tablet*, op cit, p 7; Paul Gillespie, *Irish Times*, Saturday,
8 November 2008

ternational currency transactions, to be set somewhere between 0.01 per cent and 1 per cent (Nicholas Boyle calculates that the turnover in global currency markets can run to three trillion dollars a day). His initial idea was that this tax would be a means of discouraging currency speculation. Now, however, it is being suggested that the considerable revenue this would raise could be applied to meeting the Millennium Development Goals, to funding a reformed United Nations, to setting up a stabilisation fund to guarantee the world's banking system and in general to fund the kind of sustainable development we require at global level. Is this a good idea whose time has now come?

Leading us into the Future
I want to add a final note in this section about who is best placed to lead us forward out of our present crisis. At one level this is an issue of accountability, of accepting the consequences of actions. And so, without in any way advocating some vindictive witch-hunt, it is surely right for the body politic, for all of us, that mistakes are acknowledged, that we learn from them, and that just action is taken. This will involve resignations, dismissals, and even criminal prosecutions where appropriate. With regard to politicians this can happen voluntarily (rarely the case) or, more usually, at a time of election. For leaders in the business and financial community there are other procedures to be invoked, not least the social disapproval of culpable error.

We in Ireland, in particular, already aware of the evidence, and, in some cases, findings of so many recent Tribunals of Public Enquiry, need to question searchingly the reckless practices in public life that continue to be revealed – one thinks, for example, of the Anglo-Irish Bank debacle. These practices go way beyond the merely 'inappropriate' and, if not downright illegal, are clearly wrong. This kind of questioning is necessary in order to repair the foundations and standards of public morality so necessary to restore our national and international confidence. It must extend to the appearance at least of a kind of *laissez-faire* incompetence or even collusion in these matters between sections of the political, economic and financial establishments.

However there is another, more practical side to this issue that bears thinking about. One can be sure that most of the politicians, bankers, market traders and business leaders involved in the reckless behaviour of the recent past were not themselves, for the most part, fully aware of what was going on. They were, again in Lonergan's helpful phrase, subject to a kind of individual and group bias which permeated our culture and solidified into a 'bias of common sense'. This is said not to avoid responsibility, to assert moral equivalence between leaders and led, or to absolve of all blame. It is simply to note that it became hard to argue against the encouragement to 'party on', hard not to be affected by this cult-ural bias and to avoid a sneaking regard for the 'greed is good' mantra, even when, like the Israelites of old, we were uneasily aware in a part of our minds that this was idolatry, and there was even the occasional prophet who told us so. I say occasional – it now seems, like the mythical multitudes who laid claim to being in the GPO in 1916, there is a rush of experts who tell us that they got it right, 'they told us so'!

But because these leaders were subject to this bias, and because most of us take time to acknowledge our mistakes and prefer to deny and even rationalise them, they are not always the best people to engage in the kind of fresh thinking and commitment needed to lead us into the future. Already in Ireland, for example, we have seen how government politicians reject the notion that they got anything wrong; bankers have been slow to apologise for errors; and prominent property developers (Sean Dunne, Patrick Kelly, Bernard McNamara) have defended their own conduct and that of the banks. The danger in all this is that an Orwellian narrative of self-justification takes hold in the public space, on behalf of those primarily responsible for our crisis. This simply hinders the search for solutions, since these must emerge from an under-standing and acknowledgement of past failures.

There is, besides, the practical difficulty that government in these times is beset with so many problems that ministers can scarcely have the time to think through a more radical approach, never mind what that might mean in policy terms. The remarks of Madeleine Bunting, with regard to the scene in Britain, have wider application: 'Is there anyone in government trying to work it out, or are they too busy trying to keep the old show on the road? Treasury ministers look boggy-eyed with exhaustion; it's hard to imagine them having the time to start thinking of the bold strategies we may need.'[31]

Of course one cannot over-generalise about this: some individuals have the power to lick their wounds and to bounce back again in a refocused way. Furthermore we need the memory and skill of those at the centre of that *ancien régime* which contained much that was good, as well as that which we are now rejecting. The remarks of Nobel Prize winner, economist Paul Krugman are instructive in this respect, when asked about the return to the White House of Clinton-era economists in the administration of Obama: 'Well, they're smart and relatively open-minded, so they're the kind of people who can learn from their mistakes. And you do want people who know a lot about the mechanics of finance and central banking, which is why some of the people being proposed by the left would be problematic.'[32] But we do well also to look for new faces and new ideas outside the current establishment with, above all, a commitment to justice that is non-ideological, cognisant of the common good.

PART FIVE: GOD MATTERS

I have noted that CST is bilingual, and many fair-minded but religiously agnostic commentators may well acknowledge some usefulness in the insights it offers, about our current crisis and about social reality in general, when speaking in the language of natural reason. But what about the biblical basis of this teaching, its rootedness in faith? Is this simply some kind of optional add-on?

We Christians too, all of us affected by the predominant secularism and some of us perhaps feeling on the margins of organised religion, often ask ourselves these same questions. We feel the need to understand better how God matters, and how Jesus Christ

31. *The Guardian*, 6 October 2008
32. In an online interview with Andrew Leonard – http://www.-salon.com/tech/htww/feature/2008/12/08/paul_krugman/index.html

need not be confined to the private inner sanctum of our personal spiritual life.

In what follows, I would like to propose a plausibility structure for the consideration that God is intimately and indispensably involved in our present situation, as a stimulus to questioning Christians and as a challenge to non-believers to think again, at least in the sense of thinking more positively about the religious contribution to difficult social issues.

God

Nicholas Lash[33] tells the story of the Brazilian Dominican, Frei Betto, friend of Fidel Castro who, after a visit to England in the 1980s, noted that while everyone had warned him how secular Britain had become, he disagreed. This is not a secular, but a pagan society, he argued: it just so happens that 'we do not call the things we worship "gods".'[34]

What Betto, somewhat provocatively, is drawing our attention to, is the innate human propensity to set our hearts on people or things in a disproportionate, absolute way that dominates our life and is, effectively, worship, but in this case the worship of idols.

Arguably this is what has happened in recent times in the West and, by imitation, globally: we have worshipped on the High Places at the Temples, not now of the Baals, but of the free market, and in the cathedrals of irresponsible consumerism. Our faith in science and technology has become a default religion, whose empirical methods and quantifiable results have become the template, both in popular culture and in academic circles, for all reputable knowledge and truth, heedless of the truth that most of the important realities of life (relationships, happiness, justice, love) are not measurable in this kind of way. We have idolised 'getting and spending', and engaged in the cult of celebrity and fashion – a recent survey of under-10s in Britain found that Simon

33. For what follows, cf N. Lash, *Theology for Pilgrims*, London: Darton, Longman and Todd, 2008, especially ch 2, 'The Impossibility of Atheism', pp 19-35
34. Lash, op cit, p 22

Cowell, the TV personality, was the 'most famous person in the world' – God and the Queen ran a close second and third![35] We have become enslaved adherents of success, and appearances, heedless of the egocentric and exploitative nature of what was going on.[36] In other words, the worship of gods – idolatry – is rife in our so-called secular society.

It is at the heart of what it is to be a Christian (or a Jew, or a Muslim) to be convinced that 'non-idolatrous worship is both possible and necessary'.[37] God, in this context, is not one larger and more powerful fact or thing belonging with other things to the furniture of this world, but rather that transcendent holy Mystery, in relation to which everything (including economics and science) has its origin and destiny (Aquinas, *ST*, 1a, q.1, art 7).

This means that we are radically contingent beings, vulnerable, at risk, not self-constituted. This vulnerability and risk may seem unwelcome at first, and be experienced as fear. However, in faith we believe that our contingency is rooted securely within the freely giving nature of the mystery we call God. We are creatures who are gifted into existence by God's love, and our consequent relationship of dependence is not one of servitude, but rather one of authentic freedom, with purpose and without fear.

This understanding of God as the origin and destiny of all, compatible with the notions of human freedom and truth, lays a meaningful foundation for a moral and socially just engagement with our world. Morality is impoverished when reduced to an autonomous human construction, without normative criteria. This autonomous approach, making it up, however conscientiously, as we go along, lends itself too easily to projects whose default tendency and mechanism is to favour the powerful over the weak.

We have seen how these kinds of projects have flourished historically, some of them projects with great good in them, like liberal

35. cf http://news.sky.com/skynews/Home/UK-News/Simon-Cowell-More-Famous-Than-God-Or-The-Queen-Survey-Of-British-Kids-Under-10/Article/200812315180581?f=rss
36. M. Dolors Oller i Sala, *Building a Sense of Community*, Barcelona: Cristianisme i Justicia, 131, October 2008, pp 24 ff
37. N. Lash, op cit, p 22

modernity. They have too easily degenerated into the kind of social Darwinism and neo-liberalism which have led to the extremes of *laisser-faire* capitalism at the heart of our present crisis. At their core is a 'thin' notion of the good, resulting in the kind of individualism which has avoided discussion of the deeper issues of the good life, and of the values of truth and justice. Many (for example John Rawls, Jürgen Habermas and Charles Taylor) now argue that even in our pluralist societies we must find a way to engage with a 'thicker' notion of the good, as discussed by Jesuit political philosopher Patrick Riordan under the rubric of the common good.[38]

The God question, indeed, pushes us in this other direction, on a different, less egocentric trajectory in which principles like the common good and solidarity with the oppressed come to the fore. In this scenario the whole human project, with freedom and appropriate autonomy (spoken about by *Gaudium et Spes*) intact, has its basis in transcendent meaning and in the notions of the true, the good and the beautiful. It is not that the laws of economics, science, culture and so on are denied or ignored: rather they are set within a transcendent world of meaning in which they discover their true value as creatures and are not distorted by being mistaken for that Absolute which human hearts crave.

The God question is not, then, simply an optional add-on: the use of the god word, and this word alone, according to Karl Rahner, brings 'a person face to face with the single whole of reality' and with 'the single whole of (their) own existence'.[39] Augustine's well-know comment is apposite: 'Our hearts are restless, until they rest in You' (*Confessions*, Bk 1, ch1).

The masters of suspicion of modernity – one thinks of Feuerbach, Nietzsche, Marx and Freud – have claimed to show that it is wishful thinking, a neurosis, an opium of the people given as a palliative to the oppressed to console them with vindication in an after-life – to suppose that God matters. I am advanc-

---

38. Patrick Riordan SJ, *A Politics of the Common Good*, Dublin: Institute of Public Administration, 1996; also, *A Grammar of the Common Good: Speaking of Globalization*, Continuum, 2008.
39. N. Lash, op cit, p 24

ing a plausibility structure for supposing that God is intimately, indispensably and benevolently involved in our world, and hence in our present crisis. I am, if you like, proposing that the hypothesis of God arguably makes more sense and gives more meaning to the data before us. The world of meaning and morality, so basic to the human project, is difficult to sustain rationally if its ultimate foundation is some theory of chance, in combination with a biological determinism. Why be moral if the meaning of life is simply a matter of chance, and may be different in the future? It is considerations like this that have led non-believers like Habermas to propose that the liberal project in particular, if it is to be morally sustainable, may need to re-connect with its Judaeo-Christians roots and inspiration.

Now it is certainly true that the mere profession of theism, agnosticism or atheism does not of itself settle anything – 'theism can be the mask of a concealed atheism and vice versa' (Karl Rahner).[40] Indeed, we theists, by our actions, can sometimes show that we worship a God who is just another, bigger thing of this world, as we confuse God with creatures like money, sex, success, the latest theory of human self-improvement and so on. Similarly the professed atheist who refuses to settle for the notion of reality as dull fact, but who goes on wondering and caring about our world, is in reality closer to the heart of the matter. It will always make sense, then, for all people of good will, believers and unbelievers alike, to work together for our common good.

But allowing for such ambiguities, what I am proposing to believers is the consideration that the hypothesis of God is necessary for the proper grounding of the moral life, and to believers and unbelievers alike that this notion of God can lead to constructive contributions to public debate on the way forward for our world.

Jesus Christ
The historical figure of Jesus Christ throws more light on the matter of God and its positive significance for our present situation.

First, the incarnation of Jesus Christ shows us what it is to be human. In particular it subverts our tendency to think that divinity

---

40. In N. Lash, op cit, p 34

and humanity are antithetical. In Rahner's language, humanity is not something extrinsic to God, but rather is God's mode of existence *ad extra*: 'Man is the event of a free, unmerited and forgiving, and absolute self-communication of God.'[41]

What is true of Jesus by nature, is true of us by participation: as women and men there is a spark of the divine at the heart of our humanity, we are shot through with this divinity, so it is perfectly understandable that the Greek theologians should speak of our 'divinisation'. The more divine we are, the more human we become. And thus it is also perfectly understandable that in our lives we should reach for the stars, this is the 'grandeur' of humanity, the 'yes we can' of Obama, the yearning of the world today for a way out of our crisis.

All this is, of course, the opposite of what many good people in our secular West imagine to be the notion of the good life, of human flourishing. The observations of Charles Taylor are interesting in this context.[42] Taylor judges that the issues behind secularism are perhaps not so much epistemological as cultural: we are faced not principally with a rational denial of God, but more with a moral sensibility which has persuaded itself that human flourishing is intrinsically immanent, that there is no need of a reference to the transcendent, to divinisation. The same kind of analysis is increasingly articulated by journalist John Waters in the Irish context.[43] Within this cultural framework, as the moral energy of liberalism loses force, might the Christian notion of God in Jesus Christ begin to excite imaginations again?

It might be better to say that it is Jesus Christ himself, the encounter with him, which may make the difference. Because what is involved here is not primarily a doctrine or a morality, but a relationship. In different ways in modernity and postmodernity we have put our faith in autonomy to make us happy – we believe that freedom of choice, freedom from coercion, is key to the good life. This is the kind of culture summed up by John Waters in

41. N. Lash, op cit, p 26
42. cf M. P. Gallagher, 'Charles Taylor's Critique of "Secularisation"', *Studies*, 97, Winter 2008, pp 433-444
43. See, for example, John Waters, *Irish Times*, Friday 9 January 2009

terms of the myth of eternal youth, symbolised by the aura of rock 'n' roll, in which we somehow, desperately, manage to bracket out ultimate questions of meaning often associated with middle and older age by clinging to that kind of *Tír na nÓg* mentality associated with freedom.[44] But freedom of what kind? The freedom to shop, to have sex with many partners, to take away the pain of reality through addiction?

The suggestion is that in the encounter with Jesus Christ we are offered a vision of happiness which integrates an understanding of what freedom is 'for' as well as 'from': that in this encounter our deepest searchings and longings are addressed, in a way which respects, cherishes and integrates in proportion all our other desires, relationships and commitments. The suggestion indeed is that we have been looking in the wrong place for happiness – is it not foolish to believe that happiness lies in autonomy, when even in human experience our happiest moments come when we fall in love and learn to live out that love in the mature way which draws us out of egoism towards concern for others? And if, to return to Taylor's cultural diagnosis, this love is offered in a way which transcends the immanent and which responds to the deepest desires of our hearts, does it not make sense to explore the promise of such a relationship?

This is the promise offered in the encounter with Jesus Christ. To reduce it to a doctrine is to do what the Pharisees did to the Jewish notion of God, removing it from everyday currency. To reduce it to ethics is to engage in a Pelagian moralism which misses the point. Doctrine and morality are important, but they are secondary to that vital encounter with Jesus Christ who came primarily not to teach us or improve our morals but so that we might 'have life, and have it to the full' (Jn 10:10). To reduce it to a rite of passage or to a source of consolation in troubled times is to accept that valid but impoverished notion of Christian faith which is so pervasive in our contemporary culture.

It is from that enormous love of Jesus Christ, the lodestar of our lives, the magnetic pole which draws us and shapes the whole of

---

44. John Waters, 'The Sabotage of Hope', *The Furrow*, December 2008, pp 651-661

our life, that we come to know better (doctrine) and to serve (morals). St Augustine expressed it succinctly: 'Love, and do what you will' (7th Sermon of Commentary on First Letter of John). This is the glorious freedom of the daughters and sons of God, the sisters and brothers of the God-Man Jesus Christ, a freedom worth living and dying for. To live one's life in the company of this man is to be drawn and attracted, not driven or coerced. It is to experience joy.

And this man is also God, with a divinity that surprises, that 'empties itself', that is 'like us in all things but sin', that is approachable. In other words, but now from the side of human weakness and ordinariness, it becomes clear that humanity is compatible with divinity, that Jesus can affirm the classic lines of Terence: 'nihil humanum alienum a me puto' – there is nothing that is human that is foreign to me. There is an enormous attractiveness about this notion of humanity and the relationship with Jesus which it entails.

Because Jesus too experiences life as contingent, as depending on the one he calls Abba. And, like us, like that experience of the siren call of Satan in Modernity (Milton's 'I will not serve'), he too, in the wilderness prior to his mission, is tempted to take the short-cut to autonomy, to use naked power to bring about the blessings of God. And when, instead, he goes the way of his Father, the way of vulnerable love, yet again, like us, he finds it distressing that the cost is so high, that evil seems too strong – 'Father, take this cup from me … my God, my God, why have you forsaken me?'

And so there is no dualism between the sacred and the secular in God's self-expression in Jesus Christ. Nor should there be in our imitation of Christ. Instead there is the enormous, ever-patient love of God drawing us from the exile of self-alienation and injustice, through the exodus of repentance and conversion, towards the promised land of the kingdom of God, anticipations of which we experience already in our personal and communal lives.

This love of God is universal, it extends to rich and poor, to good and evil. And yet, consonant with that original 'emptying' which grounds the incarnation, it takes the particular form of solidarity with and love of the poor, the weak, the sick, and the sinner.

These were the preferred companions of Jesus, and he was criticised by the establishment for this choice.

At stake here is a basic view of the world – riches and power
tend towards idolatry and injustice and, ironically, a certain
poverty of spirit; and, in the poor and in troubled sinners, there is a
certain openness to others, to God, there can be a richness of spirit.
This tears up the rule-books of human logic. We are invited to consider that the notion of the good life cannot be restricted to the indispensable sphere of the economic: instead it must also include
the more important aspects of love, friendship, justice, art, poetry,
nature – these are values and realities easily lost by the choking
weeds of wealth and power.

But this must not lead to a spiritualising of the evils of poverty
and injustice. And so even if Jesus himself disappointed some
potential followers by not becoming the political Messiah widely
expected, who would free the Jews from Roman rule; even if, in
his famous phrase, he said 'Give to Caesar what belongs to Caesar
…', thus opening the way for our modern understanding of the
separation of powers between church and state; still, this is the
same Jesus who roundly turned on the free market idolatry of his
day by forcibly expelling the traders and dealers at the heart of the
Temple, thus reinforcing his consistent opposition throughout his
active ministry to the establishment of his day.

And so we are faced, in Jesus, with a view of God (theology)
and of humanity (theological anthropology) which directs us, em-
powered by our relationship with God, towards a critique of abuses
of power and wealth, and towards the kind of politics which addresses these issues seriously.

But we are also faced in Jesus with a claim that we are, in principle, already saved (soteriology), that his way of vulnerable love,
as witnessed in the paschal mystery of cross and resurrection, has
achieved a definitive victory over all evil, a victory which we are
graced to appropriate.

This is what the Old Testament longed for: a definitive breakthrough from the seemingly endless cycle of God's call to justice
and peace through law and commandment, the people's resistance and refusal, the punishment of exile and then the exodus of

restoration. At last now, with Jesus, because he is that Messiah beyond expectation who is both human and divine, there has been a definitive 'yes' to this call, a breaking in principle of this wearisome cycle. This 'yes', on our behalf, has been able, in love, to endure the enormous suffering involved in absorbing in love the burden of all the terrible injustices and evil of the world which, in solidarity with victims, are gathered by the angel with his sickle and put, in that memorable phrase of the Book of Revelations, into 'a huge winepress, the winepress of God's anger' (Revelations, 14:19).

It is within this context that someone like Martin Luther King can say that 'unearned suffering is redemptive' – in Colossians the Pauline author expresses this in terms of rejoicing in his own sufferings because thereby he 'completes what is lacking in Christ's sufferings' (Col 1:24). This means that to be human is about participating in this breakthrough, this victory over evil, by sharing in the mystery of cross and resurrection that shapes our lives too. It is our call to appropriate this victory freely, a project which, despite the suffering involved, can be undertaken with certain hope (1 Pet 1:3), without fear.

But, but – can we really, without crossing that line to myth and fairytale, talk so confidently about resurrection? Cross yes, that we can imagine and have experienced too often in human history, but resurrection – now really! One hears in these incredulous questions the echoes of the sophisticated Athenians who mocked St Paul as he spoke to them about God before the Council of the Areopagus. All was going well until he mentioned the resurrection: at that the speech was over, the more polite saying 'We'd like to hear you talk about this again', with the others mocking him, bursting out laughing (Acts 17:23-34).

There is, in truth, a need for modesty, for a hermeneutic of humility and diffidence in relation to the 'how' of the resurrection. We need to acknowledge that scriptural images in relation to the next life (the eternal banquet, the heavenly Jerusalem and so on) are just that – images, metaphors, not exact descriptions or definitions. We need to be clear that by resurrection (whether of Jesus or of ourselves) we do not mean simple resuscitation, the continuation of life in the space and time of this world but now 'for ever'.

Rather, the Christian belief in resurrection involves both continuity (it is still 'I' who exist) and discontinuity (I will exist in a transfigured way, as is hinted at in the appearances of the resurrected Jesus to his disciples, who both knew and did not know him), in that sphere of eternity which is best understood as the fullness and intensity of time rather than a kind of horizontal extension of everlasting time as we know it. So we can say little enough about the 'how' of resurrection.

But we may say a little more about belief in the reality of resurrection. Ultimately, as Karl Rahner suggests, this comes down to the question about the meaning of our existence: we are all the time striving in time and history to achieve what is beyond us and what is eternal, what alone can satisfy our desires. When we act in small and big matters in this life according to our conscience, 'whenever a free and lonely act of decision has taken place in obedience to a higher law, or in radical affirmation of love for another person' something eternal has taken place.[45] Rahner's phenomenology of the human quest for meaning, adumbrated in questions like: 'Why is any kind of radical moral cynicism impossible for any person who has discovered his real self? ... why is real moral goodness not afraid of the apparently hopeless futility of all striving?',[46] leads him to assert that death cannot be the end, that if our lives are to have meaning then that striving for the beyond which shapes them only makes sense with that promise of transcendence pre-figured in the resurrection of Jesus Christ.

But why resurrection as such, why not simply immortality, understood in the Greek way as the immortality of the soul, thus eliminating all the embarrassment about the survival of corporeal materiality after the radical dissolution that is death? Judaeo-Christian anthropology understands humanity as integrally matter and spirit. There is no Platonic discourse about soul being imprisoned in body, with its more modern formulation of 'the ghost in the machine'. Rather matter – and so the whole cosmos – is hon-

45. Karl Rahner, *Foundations of Christian Faith*, New York: Seabury Press, 1978, p 439
46. Karl Rahner, op cit, p 438; and *Encyclopedia of Theology*, London: Burns and Oates, 1975, p 1440

oured. This is seen in Christian teachings about creation, incarnation, eucharist, marriage, all the sacraments, our social and political lives and so on: within this context of the unity of matter and spirit, the promise of resurrection makes sense.

I have noted that we know very little about the 'how' of the resurrection. Clearly, as outlined above, it has not to do with the resuscitation of a physical body, and it has not to do with questions of cosmology, biology or physics as we understand them. Rather, just as the hypothesis of God need not clash with evolutionary theory or indeed with science in general, and just as a Christian may believe firmly and intelligently in doctrines like creation, incarnation, God's providence which indicate divine transcendence within a respect for created realities, so we may firmly and intelligently believe in the hope and promise of the resurrection, which is the ultimate guarantor and pledge of all else – of God' victory over sin and the black hole of meaninglessness – 'If there is no resurrection of the dead, Christ himself cannot have been raised, and if Christ has not been raised then our preaching is useless and your believing it is useless ... if our hope in Christ has been for this life only, we are the most unfortunate of all people' (1 Cor 15:12-19).

It is this victory which John Donne (*Holy Sonnet*, n 10) hints at when he says:

One short sleep past
We wake eternally
And death shall be no more,
Death, thou shalt die.

We are invited to work that the fruits of this victory, known as the kingdom of God, may become evident already in our world. What is involved in this process of the coming of God's kingdom in our world?

The Life of Grace

God has come close to us in Jesus Christ: now we are the sisters and brothers of Jesus, our dignity is that of being made in the image and likeness of God. It is no wonder, then, that there is a grandeur about the human project that is God's gift to us, that we are right to use the talents given us (Mt 25:14ff) to reach to the stars.

But there is another vector at work in human hearts and human history, the vector of sin and evil, which speaks to the misery of being human. It takes so many different shapes and forms – our personal brokenness and self-alienation, our silliness, our difficulties in fidelity to those we love, never mind to those we find it hard to get on with; inter-personal and communal strife, at all kinds of levels, including the gang-warfare in our major cities, peaking in instances such as the Gomorrah-like nightmare in a city like Naples;[47] the massive global suffering and injustice which confront us daily on our TV screens.

At the back of all this is the reality of sin in all its forms – original, personal, social. Original sin exists in that we sense some kind of struggle, a contradiction at the very heart of our being. Paul knew about this: 'I cannot understand my own behaviour. I fail to carry out the things I want to do, and I find myself doing the very things I hate' (Rom 7:14-15). Often enough we are indeed conscious that 'the spirit is willing, but the flesh is weak' (Mt 26:41-42).

This power of evil, novelist Philip Roth's *The Human Stain* (2000), has powerful consequences. Using Dantesque, almost apocalyptic language, Pope Benedict refers to it as developing into a 'river of evil ... that has poisoned human history'.[48] The language is strong, but looking at the course of human history, at the enormous problems of our contemporary world, is there not some plausibility to this account?

At the personal level there is the reality that we are opaque to ourselves, and none of us is so self-transparent as to know quite where, in fact, our hearts are set. And so, even as we sin, we deny that we are doing so, we rationalise. In doing so we are sharing in that bias of individual, group and common sense to which Lonergan alluded: as bankers, politicians, property developers, citizens, we can scarcely believe that we did anything wrong – or

47. Presented on screen by director Matteo Garrone, after the book by Roberto Savino.
48. *The Tablet*, 6 December 2008, p 34

that we were so stupid and uncaring. And isn't our bewildered contemporary experience as old as Adam? Think of his reply to God's accusations: 'It was the woman you put with me; she gave me the fruit ...' (Gen 3:12).

And Eve's reply is equally instructive: 'The serpent tempted me and I ate' (Gen 3:13). We can take this as a reference to social and cosmic sin, the way that both deep within us but also in the systems and structures of our world there is a seemingly demonic resistance to order and good. This is the struggle against the principalities and powers that Paul speaks about (Eph 6:12), that struggle which we experience when we recognise the hydra-like existence of evil and its atrophying into cultures and structures that seem so strong at times as to tempt even good people into complicity. How, for example, did we as human beings live so long with the formal toleration of slavery, of the subordination of women? How have we been so blind to our worship of the gods of the free market? How can we continue to be so hardened to the glaring inequalities and injustices of our world?

It is this tide of evil, this vector of sin that Jesus Christ saves us from. This salvation is effected not by magic, not by power, but rather by that self-sacrificing, costly, redemptive love of his which respects fully our human intelligence and freedom. And so the struggle goes on. But now evil, personal and impersonal, is confronted by the wonderfully attractive face of Jesus, made present by the Holy Spirit in all its many forms of appearance in our world, healing, wooing, drawing us away from what is evil and towards what is true, good and beautiful. The poet Gerard Manley Hopkins perhaps conveys this omnipresence of Jesus Christ, even where not explicitly recognised or acknowledged, in a manner more evocative than Rahner's 'anonymous Christian':

> I say more: the just man justices;
> Keeps grace: that keeps all his goings graces;
> Acts in God's eye what in God's eye he is –
> Christ. For Christ plays in ten thousand places,
> Lovely in limbs, and lovely in eyes not his
> To the Father through the features of men's faces.
> (*As Kingfishers Catch Fire*)

And this is what grace is: not some kind of tablet or liquid or quantifiable 'stuff' that acts medicinally or to improve our perform-ance, but rather a relationship of love that is beautiful and just – a love that cries out for expression not just in personal terms, but in the kind of effective solidarity that has social and political implic-ations. These latter will involve the attempt to realise that limited common good we have spoken about earlier, with the political, social and economic structures that this entails. It will involve the kind of principled, ethical and legal behaviour that, in a fallen world, has to take account of outcomes that are less than perfect – there is a long and honourable tradition of casuistry in moral theo-logy, which reflects on how to apply principles to concrete and even hard cases. This is a love which is often mediated through so many other relationships, through events, through nature, which allows us, through the Holy Spirit, to appropriate the victory over sin already achieved for us by Jesus Christ and to bring about his kingdom in doing so.

Our lives, then, are shot through with the vectors of natural goodness, of sin, and of that redemptive self-sacrificing love that is called grace, the first word of all and, as we say with certain hope, the last one too. And so we are always tempted, we are always sinners, but we are also, and more significantly, being con-verted, being turned towards the good. This conversion will in-volve appropriate self-awareness and repentance: acts have con-sequences, there is judgement, salvation is not magic .... And so, while the unconditional love and forgiveness of the Prodigal Father is the first and last word of God to all of us (including erring politicians, bankers, property developers, priests and bishops), nonetheless the Prodigal Son needs to leave the far country of a false autonomy, needs to learn and repent – as do all of us, in part-icular our leaders, *apropos* our current situation.

This conversion involves a shift from egoism to concern for others, akin to that putting on of the mind of Jesus Christ which Paul speaks about (Phil 2:1-8; Col 3:12-15) and which CST expresses in its notion of the common good. And this is why Christianity, when it is lived properly, can be such a powerful force in terms of shifting a culture to a vision and values that are subversive of a complacent *status quo*. Within the vision of a civilisation of love characterised by justice, it can encourage and teach values such as moderation, self-control, dialogue, respect for humanity and the earth, peace and so on – values and practices which are important if democracy is to have moral authority, and if consumption is to be responsible.[49]

This shift from egoism to concern for others is a feature of all the major religions and is another reason why the Cold War between secularists and people of religion needs to come to an end: all people of goodwill need to be in solidarity if good is to triumph. Indeed this seems to be the thinking also of the Institute for Public Policy Research, the UK's leading progressive think-tank, which in a recent, pioneering study of religious faith and the public realm in Britain, advises that 'British progressives in particular have good reason to take seriously the political scientist Robert Putnam's contention that religions remains one of the most reliable and impressive sources of social capital.'[50] The Institute authors also quote the remark of the Chief Rabbi Jonathan Sachs that 'Religion is an agent of social change, the most powerful there is', and note that he proposes that religions in Britain come together to create a 'covenant of the common good'.[51]

The hardest of us – think of Raskolnikov in Dostoyevsky's *Crime and Punishment*, his evil heart melting, like snow under the sun, before the gaze of Sonia's love – may change when eye to eye with the beauty of love. The Holy Spirit is at work in our world bringing the look of love from God, from Jesus Christ to us all. We matter that much to God, who freely 'loves us to bits', loves us in fact 'to death'. Grace, as Bonhoeffer said, is costly. And God is intimately bound up with all creation but, in particular, with each one of us and with the destiny of the human race.

If Jesus Christ is the image, and in this sense, the sacrament of God, then the church, the sphere of the Spirit, may be considered as the sacrament of Jesus Christ. As such the church is not primarily

49. M. Dolors Oller i Sala, op cit, pp 24-28
50. Zaki Cooper and Guy Lodge, eds, *Faith in the Nation*, London: Institute for Public Policy Research, 2008, p 67
51. Cooper and Lodge, op cit, p 36

self-referent, but is rather a sign to the world of God's presence. The church then points to the kingdom, which is much larger than the church itself. And at the heart of the church's own sacramental system is the Eucharist, in which we participate in that sacrifice of redemptive love of the New Covenant, are even invited to be co-sufferers with Christ in offering this sacrifice; and we share too in the meal which inaugurated this sacrifice and at which the ritual washing of feet was to be a sign of that sacrament of love and service of neighbour which is the essence of Christian living.

With this kind of notion of Eucharist, recalling the 'subversive memory' of Jesus (Metz), it is easy to see why Eamon Duffy, referring to Timothy Radcliffe's study of the Eucharist,[52] can suggest that 'to go to church, therefore, is not a comforting routine for the secure and incurious, but a place of expectation, challenge and growth: the appropriate headgear is not posh hats, but crash helmets.' In the same vein Daniel O'Leary says 'we would strap ourselves to our seats' if we understand the full impact of what was happening around us when we attend Mass.[53]

Of course it also true that often we don't live out of this understanding and that, moreover, the church itself is made up of sinners as well as saints. This is reflected in its deficiencies of acts, omissions and systems, often, sadly, of a quite scandalous and shocking nature. But nonetheless, while itself living out the mystery that the wheat and tares will be together till the end, the church has to remain faithful to her mission of being a beacon of hope to our world, by daring to take out the light of Jesus Christ from under the bushel, despite her own failings. Mostly, of course, this mission is carried out without fuss or drama in the ordinary lives of Christian women and men, being a leaven in our world, the salt that gives flavour. Occasionally there are dramatic events which highlight at world level the force for good and wonder which that more usually hidden holiness may evoke only in smaller, more anonymous circles: perhaps the funeral of John

---

52. Eamon Duffy, review of Timothy Radcliffe's *Why Go to Church? The drama of the Eucharist, The Tablet* 20/27 December 2008, p 40
53. Daniel O'Leary, *The Tablet*, 20/27 December 2008, p 4

Paul II, and the respectful media attention which it evoked, was one such occasion.

The Christian attitude to the world is one of hope rather than optimism. There can be a lot of sentimental 'ooing and aahing' at Christmas time over the baby Jesus wrapped in his swaddling clothes in a crib. But, to paraphrase Irish author and playwright Aidan Matthews, this is a sad drama which begins badly and will end worse. The scriptures themselves give the lead on this: the birth is actually in a situation of poverty and vulnerability, and early on Mary is told that 'a sword will pierce your heart'.

This is all of a piece with that almost incredible sense of risk and contingency with which the human Jesus Christ (and hence God's own self) puts his fate in our hands. Think first how dependent his very existence was on the 'yes' (*fiat*) of Mary: the scene is presented in Luke (1:26-38) in a dramatic way – Mary is disturbed, she questions, this is no computer game with a pre-scripted automatic outcome. Mary had to freely say yes: what if she had said no? And if this latter is unimaginable, think how Jesus himself hoped that the Jews would accept his good news, but they didn't, there was massive resistance and it did end badly, on a cross.

And now it is our chance, and are we, like blustering Peter, so confident that we will never betray the Lord, never say 'no'? Remember what is asked is enormous: personal conversion, to love enemies, to discover the jewels of humanity in those outside my own comfort zone, to fight for a better world not in some abstract way but now, in our concrete situation of global crisis.

This is why we speak of hope rather than optimism. Hope is there precisely when things look bleak, not rosy. Surprisingly indeed it can be found in the bleakest of places (visitors to heartbreakingly difficult situations in parts of Africa, for example, are often struck by the vibrancy of hope in apparently hopeless conditions). Hope is for the long haul, it grounds human resilience. But how are we to understand the grounds for this hope itself, a hope that we are told is certain?

Hope

The myth of inevitable progress, which fuelled modernity, has had its postmodern expression in Fukuyama's *End of History* thesis when it seemed, with the fall of the Berlin Wall, that liberal democracy and free market capitalism were somehow the final and ideal expression of human government. There have been some Christian expressions of this notion of inner-worldly progress (one thinks of Irenaeus, Joachim of Fiore, Teilhard de Chardin), but the more classic Christian theology of history is more nuanced.

In this classic view history is seen as a going out (exitus) and return (reditus) to God in which the vectors of progress, decline and redemptive love constantly interact with our intelligence and freedom in a way that is far from linear, but more like a spiral of troughs, plateaus and peaks. Within this spiral it is far easier to predict progress at the level of the scientific and technical, far more difficult to be so sure about moral progress. We have gone from the printing presses and wars of Reformation times to the computers and even more savage wars of our own times.

Christian hope takes realistic account of the power of evil at all levels and is aware of the apocalyptic scenarios which this can engender. Its form is eschatological: that is to say, it believes that God's kingdom will come fully at the end, post-history, but that already we can glimpse partial, imperfect but real anticipations of it.

The hope for universal salvation at the end, including the vindication of all those who have died without any inner-worldly justice, is expressed biblically in such terms as the New Jerusalem, 'the new heavens and new earth' (2 Pet 3:8-14), the heavenly banquet and so on. Theologically it is expressed daringly in von Balthasar's image of the cross of Christ at the far side of hell, still saving. The message is clear: despite the awful weight of evil, the terrible harm we do one another, the apparently ineluctable force of vested interests and inhumane structures, still the wonderfully creative, ever compassionate and faithful love of God will find a way to achieve the divine goal of universal salvation with complete respect for our human freedom.

But what about the 'already', the this-worldly presence of the kingdom, all the human hopes for a better world now and in our historical future? The reality and experience of evil cautions us against any facile optimism. We know too that there is no claim biblically or in CST that we have a blueprint for socio-political and economic world development. We realise that the Sermon on the Mount, as Bismarck noted, is not 'fit for purpose' as an unmediated instrument of political government. We can see the sense in the separation of spheres between church and state, even if we might rightly cavil at the relegation of the church to the private sphere alone.

But, with all these caveats, there are no grounds, in the name of 'Christian realism', to put a limit to the answer that God can give to our daily prayer of 'thy kingdom come'. With intelligence, good-will, commitment, and all in consonance with God's providential plan and dream for our world, we can celebrate the partial but so wonderful successes of the end of apartheid in South Africa, the movement for Civil Rights in the USA, the peace settlement in Northern Ireland and the many other instances of communal and personal grace which we experience right through our lives. There exists an Ariadne's thread out of the Old Testament labyrinth of seemingly eternal temptation, sin and conversion, out of the enormous struggle with evil in our world – and perhaps we can already see the emerging evidence that God can write straight on the crooked lines of our contemporary fascination with the idols of wealth and autonomy.

It is worth recalling, again, that the achievements cited above are but partial and flawed, and that God's part in them is not to be understood as some kind of magical, direct intervention. God does not work in our world like some sky wizard, 'zapping' ene-mies left, right and centre, or like a cosmic engineer, ever on hand to overcome obstacles and repair damage. Rather God's provi-dential working in the world is accomplished much more along the analogy of the way a lover is affected by his or her beloved: I am drawn towards the truth and goodness of my beloved, this changes me. There is causality at work here, but not of a blunt effi-cient kind: this is more the causality of knowing and loving, of relationship. We – and analogously all creation – are drawn and lured towards the true and the good that find their absolute per-sonification in God alone. This truth and goodness are written, as it were, into the DNA of our humanity, and implicitly or explicitly we are invited to respond accordingly. Our response will involve both knowing (the search for truth) and loving (the empowerment to do what we know is required). And thus, throughout history, in response to this patient wooing by God, imperfect realisations of the common good are achieved, not least through that self-sacrifice of redemptive love which undoes the surd of evil created by us.

We do well to remember that God, through Jesus Christ and in the power of the Spirit, is the primary actor in all this, even while our whole-hearted response and effort are required. And, as in all personal relationships, our freedom is always respected. These considerations ought to make us less anxious, less fanatical in our search for a better world – its achievement does not depend only or even mainly on our efforts, indispensable though they are. And it is consoling and energising to realise that all our desires and dreams for a better world are part of our prayer to God, part indeed of God's prayer in us, that groaning which accompanies the birth pangs and first-fruits of creation in the process of liberation and is a sign of the Spirit's working within us (Rom 8:21-23).

But it does also involve our co-operative action – the intellectual conversion that shows itself in attention to data, in steady and yet inventive reflection on problems; the moral conversion that moves us from exclusive self-interest to a commitment to the common good; the religious conversion, God's love flooding our hearts that, above all, casts out fear and mobilises intelligent action.

And within this co-operative project two other particular aspects deserve mention. First, the way God works in our world, the way the kingdom comes, has a counter-intuitive dimension to it that we need to be aware of. St Francis of Assisi, according to Chesterton, after his conversion stood on his head to indicate that he now saw the world in an upside-down fashion. Jesus gave first place to the poor, he left the ninety-nine sheep to save the lost one, he was born in a cave outside a town (no room at the inn) and, to paraphrase Aidan Matthews again, he died in a public execution as a condemned criminal in a rubbish dump outside the city, far away from our leafy suburbs. Any proposed managerial solutions to our present crisis that do not take on board this disturbing solidarity with and indeed preference for the poor and oppressed is simply missing the point and lacking credibility.

Secondly there is clearly a significant role to be played by leaders of all kinds (political, business, religious) in our search for a better world. With regard to politicians in particular, the notion of public service is crucial, very much in line with the example given by Jesus at what we call his Last Supper.

With the appearance of a leader of the stature of Barack Obama in the United States, many people throughout the world have grown in hope, even according him an almost messianic devotion. We need of course to be careful here. Jesus as the unique God-Man is the only one who can perform the decisive act which can bring about our salvation. Nonetheless, with all due respect for the inevitable obstacles and even failures which characterise the efforts of even great women and men, we do well to acknowledge that all leaders in some way participate in the Lordship of Jesus Christ, and to rejoice in the hope which gifted and graced leadership can inspire in us.

I note, finally, that the structure of our hope is trinitarian. The God who matters, origin and end of all, is revealed as our Father; Jesus Christ is the Son, our brother; the Holy Spirit is the bond of love uniting this diversity of relationship into that profound unity which permits us to speak of the mystery of the One God. We are called into this life of God, by the initiative of the Father, through the decisive *kenosis* or emptying of the Son in taking on humanity to the point of cross and resurrection, and in the power of the Spirit. This is the Trinity of St Ignatius of Loyola, presented to our imaginations as seated on the Divine Throne, looking down on our troubled world and saying 'let us work the redemption of the human race' (*Spiritual Exercises*, 106).

This Trinity of unity-in-diversity allows for the presence of the Spirit and seeds of the Word that is the Son to be present in the many world religions other than Christianity. The approach here has been from a Christian perspective. This perspective is increasingly aware and accepting of the presence of God working through all religions. The theological understanding of this truth is perhaps in an early stage of development, but already it has become apparent that the dialogue of theological ideas will learn from the other dialogues of life, action and religious experience which point the Christian towards the need to engage with devotees of other faiths in our search for a better world.

This is also a Trinity of *kenosis*, of self-emptying, of solidarity. And this *kenosis* for the Christian will involve too the movement away from another comfort zone, that of engaging solely with fellow-religionists. Instead we are called to engage and work not just with those of other religions, but also with agnostics and atheists, within that widespread culture of secularism in which there are often so many examples of that 'civic grace' which James Hanvey speaks about. Even with that bi-lingual approach of CST, in which secular language finds a home, this can be a difficult task because of the in-built resistance in the dominant liberal culture to the notion that people of faith might have a constructive and substantial contribution to make to the issues of the day. We need to avoid wallowing in a kind of victimhood in this matter (the media as anti-Christ!), and instead take our courage in our hands, be a bit more daring, and believe that in the end truth has its own powers of persuasion (and indeed, that we, as Vatican II articulated so well, have a lot to learn about the truth from our secular co-citizens).

Modernity prized the value of freedom greatly, and understood it predominantly in terms of a strong individualism with weak social ties. Postmodernity seems to allow more scope for the group or community, but with a weak, de-centred notion of the subject. Taken together they have been a fertile breeding ground for the recent dominance and excesses of the neo-liberal brand of capitalism. God, it might be agreed, is the ultimately free, autonomous Subject. And yet God is revealed to us as the trinitarian mystery, a symbol of interdependence. We, who are made in God's image and likeness, do well to take notice.

Conclusion

> '*It was an ideology, not an act of God, that made this crisis possible*' – Paul Krugman, 12 December 2008

> '*But in the words of scripture (1 Cor 13:11) the time has come to set aside childish things ... to choose our better history ... the God-given promise that all are equal, all are free, and all deserve a chance to pursue their full measure of happiness*' –President Barack Obama, Inaugural Address, 20 January 2009

We are experiencing what seems like another Babylonian captivity in the form of our current global crisis. Bewilderment, fear and anger are common: we are even tempted to lose hope.

We are in a human situation not unlike that of the two disciples on the road to Emmaus. There the stranger who joined them on the way helped them to reflect on the meaning of the past so as to open up a future full of hope.

While detailed technical solutions have been beyond the scope of this essay, it seems that there are fairly clear and agreed broad lines along which our future should go, if we can learn from our past. These involve a more socially responsible economic paradigm, with greater regulation at national but also global level.

However, it has also been proposed here that this consensus does not go far enough. There needs to be a real effort at cultural change, so that we begin to live the kind of sustainable life compatible with moderate growth expectations, respect for the environment, and an effective solidarity which rejects the gross inequalities within and between nations. We need to place the common good at the heart of our concern and to search for the new kind of economic and political models which may embody this concern. At a time of crisis we have an opportunity for this new kind of thinking, vision and values. High-flown rhetoric, a return to the heady 60s and the notion that the 'future is socialist', will not be adequate. We need intelligent problem-solving, but within a wider conceptual framework than a simple return to 'business as usual' model.

I have suggested that CST gives some pointers as to how this might be achieved. In this context we need the church itself to appropriate this teaching more fully and engage with our world accordingly. In this era of postmodernity in the West in general, but perhaps in particular because of our Irish experience of secularisation and clerical scandal, the church can seem quite timid, focused excessively on its own identity or seemingly exclusively on socially conservative issues. We seem to be somewhat complacent about the great issues of our day, complicit rather than subversive, lacking, as an institution, that passionate engagement which characterised our founder in his own day.

Obviously we need to work to change this, even if it will take time. Of more immediate prospect is the formation of clusters, movements, coalitions, campaigns, networks, even at some stage perhaps political parties, from people with a shared concern for our future. Some of these people will be inspired by religious faith, others not. Not all will agree on specific policy issues. But we can realistically hope for this kind of alliance at the level of civil society, within the kind of respectful pluralism which allows for different (religious and non-religious) sources of inspiration, but which shares the same basic concern for a more adequate expression of our common good.

And, of course, there is no simple connection between the mystery of the Blessed Trinity and fiscal stimulus packages. But I hope to have shown that 'scrutinising the signs of the times' leads to the conclusion that religion is properly and intimately concerned with this crisis of our day, in all its aspects. That while God is active – indeed is the principal actor – in our world, this is not to be conceived along the 'act of God' lines which insurance companies use to invoke the occurrence of seemingly inexplicable natural events, but rather along the lines of that transcendent origin, sustainer and end of all creation, completely respectful of human freedom, wooing us towards that relationship with the divine which people of faith acknowledge as the only ultimate satisfaction of human desire, and towards that multi-layered expression of our common good sought by all people of goodwill. And I hope to have shown that our religious faith can help us to be less afraid, give us hope, offer insight and harness energy for the next, so-important, steps of our journey, to be taken together with all fellow-citizens and fellow-human beings.

Throughout this journey we are held by the safe and loving embrace of our God, and in this gift we may trust absolutely. It is a gift presented to us above all in the person of Jesus Christ, made accessible now by his Spirit. This is precisely the point where prayer and worship, redolent of gratitude and joy, combine with an intelligent commitment to a politics that will engage in that difficult and sometimes even ferocious search and struggle for what is good. It is why French poet Charles Péguy could say that 'everything begins in mysticism and ends in politics'.

CHAPTER TWO

How Much Equality is Needed for Justice?

Critics of Ireland's decade-long economic boom often, with an eye to justice, express considerable concern about 'rising inequality and about the core features of the strategy adopted by the government to combat poverty'.[1] This is so despite the fact that since 1994 the percentage of the population living in 'consistent poverty' appears to have fallen from 16 per cent to 7 per cent.[2] However, since the late 1990s, 'relative income poverty' has persistently remained around 20 per cent, higher than it was in 1994.[3] Would it be more just to return to a poorer but more equal Ireland, or is this the wrong kind of question to ask? Can we say instead that this is not a choice Ireland needs to make?[4]

While we have systems in place to measure 'consistent' and 'relative' income poverty on a regular basis, we have no systems that routinely measure relative poverty in terms of access to health, housing, education, social supports and transport.[5] If, over the next decade, the government moved to address the issue of inadequate public services and social supports, would this satisfy critics, even if considerable relative disparities in income and

---

1. 'Poverty and Inequality', *Working Notes*, Issue 55, May 2007, p 5
2. Central Statistics Office, *EU Survey on Income and Living Conditions* (EU-SILC) 2005, Dublin: Central Statistics Office, 2006; 'Poverty and Inequality', *Working Notes*, Issue 55, May 2007, p 7. 'Consistent poverty' is defined as falling below an income poverty line (set at 60 per cent of median equivalised income) and lacking two or more items from an index of deprivation. (These items include being able to keep one's home adequately warm, being able to afford two pairs of strong shoes, having enough money to buy presents for family members at least once a year.)
3. Ibid. 'Relative poverty' is defined as having an income that is lower than 60 per cent of median equivalised income.
4. 'Poverty and Inequality', *Working Notes*, Issue 55, May 2007, p 7
5. 'Voting in Pursuit of Justice', *Working Notes*, Issue 55, May 2007, p 3

wealth remained? Or do we also need to address more directly these relative disparities, by means, for example, of greater tax equity?

And what if one goes beyond Ireland and considers the issues of equality and justice in the world at large – how are they and ought they to be linked?

Contrasting Perspectives

In a provocative piece from an avowedly Christian perspective, Mary Kenny argues that equality – except in respect of the unique value of every human person – is not Christian doctrine but rather a notion ushered in by the French and Russian Revolutions.[6] In fact, she argues, parables such as the Prodigal Son, the labourers in the vineyard, the unequal distribution of talents, all show that life is not fair, and what matters is not equality but the way you use what you have been given. And so, she asserts, what Christianity teaches is kind and loving behaviour towards everyone, as well as issuing a warning to rich people not to be greedy, cruel and arrogant, since it is true that riches often lead people astray. So, concludes Kenny, at a secular level equality theory sets people up for a life-time's unhappiness: 'If you are always comparing yourself to others on the grounds of a lack of equality, you will certainly be miserable', while in the scale of Christian values the doctrine of equality is 'historically heretical'. Is she right?

In a very different analysis, John Baker argues for the intrinsic connection between equality and poverty (and by implication justice).[7] His definition of equality is wide-ranging: it includes the egalitarian (if not strictly equal) distribution of resources, equality of opportunity, equal respect and recognition, equality in power relations and equality in relations of care, love and solidarity. Does Christianity, *pace* Kenny, entail something like this strong definition of equality?

6. Mary Kenny, *The Irish Catholic*, 19 April 2007, p 15
7. John Baker, 'Poverty and Equality: Ten Reasons why Anyone who Wants to Combat Poverty Should Embrace Equality as Well', in Combat Poverty Agency and Equality Authority, *Poverty and Inequality: Applying an Equality Dimension to Poverty Proofing*, Dublin: Combat Poverty Agency and Equality Authority, 2003, pp 12–25

CATHOLIC SOCIAL TEACHING ON EQUALITY

Human Dignity and Equality

Fundamental to Catholic social teaching is the assertion of the basic dignity and equality of all human beings. This basic equality – also asserted in secular human rights discourse, even if more as a self-evident truth than one which can be proved – is said in Catholic social teaching to be grounded in two revealed truths of the Christian faith: the creation of humankind in the image and likeness of God (Gen 1:26) and the taking on of human flesh and nature by God in the human being that is Jesus Christ. Every human person is gifted into birth by God, is called to be a sister or brother of Jesus Christ and to become part of the rich love-life of our God who is not solitary but is, by nature, relational, Trinitarian.

For Christians, this deep earthing of human dignity in the ulti-mate reality that is God explains and justifies secular human rights discourse, not to mention that instinctive grasp of human-kind's misery and grandeur which characterises literature, phil-osophy, and the human sciences down through the ages. 'Sceptre and Crown must tumble down …': in the end, beggar or king, the wonder and mystery that at our best we instinctively grasp in every human being entails a basic equality that is due to our ident-ity as beings who are from and for God.

A Framework of Principles

Given this basic equality, Catholic social teaching develops a framework of principles and values which it believes can help to structure our lives together.

We ought to live according to the principle of *the common good*, a principle which, in contrast to any notion of isolated individual self-fulfilment, entails 'the sum total of social conditions which allow people either as groups or individuals to reach their fulfil-ment more fully and easily'.[8]

This is complemented by the principle of *the universal destin-ation of goods*: even if there is a right to private property, still in

---

8. Pontifical Council for Justice and Peace, *Compendium of the Social Doctrine of the Church*, Dublin: Veritas, 2005, n 164

some basic sense the goods of the earth are for all and the use of private property involves a social responsibility.[9]

Catholic social teaching involves in particular a *preferential option for the poor*: all, including those who are poor, must have access to the level of well-being necessary for their development.[10] There must be also effective conditions of equal opportunity for all and a guarantee of objective equality before the law.[11]

The *principle of solidarity* – not a 'feeling of vague compassion or shallow distress at the misfortunes of so many people … but a firm and persevering determination to commit oneself to the common good'[12] – makes it clear that the unity and equality of humankind is marred by the existence of stark inequalities.[13]

The *principle of subsidiarity* preserves the right of consultation and decision-making at appropriate lower levels of society, avoiding the excesses of totalitarian state intervention.[14] Complemented by the values of truth, freedom and justice, the principle of subsidiarity reminds us of our role as citizens in civil society as we play our part in founding what Catholic social teaching boldly, and in almost utopian vein, calls the 'civilisation of love',[15] towards which all human striving tends.

Diversity and Inequality

Given this basic framework, with its strong presumption of equality, there is room, however, for diversity and even inequality. We know that, controversially, this notion of equality in diversity (familiar to us in Ireland in the context of the politics of Northern Ireland) has been used by the Catholic Church to defend the non-ordination of women. But even if this particular application is contentious, the principle itself need not be: so, for example, men

9. Ibid., nn 171-81
10. Ibid., n 172; n 182
11. Ibid., n 145
12. Pope John Paul II, *Sollicitudo Rei Socialis* (The Social Concern of the Church), Encyclical Letter, 30 December 1987, n 38
13. *Compendium of the Social Doctrine of the Church*, n 192
14. Ibid., nn 185-88
15. Ibid., nn 575–83

and women are different in many ways but are equal, and the world is the richer for having all kinds of other examples of equality in diversity (colours, sounds, physical characteristics, personality traits and so on).

Matters begin to get a bit more difficult and complicated when we come to the notion of the kind of diversity that is accompanied by inequality. In a comment on the remark of Jesus that 'You will always have the poor with you ...' (Mt 26:11) the *Compendium of the Social Doctrine of the Church* notes that: 'Christian realism, while appreciating on the one hand the praiseworthy efforts being made to defeat poverty, is cautious on the other hand regarding ideological positions and Messianistic beliefs that sustain the illusion that it is possible to eliminate the problem of poverty completely from this world'.[16]

These remarks do indicate that poverty is to be combated, and we may suppose that the caution expressed relates to historical experiences like the project of communism, which is criticised for its false anthropology in that basic human values, such as freedom and truth, were sacrificed in the name of a justice and equality that were not achieved. In his encyclical, *Centesimus Annus*, marking the hundredth anniversary of *Rerum Novarum*, Pope John Paul notes Pope Leo XIII's prescience in pointing up the dangers of 'socialism' – that 'The remedy would prove worse than the sickness ...'– and in warning that encouraging 'the poor man's envy of the rich' is not an adequate way to address the social question.[17]

More blunt is the comment of the US Catholic Bishops in their much-praised 1986 Pastoral Letter, *Economic Justice for All*:

> Catholic social teaching does not require absolute equality in the distribution of income and wealth. Some degree of inequality not only is acceptable, but may also be considered desirable for economic and social reasons, such as the need

16. Ibid., n 183
17. Pope John Paul II, *Centesimus Annus* (The Hundredth Anniversary), Encyclical Letter, 1 May 1991, n 12, in David J. O'Brien and Thomas A. Shannon, *Catholic Social Thought: The Documentary Heritage*, New York: Orbis Books, 2005.

for incentives and the provision of greater rewards for greater risks.[18]

Maybe Michael McDowell is closer to Catholic social teaching than we might have thought!

Wealth Creation
There is indeed in Catholic social teaching some considerable encouragement of wealth creation in terms which are rarely cited. So, there is a defence of the right of private initiative in economic matters against those who have wanted to limit it 'in the name of an alleged "equality" of everyone in society', which has resulted 'not so much in true equality as in a "leveling down"'.[19] Business planning, innovation, risk taking, wealth creation, entrepreneurial ability are all praised.[20] The church recognises the 'proper role of profit as the first indicator that a business is functioning well'.[21] There is reference to an 'authentic concept' of business competition.[22] The free market is praised as in many circumstances being 'the most efficient instrument for utilising resources and effectively responding to needs … a truly competitive market is an effective instrument for attaining important objectives of justice.'[23] All this needs to take place in the context of environmentally sustainable development.[24]

This approval of wealth creation, this utilisation of talents which are unequally distributed, must, according to Catholic social teaching, occur within a context which respects that basic framework of principles and values outlined above. And so the

---

18. National Conference of Catholic Bishops, *Economic Justice for All: Pastoral Letter on Catholic Social Teaching and the U.S. Economy*, Washington DC: Office of Publishing and Promotion Services, United States Catholic Conference, 1986, n 185
19. Pope John Paul II, *Sollicitudo Rei Socialis* (The Social Concern of the Church), Encyclical Letter, 30 December 1987, n 15, in O'Brien and Shannon, op.cit.
20. *Compendium of the Social Doctrine of the Church*, nn 336–37
21. Ibid., n 340
22. Ibid., n 343.
23. Ibid., n 347
24. Ibid., nn 461-87

US Bishops, after their remarks on the admissibility of some inequality, go on to say:

> However, unequal distribution should be evaluated in terms of several moral principles we have enunciated: the priority of meeting the basic needs of the poor and the importance of increasing the level of participation by all members of society in the economic life of the nation. These norms establish a strong presumption against extreme inequality of income and wealth as long as there are poor, hungry and homeless people in our midst. They also suggest that extreme inequalities are detrimental to the development of social solidarity and community.[25]

Love and Justice

Again and again, faithful to principles such as the common good and solidarity, Catholic social teaching condemns stark and extreme inequalities whether they exist within or between nations. Even if there are different talents, still each person and each nation has a right 'to be seated at the table of the common banquet' instead of lying outside the door like Lazarus, while 'the dogs come and lick his sores'.[26]

And so, if wealth itself is not condemned, but rather 'immoderate love of riches or their selfish use',[27] there is an obligation on the rich to act always with love for the poor, a love that involves not just almsgiving but also the social and political aspects of poverty as well as the demands of justice.[28] This will even mean that the rich, the more fortunate, 'should renounce some of their rights so as to place their goods more generously at the service of others'.[29] There is also a warning that an excessive affirmation of equality of rights 'can give rise to an individualism in which each one claims

---

25. National Conference of Catholic Bishops, op cit, n 185
26. Pope John Paul II, *Sollicitudo Rei Socialis* (The Social Concern of the Church), n 33 in O'Brien and Shannon, op cit.
27. *Compendium of the Social Doctrine of the Church*, n 184
28. Ibid., n 184. 29
29. Ibid., n 158

his own rights without wishing to be answerable for the common good'.[30]

There are several reasons given why serious disparities, inequalities, imbalances of any kind (economic, social, political, cultural, and religious) are to be avoided. When they involve the denial of basic human needs and rights, such inequalities are an offence to the basic dignity of oppressed people. When they involve an excessive gap between different sections of society or between different countries, there arises a lack of social solidarity and real community, with dangerous consequences for all (not least, by implication, the threat of violence).[31]

In more positive terms, social solidarity will bring benefit to the richer nations, both within their own countries and in their dealings with the rest of the world. Without it, they live 'in a sort of existential confusion ... even though surrounded by an abundance of material possessions ... a sense of alienation and loss of their own humanity has made people feel reduced to the role of cogs in the machinery of production and consumption'.[32]

Something of this sense of alienation can surely be observed in contemporary Ireland, as we struggle to find meaning in so much affluence, when around and about us, in Ireland and more visibly in other parts of the world, so many are clearly not 'seated at the table of the common banquet'.

IMPLICATIONS

It seems to me that a prophetic but also a wise perspective issues from Catholic social teaching on equality. The fundamental equality of all ought to result in ways of living together that ensure basic human needs are met and that relative inequalities are not so excessive as to wound solidarity and be a blight on human dignity and respect.

There is no precise measurement given in Catholic social teaching as to what might constitute excessive inequality, but plentiful indicators are provided to help in the discernment of

30. Ibid., n 158
31. Ibid., n 192
32. Ibid., n 374

particular situations.[33] Envy at the existence of a certain degree of inequality is not a sufficient indicator that there exists injustice.

Throughout an exploration of Catholic social teaching on equality, one is conscious that this is no mere abstract, academic exercise but involves real people often living in intolerable situations: there is real urgency about getting the analysis right.

Certain implications flow from the preceding discussion of Catholic social teaching. Clearly, there do exist stark and even death-dealing inequalities in our world, and in prophetic mode we need academics and activists of all kinds to engage with this evil. At the same time, there is a cautionary or wise undertow to the prophecy: a utopian advocacy of what is not achievable can result in a levelling down that is worse than what went before.[34]

In this sense, I would suggest that the Christian values of altruism, preferential option for the poor, solidarity and *kenosis* (self-emptying) are not sufficient criteria on their own for sound social and economic policies: within the notion of the common good, there must exist too a healthy respect for self-interest, wealth creation, profit, entrepreneurial risk-taking, as well as an ethic of consumption.[35]

When applied to Ireland this suggests an interesting scenario. It is certainly the case that poverty still needs to be tackled, that inequality (particularly when compared to levels in some other wealthy EU countries) is excessive, that one way to address this situation is to realise the so-called social dividend accruing from this time of affluence. And in this context there is always the

---

33. I could find only one explicit reference in Catholic social teaching to the notion of 'relative poverty' – cf *Compendium of the Social Doctrine of the Church*, op. cit., n 362

34. See also Seamus Murphy SJ, 'Utopianism, Advocacy and Consequentialism', *Milltown Studies*, No 28, Autumn 1991, pp 5-23

35. In a 1999 Pastoral Letter, the Irish Catholic Bishops' Conference argued that there is an urgent need to develop 'an ethic of consumption'. (*Prosperity with a Purpose*, Dublin: Veritas, 1999, p. 139-144) The Pastoral Letter acknowledges that this is 'probably the least developed area of the church's social teaching ...' (p 139). See also Padraig Corkery, *Companion to the Compendium of the Social Doctrine of the Church*, Dublin: Veritas, 2007, Chapter Eight.

imperative for poverty and justice lobbies to denounce injustices and skewed ways of proceeding: the default position of governments and indeed societies very often is to favour the well-off.

Constructive Dialogue

Perhaps it is also important for those of us who are inspired by Catholic social teaching to engage more constructively with the wealthy and powerful, some of whom may very well be susceptible to what Christian teaching has to say about the conduct of business, social affairs and politics.

Do we too easily fall into an exclusively oppositional mode of discourse? There is a discernment of spirits needed here: how to be true to the gospel condemnation of the danger of riches without falling into that begrudgery which is often the Irish form of envy?[36]

The preferential option for the poor cannot be discharged responsibly by prophetic condemnation only: it requires engagement with the powerful to come up with good solutions for all. The rich and powerful need to be persuaded and wooed as well as condemned; they need to be engaged with on their own turf, with respect for the issues they face: this, it seems to me, is what Catholic social teaching on equality suggests and it is what we in the church often fail to do. Constructive engagement of this kind is needed to translate values, however admirable, into workable policies.

With regard to the wider world and its scandalous inequalities, we in Ireland do well with respect to aid and issues around debt relief, but seem less aware that our trade policies are an intrinsic part of this picture. We need to move to a situation for ourselves and others in the western world where such policies are less protectionist and self-serving and more just to developing nations. And in an increasingly globalised world we need to actively seek to establish the kind of international institutions that can effectively deal with the challenges of a more equal model of

---

36. Andrew Greeley, 'Will Success Spoil Cathleen Ní Houlihan?', *Doctrine and Life*, Vol 57, No 8, October 2007, pp 46–52

globalisation at all the requisite levels – economic, political, cultural, social and religious.[37]

Conclusion

It is interesting, given the church's negative experience of the
French Revolution in particular, that equality is endorsed so
strongly. That negative experience is perhaps reflected in the careful situating of equality in the context of other values and the dislike of terms such as 'class struggle', even if, of course, there are
other, more positive reasons for such a nuanced approach.

I wonder, even if he had cared enough to bother about Lazarus
at all (Lk 16:19-31), would it ever have been possible for Dives to
literally sit down with him at 'the table of the common banquet'?
Perhaps too much divided them at all kinds of levels; perhaps this
would not have been what Lazarus himself wanted? Dives is condemned because he did nothing – a sin of omission, perhaps a
rationalisation on his part that, given all the complications, there
was nothing that he could do to make the situation better.

We are urged not to fall into the same trap of self-serving
rationalisation. No human being ought to be deprived of basic
human rights, and the gap between the better-off and the less
well-off ought to be such that, at least metaphorically, we are open
to sitting at the same table. This end-point is more likely to be at-
tained by an evidence-based approach than an ideological one, be
that ideology a discredited socialism or the predominant and dysfunctional neo-liberalism. It is an end-point worth giving one's
life to, not so much to avoid condemnation, but rather to honour
the wonderful gift to us all, rich and poor, of being created in the
image and likeness of God, called to be a sister or brother of Jesus
Christ.

---

37. 'The architecture of global governance has massive gaps in its coverage', John Palmer, 'European Integration: A Vital Step on the Road to a
New World Order', in Jesuit Centre for Faith and Justice, *The Future of
Europe: Uniting Vision, Values and Citizens?*, Dublin: Veritas, 2006, p 136;
also *Compendium of the Social Doctrine of the Church*, n 369; n 371; n 441.

CHAPTER THREE

Crime and Punishment: A Christian Perspective

At the height of the Northern Ireland Troubles, it was usual to distinguish between paramilitary prisoners and ODCs – 'ordinary decent criminals'. The terminology is suggestive, even provocative: is it ever right to consider criminals as 'ordinary', much less 'decent'? Certainly, it would be altogether wrong to trivialise the plight of victims, and especially victims of violent crime, by too lightly using a euphemism like 'ordinary decent criminals'.

Yet there are significant issues that arise concerning the current emphasis in the state's response to crime and those who perpetrate it. In a context where official figures indicate that there has been a fall in the overall level of crime over the last decade – although there has been an increase in the incidence of crimes of violence – there are more people in prison than ever before.[1]

These prisons are often over-crowded, with too little in the way of rehabilitative facilities or follow-up from other state

---

1. It is widely acknowledged that it is difficult to get a true picture on the extent of crime, due to the complexity of the phenomenon of crime, and the methodological problems in measuring it, such as under-reporting of incidents to the authorities. The official figures indicate that there has been a fall in the overall level of crime in the last decade. For example, total recorded offences in 1995 stood at 581,217 whereas the figure for 2006 was 406,163. Within this overall figure there have been increases in some forms of crime and decreases in others. What is of particular concern to the public and the authorities is the significant increase in the number of murders in the past ten years: whereas there were 43 murders in 1995, by 2006 the number had risen to 60.

With regard to imprisonment, the daily average number of people detained in Irish prisons in 2006, the most recent year for which there are official statistics, was 3,331. In 2003, the daily average was 3,176 and in 2000 it was 2,919. The daily average in this decade is significantly higher than in previous decades: in 1990, the figure stood at 2,108; in 1980 it was 1,215 and in 1970, 749.

agencies when people who have been in prison return to society 'on the outside'.[2] And since it is not clear that imprisonment 'works' – in the sense that it prevents re-offending – this would seem to indicate a predominantly punitive ethos, which is found also in Britain and the USA. This punitive ethos is encouraged by the tabloid description of the perpetrators of more egregious crimes as 'monsters' or 'scumbags': no longer human, in other words.

It is also true that the majority of those in prison come from disadvantaged backgrounds: perhaps the issue of crime is not simply a matter of 'just deserts', but is also a matter of how fairly we organise our society? Governments speak easily of a 'war on crime', but the war can often seem quite selective: it is interesting that 'white collar' crime, despite its enormous downstream implications, gets relatively little attention. Financial institutions are often subject to regulation rather than criminal law, and tax evasion is not treated like shop-lifting or any other form of stealing.

In the face of the many and complex issues involved in our concern about crime, especially the issue of the suffering of victims, how ought we to respond? Looking at this question from a Christian perspective, how might the demands of justice be satisfied in a way that transcends an exclusively punitive ethos and reaches out towards recognition of our common humanity?

In an article in *Working Notes*, Brian Grogan has very ably outlined many of the features of a Christian vision which may 'raise questions in a few minds'.[3] God wants us all to be saved; God has a special regard for the sinner (who may also be the criminal); we are asked as Christians to put on the mind of God and act accord-

---

2. For some background reading on the Irish criminal justice system, see Ian O'Donnell and Eoin O'Sullivan, *Crime Control in Ireland: The Politics of Intolerance,* Cork: Cork University Press, 2001; Ian O'Donnell and Finbarr McAuley, *Criminal Justice History,* Dublin: Four Courts Press, 2003; *National Crime Forum Report,* Dublin: Institute of Public Administration, 1998.

3. Brian Grogan SJ, 'What Does God Think of Irish Prisons?', *Working Notes,* 58, 2008, pp 9-12. See also Christopher Jones, 'Punishment and Justice', in Christopher Jones and Peter Sedgwick (eds), *The Future of Criminal Justice,* London: SPCK, 2002, pp 43-56

ingly; there is a basic solidarity which unites us all, despite the most extreme differences and opposition. The great Christian symbol of this vision is the Blessed Trinity, with the cross of Jesus Christ at its core: God understood as love, as relationship, with a profound unity, which can yet embrace plurality and diversity, and even the diversity of sin and criminality.

This is a vision which respects the demands of justice, but tempers it with mercy, and locates it within the wider context of love. The cross of Jesus 'is the overwhelming encounter of divine transcendent justice with love: that "kiss" given by mercy to justice'.[4] We are helped in an attitude of respect for the sinner, while repudiating the sin, by a truthful recognition of our own vulnerability to sin: we live in a world which God created and saw was good, but which is infected by what Christians refer to as Original Sin, so that Augustine could say without any false humility, 'There go I, but for the grace of God'.

We are helped too by the theological categories of social sin and social grace first adopted by liberation theologians. These refer to situations and structures (be they economic, social, cultural, political) which by their nature facilitate grace or, to the contrary, disgrace and sin. And so, for example, God's justice in the Old Testament is a saving justice which has particular regard for the poor, calling the rich to conversion and to an observance of the Jubilee remission of debts. The passion of Jesus for the kingdom of God is shot through with that preferential option for the poor, which Catholic social teaching identifies as intrinsic to the community of peace and justice which God wants to establish among us.

God's justice then has regard not only for acts of individual responsibility, but also for the kind of society that forms the backdrop to such acts. The inequalities in Irish society, mirrored in our treatment of crime, must rightly disturb any complacency we might feel with regard to our criminal justice system.

The Christian Vision and the 'Reality on the Ground'
Bismarck is supposed to have said that one couldn't run a state by

4. Pope John Paul II, *Dives in Misericordia*, 13 November 1980, n 9

the principles of the Sermon on the Mount. In this he was merely reiterating what Augustine (with his notion of the Two Cities) and Luther (with his notion of the Two Kingdoms) had already stated: while one could expect the individual or the church to be 'holy', or 'justified', this was not a legitimate expectation *apropos* the state. And the failed Calvinist experiment in Geneva of a theocratic state seemed to bear this out, as today do the more extreme manifest-ations of Islamic Sharia states. Indeed, this kind of position is music to the ears of many contemporary liberal secularists, who would prefer the church to limit itself to the private realm.

However, mainline Christianity and Catholic social teaching in particular think differently. There is no claim that Christianity has some blueprint for the organisation of society. But there is con-fidence that the Christian vision may offer a significant lens through which ways forward may be discerned – what T. G. Gorringe refers to as a 'structure of affect'.[5] And so, with regard to the criminal justice system, there is needed what Brian Grogan refers to as a dialogue 'among the concerned parties on possible ways forward in the highly complex and emotional arena of crime and punishment'. This dialogue must take account of all relevant factors – the responsibility of criminals, even within an unjust society (only a very small minority of poor people resort to crime); the debt owed to victims; the nature and purpose of our response to crime, including wider societal factors, and so on.

What kind of ways forward might this dialogue be expected to produce?

WAYS FORWARD

The Nature of Punishment

A dialogue might, firstly, produce a more holistic understanding of the vexed and somewhat controversial question concerning the nature of punishment as a response to crime. At a popular level, it can sometimes seem that this understanding is not so far removed from the Old Testament '*lex talionis*' of 'an eye for an eye' – a mea-sured vengeance which, at best, shades into a notion of 'just

5. T. J. Gorringe, *Crime*, London: SPCK (Changing Society and the Churches Series), p 128

deserts'. Instead, it would seem better to grasp punishment from diverse viewpoints, which taken together yield a more fruitful understanding.

So, punishment can be seen to involve:

Judgement on crime – a denunciation of what is wrong;

Retribution – in the sense of a proportionate response to satisfy the demands of 'just deserts', which might include restitution (in so far as this is possible) to the victim of crime, and a certain symbolic balancing of the injury done to the rule of law and the common good of society;

Deterrence – although the common-sense view, that this is a major factor is disputed by criminologists;

Restraint and incapacitation – in the case of criminals who are dangerous to society;

Repentance, reform, rehabilitation, leading to atonement and full re-integration into society.

In the parable of the Prodigal Son, the young man suffers the humiliation of a life of poverty abroad and the shame of returning to his father – this is his 'punishment'. But it is a punishment which is completely subordinated to the over-riding dynamic of the parable which is the unconditional love of the father and his desire to accept the erring son back into the bosom of the family.

This aspect of the Prodigal Son story suggests a challenge to us to allow the retributive aspects of punishment be subordinated to the overall purpose of reintegration and restoration. To do otherwise is to lock ourselves into the iron logic of a strict 'just deserts', which is the breeding ground for the resentment of the elder brother in the parable and, in the manner of the Pharisees, may easily become a hypocritical cover-up for our own sinfulness and need of mercy.

Societal Factors
This more holistic notion of crime and punishment must, secondly, take account of the wider societal context. Politicians find it easier to be 'tough on crime' than 'tough on the causes of crime'. I have noted that the vast majority of prisoners come from disadvantaged backgrounds: it makes sense to suppose that where society

is organised in a more just and equal way, with all being able to feel that they are stakeholders, there will be a decrease in levels of crime.

In Ireland we know that despite the great gains of more than a decade of economic success there have been downsides as well, including the lack of a social dividend in areas such as education and health (think of drug prevention and rehabilitation programmes) that impact on crime levels. There is the re-balancing to be done in terms of tackling white-collar crime with more serious intent. And there is the worrying coarsening of our society, perhaps attendant on such rapid economic success without an accompanying moral or spiritual compass, which has led to a trivialisation of sex, an upsurge in the recreational use of drugs, a widespread abuse of alcohol, a fragility in relationships and family, and, worst of all, a de-humanising violence which sees the ganglands replacing the paramilitary no-go areas. We need not exaggerate: compassion, fairness and generosity are present too in Irish society, often nourished by deep roots of spirituality and faith. Nonetheless, we do well to recognise the crude forces of a kind of social Darwinism at play in Ireland today, trumpeting the survival and flourishing of the strong and fit.

There is a wide agenda here for government, and indeed for civil society as a whole, and not just for the Minister for Justice, Equality and Law Reform: the issue of crime and punishment cannot be solved without attending to this wider context. It will not do, for example, to use prisons as a kind of 'out-of-sight dumping ground', and prisoners as scapegoats who carry our anger about crime. And it will not do either to allow ourselves to remain undisturbed by questions about societal injustices or how prisoners are to be re-integrated into a hopefully more just society.

One does not have to excuse or condone criminality to acknowledge that many criminals are themselves damaged and vulnerable individuals, victims in this sense of injustices perpetrated by individuals as well as by society.

Prison: A Place of Redemption?
Thirdly, it is sadly the case that prisoners themselves rarely exper-

ience the hope expressed by Pope John Paul II that prison might be 'a place of redemption'.[6] Despite some efforts at rehabilitation, our prisons are in general shot through with a punitive ethos. Several factors need to change here if the reality of imprisonment in our society is to be in harmony with the Christian vision.

We need, first of all, to use imprisonment as a sanction of last resort. It is a form of violence to deprive someone of their freedom. Sometimes violence may be justified – one thinks of self-defence, for example. But there are other sanctions – fines, community service, problem-solving approaches which try to tackle the underlying causes of criminal behaviour. Judges, and we as a society, need to reconsider sentencing policy in the light of the reality of a growing number of prisoners and of calls for more prison spaces, and the clear evidence that in most cases imprisonment simply does not work. This is particularly true where non-violent crime is concerned as, again, is the case predominantly with female prisoners, where the sanction of imprisonment has such drastic consequences for dependent family members and thus for society as a whole.

Furthermore, the prison experience itself ought to be one which is geared predominantly towards rehabilitation. This will mean, *inter alia*, the avoidance of over-crowding (over the last two decades we have rowed back from a century-long practice of single-cell provision); an attitude of respect on the part of all staff; the provision of educational and rehabilitative facilities (such as counselling services and drug treatment); permeable prison walls, in the sense of controlled access to and from the local community, involving fairly remunerated jobs and proximity to family members; and a chaplaincy service that relates to prisoners with those Christian virtues of courtesy, non-condemnation of the person, hope and understanding that God's power is made perfect in weakness.

None of this need be starry-eyed and soft in an unrealistic kind

6. Pope John Paul II, 'Message for The Jubilee in Prisons', 9 July 2000, quoted in The Catholic Bishops' Conference of England and Wales, *A Place of Redemption*, London: Burns and Oates, 2004, p 79. See also: www.vatican.va

of way: there is need for coercion and firmness, particularly in dealing with hardened, violent criminals. Nonetheless, we know that violence on its own simply breeds more violence. We need to create the kind of space where the person who has committed a crime can come to judge him/her self and to repent, and in doing so we need to trump the predominantly fearful ethos of a criminal justice system that looks to the past and to retribution, with a more hopeful scriptural approach, which sees justice in the context of a resurrection forgiveness that looks more to the future. From the Christian perspective, it will never do to write someone off as less than human, as incapable of free conversion and repentance. In this context too it will be important to employ a multi-agency approach in the re-integration of the person into society after the prison term has been served.

If one adds to all this the conventional best-practice wisdom that imprisonment with a view to rehabilitation is best realised in smaller-sized units, close to local community and family members, and that women, young people, and people with mental illness should not be co-located with adult male prisoners, then one can see that many disturbing questions are raised about the prospective Thornton Hall project now under way in our state.

Victims
Fourthly, we need to respond much more sensitively and effectively to the needs of victims of crime. It is true that we have become more aware in recent years of the trauma experienced by victims and the support they require to get their lives back on track, in particular where there has been violence involved. The parable of the Good Samaritan indicates the kind of practical and loving response which can make a great deal of difference to victims of this kind.

There is, however, also an issue in justice regarding the way our criminal justice system operates. The professionalisation of this system, and its specialised, formal, and to the lay person often very abstruse, ways of proceeding can result in an alienating distancing of the victim from judicial proceedings. This arises above all because, in contrast to some traditional legal systems, the state takes the place of the victim in criminal law so that the process can become a contest between state and offender with the victim as an almost incidental witness.[7] The introduction of victim-impact statements was clearly an attempt to address this problem.

Restorative Justice
Fifthly, we need to explore fully the potential of the various modes of restorative justice (including elements of mediation, re-integrative shaming, and reparation) which bring victim and offender, voluntarily, together in a controlled and respectful way, with the fall-back position of recourse to the conventional means of proceeding within the criminal justice system if this does not work.

One interesting feature of the success to date of this approach in other jurisdictions is the perhaps counter-intuitive finding that what victims want is not simple revenge or punishment but rather recognition, explanation, and some reassurance that no one else will suffer in the same way that they have. But then, again, perhaps we (and judges, who after all, are human and therefore responsive to public opinion) are over-influenced by tabloid vitriol when it comes to offenders: more considered attempts to establish what is public opinion have shown that the public is more interested in a justice that embraces reparation and rehabilitation than any simply punitive model.[8]

Indeed, it would seem that some kind of restorative justice model might work best not just for victims but for offenders and society as a whole, and be more in tune with the Christian vision of justice. To this end, one looks forward with interest to the outcome of the work of the seven-person National Commission on Restorative Justice, chaired by Judge Mary Martin, whose interim report was submitted in March 2008.[9]

7. Gorringe, op. cit., pp 116-117; p 124
8. Irish Penal Reform Trust, 'Public Attitudes to Prison', February 2007 (www.iprt.ie); O'Donnell and O'Sullivan, op cit, p 73; *Report of the Committee of Inquiry into the Penal System* (The Whitaker Report), Dublin: Stationery Office, 1985.
9. National Commission on Restorative Justice, *Interim Report*, March 2008, Dublin (www.justice.ie).

Conclusion

I have noted that the Christian vision of justice does not admit of any simplistic application to the secular sphere, nor does it provide a blueprint which gives all the answers. However, it does provide an orientation which can be helpful in reinforcing our better instincts and taming our more savage ones. In this case, it points in a direction of a criminal justice system which legitimates proportionate punishment and the demands of victims for justice, but which locates crime in the context of society as a whole and prioritises the rehabilitation of criminals, with a reduced and more humane use of imprisonment as a sanction. This is a radical position, one which we are failing to take in this state.

I have indicated how this might affect current policy in a number of areas: one could apply the same logic of inference to all other areas of the criminal justice system, including, for example, the need for fair legislation and the resourcing and accountability of the police force.

The radical position indicated above would require a good deal of re-thinking of present theory and practice, but it is a position that, apart from being more just to all concerned, would also be to the benefit of all, for our common good. We are then, as often, faced with a choice: do we, like the Priest and Levite, pass by on the other side, and drift on? Do we care enough?

There does seem to be something like this kind of 'drift' operative often in government policy and in our public response – instead of facing problems head-on, analysing them carefully, consulting all the interested parties and coming up with solutions which have widespread support, we tend to get 'solo' runs, with resultant adversarial recrimination and defensiveness. One thinks of issues such as the decentralisation of government departments and agencies; our health service in general and the co-location of private and public hospitals in particular; and now, in the justice area, the Thornton Hall project. And one contrasts this with the meticulously painstaking, intelligent, dedicated approach to a solution of the Northern Ireland problem. We are capable of better.

CHAPTER FOUR

Some Christian Perspectives on Health and Sickness

Introduction

'There's nowt so queer as folk' – this, now non-politically correct, maxim from the North of England applies pretty well to the common human experience of taking good health for granted, while becoming anxious at the onset of illness. But, of course, there may be good reason for such anxiety – even minor ill-health causes inconvenience and loss of energy, while major illness, chronic or acute, brings great suffering and raises serious life and death questions. In what follows, I want to propose some Christian perspectives on health and sickness that may help to address some of the questions that arise at both a personal and a societal level.

Jesus Christ and Health and Sickness

We are not told if Jesus ever caught a cold or suffered from a migraine. We do know, however, that he experienced human weakness; that 'he was like us in all things except sin' (Heb 4:15); that he wept at the news of the death of his friend Lazarus; that, in one version of Luke, in his anguish at Gethsemane 'his sweat fell to the ground like great drops of blood' (Lk 22:43-44).

Moreover, we do also know that when he preached his central message of the coming of the kingdom of God, he accompanied it with many miraculous healings. When the disciples of John the Baptist came to enquire if he really was the Messiah, he answered by saying: 'Go back and tell John what you have seen and heard: the blind see again, the lame walk, lepers are cleansed, and the deaf hear …' (Lk 7:22). And he could also have mentioned the healing of the many people the society of the time deemed to have 'evil spirits', who we may conjecture were suffering from mental illnesses of various kinds or epilepsy.

HEALING MINISTRY OF JESUS

There are several aspects to the healing practice of Jesus that give us an insight into his – and so, we believe, God's – attitude to health and sickness.

Compassion

First, Jesus always agrees to heal, and we are often told that he does so because he has compassion. Of course, one might say, this is only what could be expected: if he was a good person, if he had this power, then why not? But there is a deeper layer of meaning involved here. Jesus is implicitly telling us that our salvation, that deep friendship with and love of God which is our destiny, that 'life to the full', includes physical and mental health as values to be cherished. Ill-health, then, is at least a pre-moral evil, and is to be avoided.

This attitude is a far cry from a notion of salvation that is purely spiritual or, indeed, from a notion of illness (present in parts of the Old Testament tradition) as a punishment from God – 'Rabbi, who sinned, this man or his parents, for him to have been born blind?' 'Neither he nor his parents sinned,' Jesus answered (Jn 9:1-2). Of course, we may bear some responsibility for illnesses which afflict us – individually because, for example, of our choice of poor diet or lack of exercise; communally, for example, because of our creation of a hazardous environment or our tolerance of social and economic conditions that damage health. But good people sometimes needlessly compound their own anxiety with the often unspoken notion that their illness is due to the fact that God is 'out to get them'. Nothing could be further from the attitude of Jesus in the gospels. Jesus wants to heal and it is part of his mission to his disciples that they continue his ministry of healing.

Need

Secondly, it is clear that the ministry of healing which Jesus exercises is conditioned by need, not by class, nationality, or ability to pay. We can suppose that those he healed were mostly poor: this, of course, was the largest social group at the time, and the group with which Jesus most identifies. Nonetheless, he is not deaf to the plea of the synagogue official, or to the faith of the Roman centurion. The only time that Jesus even questions this universal, inclusive approach is in relation to his encounter with the Syrophoenician woman whose daughter had 'an unclean spirit' (Mk 7:24-30) but, perhaps learning from the insistent need of the woman herself, he decides firmly in her favour and in favour of inclusivity.

The Kingdom

Thirdly, the kingdom that Jesus preaches is to come in the future and yet is already among us. Theologians use the term *eschatologi-cal* to express this reality: the fullness has yet to come, but there are anticipations, given as a pledge of that fullness, already present. Jesus, then, did not cure everyone who lived in Palestine in his day. In fact, according to St Paul, sickness and weakness may sometimes have a beneficial effect in God's plan for us: '… I was given a thorn in the flesh … about this thing I have pleaded with the Lord three times for it to leave me, but he has said, "My grace is enough for you: my power is at its best in weakness" … so I shall be very happy to make my weakness my special boast … for it is when I am weak that I am strong' (2 Cor 12:7-10).

This surprising slant on what we spontaneously view as nega-tive is quite often borne out in our experience, and not just in a faith that 'hopes against hope'. So, for example, you will hear someone who has recovered from a serious illness express the conviction that now they appreciate life in an altogether different, more profound way, while others will testify to the life-changing experience of being loved as never before in their situation of ill-ness and vulnerability.

This perspective is reinforced by the remark elsewhere in Paul that 'it makes me happy to suffer for you, as I am suffering now, and in my own body to do what I can to make up all that has still to be undergone by Christ for the sake of his body, the church' (Col 1:24). This line of thought is re-captured in the intuition of Martin Luther King that 'unearned suffering is redemptive' – the intu-ition that at the heart of the world is a struggle between good and evil which only a redemptive love involving sacrifice and suffer-ing can resolve, that Jesus Christ is the one who brings about this resolution, but that, graciously, he has allowed us a part in this resolution through our own offerings of a love that will sometimes suffer.

This third aspect makes it clear that sickness, and even death, are best understood according to the premise of St Augustine's theodicy that God 'judged it better to bring good out of evil than not to permit evil to exist at all'.[1] Nonetheless, there is real negativity here, at least a pre-moral, physical evil, and the predominant tone of the New Testament is to encourage prayers for good health and healing, which are regarded as symbolic anticipations of the final coming of God's kingdom.[2]

Social Aspects

Fourthly, it needs to be noted that there are inherently social aspects to the healing practice of Jesus. What I refer to here is not just the inclusivity of his ministry, but also the reality that, for poor people in particular, illness could involve the stigma of being 'unclean' in a way that cut them off from the worshipping community. We are told that there were as many as 248 commands and 365 prohibitions making up the Law, many of them to do with dietary matters and hygiene.[3]

Apart from the fact that knowledge of the Law became the prerogative of scholars and the establishment, the poor, as always, were more likely to suffer from illness. And so, when Jesus cures a leper, for example, or casts out an 'evil spirit', one needs to reckon with the fact that what is involved here is not merely a personal matter but also the re-integration of that person in the community. Leprosy, in particular, is often a 'catch-all' title for various skin diseases, often due to poor diet and hygiene, which resulted in automatic expulsion 'outside the camp' – precisely where Jesus himself ended up at his crucifixion, such was his identification with the poor and sick.

---

1. Gabriel Daly OSA, *Creation and Redemption*, Dublin: Gill and Macmillan, 1988, p 161
2. Dermot Lane, *Christ at the Centre*, Dublin: Veritas, 1990, pp 30-31
3. Gerald O'Collins, *Interpreting Jesus*, London: Chapman, 1983, p 51

Discipleship of Healing

There is, fifthly, the way in which the healing practice of Jesus ought to be understood today. While living in Northern Ireland in the 1980s, I attended many Protestant Pentecostal and Evangelical services which often included a healing dimension: one was encouraged to believe that if one had faith, one would be healed. On the Catholic side, there has been a resurgence of interest in this kind of healing service through the Charismatic Renewal movement, while there has been a more constant belief in the power of healing associated with holy places such as Lourdes and Knock, not to mention the intercession of saints and holy people like Padre Pio and John Sullivan. And why not – after all, did not Jesus give this mission to his disciples, did he not say, in sending them out to the whole world, that 'they will lay their hands on the sick, who will recover' (Mk 16:18)?

There are two dangers in any simplistic reading of this understanding of what discipleship might involve. One concerns the so-called prosperity gospel approach, popular in parts of the United States in particular but often exported more widely. This approach teaches that if you have faith – if you *really* have faith – then life will be good, you will make money, and you will have good health. Well, apart from this being a mis-reading of the sense of the Bible taken as a whole (neither money nor health is the ultimate criterion of the good life) it also can be psychologically very damaging – think, for example, of the seriously ill person who does not experience healing after prayer, and who now may feel the burden of guilt and depression at his or her presumed lack of faith, or may doubt in the very existence of the God who could comfort at a time of suffering.

The other danger is that this approach ignores, or undervalues, the principal way in which God works in our world through us. St Irenaeus liked to speak of Jesus Christ and the Holy Spirit as the two hands of God the Father. Carrying on this theme of instrumental causality, St Ambrose spoke of every worker being 'the hand of Christ'. In other words, the principal way in which God is present in our world, in which his kingdom comes, is through the conscientious, competent, inventive work of us human beings.

And so there is the human desire to help the sick, the medical skill that is required, the social and bureaucratic policy and organisation that can make those desires and skills as universally available as possible – this is at the heart of Christian discipleship of the healing Jesus in our world of today, a mission we gladly share with those of all other and no faiths.

None of this ought to be taken as denying the rightful place (and the power) of prayer, or of the turn to holy places and people for help. The Catholic Church, in particular, has made a sacrament of this 'turn to God' for help, the Sacrament of the Anointing of the Sick (still, it seems, too closely associated only with the kind of sickness which is close to death, and so still in practice often conjuring up the older title of the Sacrament of Extreme Unction). We are talking about 'both/and', not 'either/or' – as applies, indeed, across a whole range of related topics which are often reduced to alternatives of separation rather than distinctions of relationship (for example, religion-science; religion-politics, and so on).

This more inclusive approach makes intellectual sense because ultimately all is 'in God's hands'. God is working through the skilled individuals and systems that are the professional healers of today. There is also a great deal that these professionals don't know, strange things happen (as is evidenced, for example, in the old tradition of faith-healers), and the believing Christian will have faith not just in the God-inspired professionals but in the mysterious irruptions of the kingdom into our 'now' that accompanied the ministry of Jesus and that can, as St Ignatius put it in a different context, occur today as instances of 'consolation without cause'.

Vision and Values
From this consideration of the healing practice of Jesus, to which we might add his other prescriptions regarding a moderate lifestyle, we may extrapolate a notion of the person and society in which health of mind and body – a holistic model of health care, in today's jargon – is intrinsic to the Christian vision. In an earlier study, the Jesuit Centre for Faith and Justice along with the Adelaide Hospital Society outlined four principal values which

we argued ought to accompany this vision: care, excellence, justice and freedom.[4] It remains to comment briefly on some perti-
nent implications of the social implementation of this vision and
these values.

Social Implications
The principal source of the nuanced application of the teaching of
Jesus to the social arena is to be found in our day in Christian
social ethics, and for Catholics in Catholic Social Teaching. I limit
myself to two observations taken from this corpus of teaching.

First, with reference to the question of introducing a system of
universal health insurance, the attitude of Catholic Social
Teaching to the free market is worth recalling.[5] On the one hand,
the teaching is appreciative of the positive value of the free market:

> It would appear that, on the level of individual nations and
> of international relations, the free market is the most effic-
> ient instrument for utilising resources and effectively re-
> sponding to needs.

However, the teaching is also acutely aware of the limits of the
market:

> But this is true only for those needs which are 'solvent', in-
> sofar as they are endowed with purchasing power, and for
> those resources which are 'marketable', insofar as they are
> capable of obtaining a satisfactory price. (*Centesimus
> Annus*, n 34)

The market, then, is never sacrosanct, but rather:

> It is a strict duty of justice and truth not to allow fundamen-
> tal human needs to remain unsatisfied, and not to allow
> those burdened by such needs to perish. (*Centesimus
> Annus*, n 34)

4. The Adelaide Hospital Society and the Jesuit Centre for Faith and
Justice, *The Irish Health Service: Vision, Values, Reality*, Dublin: 2007.
5. For what follows, see Pope John Paul II, *Centesimus Annus* (On the
Hundredth Anniversary of *Rerum Novarum*), Encyclical, 1 May 1991.

And so, useful though the market is, 'there are important human needs which escape its logic', and an 'idolatry' of the market 'ignores the existence of goods which by their nature are not and cannot be mere commodities' (*Centesimus Annus*, n 40).

One needs to avoid a fundamentalism in applying Catholic Social Teaching, just as one needs to avoid a biblical fundamentalism. And so the application of this teaching concerning the value and limits of the free market to the issue of health care in any particular context needs, as always, to be guided by prudent political judgements and not some *a priori*, however sacred in source, ideology. However, given what we know about the workings of the free market in our world today, given in particular the experience of the United States of America (following a free market approach) with the highest expenditure *per capita* in the world for health care and the worst outcomes of all developed countries, then it really does behove us in this country to ask whether indeed it is better to be closer to 'Boston rather than Berlin'. Our two-tier health system in Ireland is a scandal; it offends against justice and the socially inclusive practice of Jesus Christ, and it requires radical reform.

Secondly, with the increasing professionalisation of health care, its tendency to be seen nowadays as a job rather than as a vocation, there is real need for the value of care to be understood as going beyond technical expertise. When people are sick, 'they may be vulnerable, dependent, needy, and issues of intimacy and trust come to the fore'.[6] In this context, it is wise for civil authorities to attempt to integrate this aspect of care into professional training, but also to allow, and indeed where necessary (one thinks of chaplaincy services) subsidise, the more explicitly vocational approaches of voluntary and religious groups which address this real need.

Conclusion
There are many positive realities in the Irish health service, not least the competence and dedication of those working within it,

---

6. The Adelaide Hospital Society and the Jesuit Centre for Faith and Justice, op cit, p 3

and there have been real improvements too – one thinks, for example, of what is happening in the provision of more reliable can-
cer diagnosis and treatment. However, a Christian perspective
would also identify severe shortcomings, which include the basic
model employed which, with over-reliance on the free market,
perpetuates the private-public divide, widening and deepening
the two-tier nature of the service. And, in the holistic context that
this Christian perspective offers, it is also appropriate to ask questions about the level of provision of social care and support services
and our society's commitment to addressing the income inequality
and lifestyle factors which endanger public health.

CHAPTER FIVE

Europe and the Roman Catholic Church

The political mood in Europe at time of writing (2006) is rather querulous. The proposed Constitutional Treaty has been rejected by referenda in France and The Netherlands. There is a tetchiness over budgetary matters (including different approaches to reform of the Common Agricultural Policy and to allocation of funds to accession states), and there remains a distinct cooling of attitude on the part of some to Turkish accession. Because of fears about terrorism, there is a tendency to get tougher on immigration control and there is a new uncertainty about integration policies in countries such as France and the United Kingdom. Real differences are apparent on how a social model of Europe can be balanced with the workings of the free market. And all the time there is the impression that ordinary citizens find it difficult to engage with European issues, so that the 'democratic deficit' is in danger of leading to the kind of self-interested and isolated nationalism which the founders of the European Union sought to combat and which is all the more out of place in our increasingly globalised world.

One gets the sense of the need for a new vision and for a more shared commitment to that vision. *The Tablet* (26 November 2005) reported that: 'Catholic Bishops meeting in Brussels have welcomed the European Commission's renewed efforts to bring Europe closer to its citizens through a more coherent communications strategy.' (p 33) Bishop Josef Homeyer, President of the Commission of the Bishops' Conferences of the European Community (COMECE), is quoted as saying: 'People are very insecure at the moment. The EU is faced with a very serious situation – perhaps the most serious since it came into being 50 years ago ... yes, we are in a deep crisis ... But this is an opportunity to relaunch Europe.' And, in this context, he signaled the willingness of COMECE and the Roman Catholic Church to make a positive contribution.

It might seem surprising to many that the Catholic Church sees itself in a position to make a positive contribution to a re-launch of the European project. What resources does the church bring to this relaunch and how credible is its contribution likely to be?

The Roman Catholic Contribution

Churches have an important role to play in European civil society and do so in many ways – through schools, universities, hospitals, publications, and so on. I want to focus on one, albeit central, as-pect of the Catholic Church's contribution, namely its teaching on Europe. The most authoritative contemporary document articu-lating this teaching is the Apostolic Exhortation, *Ecclesia in Europa*, of the late Pope John Paul II (2003), which followed on from the Synod of Bishops' Second Special Assembly for Europe in 1999. The members of the church itself are the primary target audience for the document, but its content has relevance to a wider public.

What emerges from this document is Pope John Paul's under-standing that Europe is going through a difficult time of fear and his desire to offer it hope for the future. He does so because he clearly values the European project, seeing in it an 'affirmation of the transcendent dignity of the human person, the value of rea-son, freedom, democracy, the constitutional state and the distinc-tion between political life and religion'. (n 109) He notes positively the adherence to values of solidarity and subsidiarity in the European Union (n 110), so that at least normatively it wants to in-clude the poor and less strong, and respect national and cultural differences. He does so, too, because he is conscious of the responsibility and great potential Europe has for the rest of our world: 'Saying "Europe" must be equivalent to saying "open-ness"' (n 111) – and this means openness not just to immigrants but also to the rest of our increasingly globalised world so that we need to rethink 'international co-operation in terms of a new cul-ture of solidarity'. (n 111) To this end, he encourages the different

European institutions to continue to develop in ways that can better promote values such as solidarity, justice and peace in our world.

Much of this could, of course, be written by a non-religious person, as the late Pope implicitly acknowledges when he states that the solid foundations needed for the building up of the new Europe are those authentic values grounded in the universal moral law written on the heart of every man and woman. He quotes from his letter of October 2000 to Cardinal Miloslav Vlk, President of the Council of European Episcopal Conferences: 'Not only can Christians join with all people of good will in working to build up this great project, but they are also called to be in some way its heart, revealing the true meaning of the organisation of the earthly city'. (n 116) There need not be any triumphalism involved in this specification of the Christian role: Pope John Paul does not want a return to the confessional state (n 117), only a respectful dialogue between the European Union and religious confessions which can be to mutual advantage (n 114). And if Europe itself must learn from its failures to handle conflict well, from its history especially in the last century 'of totalitarian ideologies and extreme forms of nationalism' (n 112), then the church, too, must be careful not to be seen as a factor of division and discord: 'Would this not be one of the greatest scandals of our time?'(n 119)

However, John Paul does, of course, want to say that Christianity has specific resources to contribute to this project which will be realised together with all men and women of good will. He is certainly referring here to various international, European, and national institutions through which the Roman Catholic Church acts in our world (n 116-119 especially). But more particularly he is referring to Jesus Christ and the gospel itself, with the good news there that we need not be afraid, that our grounds for hope are sure, and that values such as freedom, justice, peace and forgiveness as found in the Christian tradition (not least in Catholic social teaching) can be a powerful reinforcement of humanitarian efforts towards a better world. And so, 'in keeping with a healthy co-operation between the ecclesial community and political society, the Catholic Church is convinced that she can make a unique contribution … by offering the European institutions, in continuity with her tradition and in fidelity to the principles of her social teaching, the engagement of believing communities committed to bringing about the humanisation of society on the basis of the gospel, lived under the sign of hope.' (n 117) From the gospel then can come a new enthusiasm for Europe. (n 120)

The Pope, therefore, is offering the church's support for those humanitarian values consonant with the gospel, which can form the basis for a vision of Europe into the future. He goes further, of course, in diagnosing the current fear and lack of energy in relation to the European project as due to the loss of its spiritual roots, and in prescribing a new evangelisation of Europe as being the way to reinvigorate the project: 'Do not be afraid! The gospel is not against you, but for you. This is confirmed by the fact that Christian inspiration is capable of transforming political, cultural and economic groupings into a form of coexistence in which all Europeans will feel at home and will form a family of nations from which other areas of the world can draw fruitful inspiration.' (n 121)

Value of this Contribution
Ecclesia in Europa threads a fine line between allowing for the rightful autonomy of earthly affairs, as articulated in *Gaudium et Spes* (Vatican II, 1965, n 36), and yet refusing to countenance any dualism between the gospel and public life. It does so well: the separation of church and state is clear, while the potential for constructive dialogue is also asserted.

For Christians the content is helpful, and even inspiring. This is a wake-up call to rouse us from apathy about the European project, to appreciate its great potential to realise important gospel values, not least the peace that has come to the original EU members through the workings-out of the Franco-German alliance and the freedom and justice, long overdue, which are characteristic of the new accession states of Eastern Europe. It remains to be seen whether the more cautious tone of the document concerning Islam might not change as the injunction to grow in knowledge of other religions is realised (n 57) – and certainly this remains a key task for the churches, not least in the context of talks leading up to the possibility of Turkish accession to the EU.

But there is also an opportunity here for secular humanitarians from the liberal and social traditions to respond positively. For many secularists, religion can be almost synonymous with superstition or divisiveness or indeed both. And so there can be a tendency among liberals to be less than tolerant – in fact illiberal – towards the religious viewpoint, be it fundamentalist or more mainstream. Many are now questioning the wisdom of this stance. They are doing so, firstly, because, stubbornly, religion has not and will not go away: it remains a potent force in many people's lives, and so politically it is important to try to understand it. And if at its worst (the religious wars in Europe of the past, the appeal to Islam in support of terror in the present and the misuse of the gospel by the 'religious right' in the USA in response) this potent force is destructive, then at its best it is liberating: the influence of religious factors, starting in Poland, on the fall of communism was considerable. In either case, it needs to be understood, not dismissed or denied. Secondly, and more significantly, post-modernism has trenchantly criticised what it diagnoses as the bias of modernity's rejection of the transcendent and is calling for a re-enchantment of our world. In this context, the poignant words of Nietzsche are apt: 'Where has God gone? … I will tell you. We haved slain him – you and I … but how did we do it? How could we drink up the sea? Who gave us the sponge to wipe out the whole horizon? What did we do when we unchained the earth from its sun? … Do we not now wander through an endless nothingness? Does empty space not breath upon us? Is it not colder now? Is not night coming, and even more night? Must we not light lanterns at noon? God is dead. God stays dead. And we have slain him …'. (Quoted in Thornhill, 2000, pp 31-32)

If this existential loneliness and sense of demoralising aimlessness can be assuaged by a divine presence that is not simply wish-fulfilment but, rather, is true, then surely our situation is so much better? And, if this is a step too far, too quickly, then at least it surely makes sense for religious and secularists to come to some kind of respectful settlement of their dispute so that together they can get on with their common aim of striving for a better Europe and a better world? Cannot religion be a help in replenishing the moral capital of liberalism, be it in its modern or postmodern form and without threat to the gains of the enlightenment? (Vallely, 2005)

Credibility of the Church's Contribution

The content of a teaching may propose what is true and good and yet for different reasons, not least the credibility of its source, it may not be heard. It seems that many people, including those who might describe themselves as being on the edges of the Roman Catholic Church, no longer listen sympathetically or at all to what the church officially teaches. What can the church do to enhance its credibility?

The late Pope himself has some ideas on this topic. He notes the need for conversion within the church itself: 'One sees how our ecclesial communities are struggling with weaknesses, weariness and divisions. They too need to hear the voice of the Bridegroom, who invites them to conversion ... In this way Jesus Christ is calling our churches in Europe to conversion ...'. (n 23) This need for conversion, for a lived, intimate contact with Jesus Christ will, of course, be central to the 'new evangelisation' which John Paul II called for so insistently. It is what distinguishes the church from being just any other well-meaning NGO. The Pope's own transparent faith was exemplary in this respect. We as church in Europe need to pray for this conversion and to appreciate its centrality for our mission. Holiness has a certain transparency, which carries its own conviction even to non-believers.

But holiness – which is what conversion is about – is one among several factors which are likely to impact on church credibility. As well as the centrality of the spiritual in the lives of human beings, several other dimensions spring to mind as being so important as to affect the credibility of any institution which claims to teach about what it is that makes up a good and happy life. I refer in particular here to the dimensions of money, sex and power. With regard to the economic dimension, while there are negative comments sometimes about the wealth of the church, it seems to me that its teaching on wealth is well-respected and the witness of many individual Christians reinforces this teaching in a way that prevents this becoming a major stumbling block to credibility. It is different with respect to sex and power, however, so that I wish now to focus more particularly on these two important dimensions of human living.

The Church and Sex

For most human beings the search for meaning in life – and so for God – is most real in the struggles and joys surrounding the attempt to relate to and love significant others – parents, siblings, spouses, children, and so on. Because this is so, for Catholics the credibility of the church will depend significantly on the extent to which they can expect wise counsel with respect to this central aspect of life. The richness of church teaching concerning the fundamental principles that should inform such key relationships – respect, commitment, fidelity, love, for example – is overshadowed by the fact that many Catholics are disappointed, not to say dismayed, with what the church has to say with regard to aspects of sexuality. This inevitably leads to a lack of confidence in church teaching generally.

What is at issue here? In conversation with committed Catholics over the years many points have been put to me on this matter. Let the eponymous Deirdre act as spokesperson for these views. Deirdre is in her thirties, believes in God, has been baptised a Catholic, has studied some theology and 'hangs in' with the church even though she disagrees with important aspects of church teaching in the sexual area. She respects greatly the church's wisdom in locating the powerful drive of sexuality within a more integral emotional and personal context, and within the parameters of a relationship of exclusive commitment. She appreciates also the condemnation of the exploitation of women in church teaching, and agrees with the cautions against the development of a 'contraceptive mentality'.

Nonetheless, Deirdre cannot understand or accept the normative weight and value given to the distinction between natural and artificial methods of birth control. It seems to her that this distinction relies on an excessively physicalist interpretation of natural law, which is not applied with the same absoluteness to other areas of life – for example, to the use of medication or to the judgements to be made about genetically modified food. She knows that the church has only relatively recently accorded equal value to the notion that sex is important for the good of the relationship of a married couple (the unitive dimension) as well as for purposes of fertility (the procreative dimension), and she is concerned that there remains apparent in the church an excessively fearful and controlling attitude to sexuality in general and to women in particular. She wonders if this attitude is not due, in part at least, to the fact that the teaching authority of her church is still very much in the hands of male celibates.

And this doubt about the reliability of church teaching in the area of contraception – which she is aware is widely shared by many other Catholics and, indeed, by many theologians – leads her to question the wisdom of teaching in related areas. She appreciates the value of church teaching on abstinence in the context of the fight against HIV / AIDS, but is aghast that there is not a more open acceptance of the morality of condom use in the context of disease prevention. She has some friends who are divorced and are now in stable second unions but are not welcome to participate fully in the Eucharist. She wonders in this context if the church has not over-emphasised its theology of Eucharist as a *sign* of unity over the other tradition of Eucharist as a *means* to unity – a tradition which, she understands, is normative in the Orthodox Churches and which Rome has never seen as a stumbling block to unity with these churches. She thinks it is odd that these friends of hers are made to feel less comfortable joining the line of people going up to receive communion than people who have been involved in corporate greed, racism and tax evasion.

Deirdre wonders if the designation of homosexuality as 'objective disorder' is not again due to a one-sided interpretation of the natural law, as well as being a nightmare in terms of communicating a message of respect for people who are homosexual. She values the gift that celibacy is for the church and is aware that a married clergy is not without its own problems, but wonders nevertheless if the discipline of the Western church concerning compulsory clerical celibacy is desirable or indeed sustainable, given the needs of the church and the drop in priestly vocations, not to mention the good in itself of having clergy who are married.

She is incredulous and angry at the church's refusal to consider the ordination of women and at its attempt to stifle discussion on the topic. She is aware that already in the 1970s the Pontifical Biblical Commission had stated that there is no absolute ban on women priests from a scriptural point of view. While acknowledging that there is a long tradition of priesthood being reserved to males, she knows that other venerable traditions of the church have changed over time, often due to shifts in cultural and moral sensibility (for example, the teaching on slavery), so the length of the tradition is not in itself an insurmountable obstacle to change. And if the argument for the *status quo* is to be sought in a theological anthropology, which asserts that male and females are equal but different in a complementary way, which suggests the suitability of priesthood for men and not women, then Deirdre begs to demur. She knows that this anthropology is controverted and is not convinced by it.

Even allowing for the notion that the equality between women and men does contain within it a difference between male and female that is not simply biological, Deirdre, relying on her own experience but aware too of the body of academic work which supports her view, would want to interpret this difference less rigidly. She affirms that women too are made in the image and likeness of God, women too can exercise leadership roles, and only a very paradoxically literalist understanding of symbolism would deny that women too can represent Jesus Christ in his love for us unto death. If scripture, tradition and theology can offer no conclusive obstacle to the ordination of women she finds it unacceptable that the church wants to curtail further discussion of this matter. All these issues coming together create a doubt for Deirdre about the reliability of church teaching in the contested and highly significant field of bio-ethics in general.

Apart altogether from the particular answers to any one of these difficult and extremely relevant questions, Deirdre senses what she can only describe as a controlling approach and a reliance on a particular form of natural law and anthropological essentialism which result in a stance that lacks compassion and even wisdom. So, for example, because the physical act of intercourse can, and sometimes gladly does, lead to conception does not mean, in her view, that it should always, even in principle, do so. The meaning of that physical act has to be understood, in her view, in a wider context, which takes account of many factors other than the physical alone. And similarly, as already indicated, she is not convinced that, given all we know nowadays about gender and about the new roles which women have assumed, maleness and femaleness should be differentiated in such an absolute way as to indicate so clearly that God cannot call women to ordination in the church.

Deirdre knows that in expressing these disagreements and doubts she will be understood by some as taking the easy way out, unable to accept the 'hard sayings' of the gospel, asking the church to accommodate revealed truth to modern and post-modern culture in a reductive way. But she rejects this understanding. She says simply that she believes the church is wrong on some of these issues, may be wrong on others, and has changed many times in the past. She argues that 'hardness' and 'softness' are not properly criteria of truth and so do not come into the question – she adheres to the wonderful good news of Jesus Christ about love of friend and enemy. This good news brings its own suffering and joy and is at the centre of the bigger picture which, she believes, is too often obscured by excessive attention to and insistence on relatively insignificant details of sexuality which somehow seem almost divorced from the wider context of love in which they belong.

In fact, Deirdre is only too well aware that our overly-sexualised culture is all at sea and that the church has some wonderfully wise and helpful things to say in this area, but she believes that because its stance on particular issues is so mistaken then it loses much of its credibility. She herself now listens to the latest church pronouncements on sexuality with something of a sigh and half an ear, and this has begun to affect her respect for the authority of the church in other areas too.

Deirdre's position, then, does bring up the related issue of power and authority, to which we now turn. Her hermeneutic of mistrust in the sexual area has been reinforced by the revelations concerning clerical sexual abuse of minors and in particular by the inadequate response of church authorities.

The Church and Power

In *Ecclesia in Europa*, Pope John Paul II recognises that the credible proclamation of the gospel to Europe depends, among other things, on the service of theologians who are encouraged to 'persevere in the service which they render, to combine their scholarly research with prayer, to engage in attentive dialogue with contemporary culture, to adhere faithfully to the *magisterium* and to co-operate with it in a spirit of communion in truth and charity, immersed in the *sensus fidei* of the People of God and helping to nurture it.' (n 52) It is wise that the theologian pays attention to these several sources – and there are others too – of theological truth rather than playing a solo game. It is wise in particular that theologians have a real desire to think with the church, to have a positive attitude towards the acceptance of church teaching, without, of course, suspending all critical faculties.

However, a difficulty arises when there is a conflict between the different sources of theological truth. Such a conflict clearly arises in the sexual area, in particular with the teaching in the encyclical, *Humanae Vitae* (Pope Paul VI, 1968). The eponymous Deirdre is not an isolated figure: there is 'the virtual non-reception by many theologians and a large percentage of the laity in some countries of *Humanae Vitae* on contraception.' (O'Donnell, 1996, p 401) Of course it is true that the 'sense of faith' of the faithful and their reception of truth – both significant technical terms within theology – are not a simple matter of counting heads, nor are they a precondition of true magisterial teaching. However, reception – the acceptance by the faithful that what their pastors teach is authentic and life-giving – is an important sign that teaching is definitive. Where there is non-reception serious questions must be asked, even if it is not always immediately clear what the reasons might be. These reasons might have to do with human perversity, blindness, hardness of heart on the part of the receiving faithful, but they might also have to do with a teaching that is false in whole or in part, and so cannot be binding (O'Donnell, 1996, p 401).

Perhaps the task of a bishop was never easy, but certainly it is true that few people in Ireland today would envy those who have been called to serve the gospel in this way. How might bishops, many of whom would claim no special theological expertise, respond to someone like Deirdre? I think the issue here is not so much one of theological expertise *per se*, but rather a decision to listen carefully to what people are saying, to try to sift and discern what is genuine and true from what may be more superficial, and then to bring this to the table of the Episcopal Conference and higher. Of course, that decision – to listen, discern, represent – does imply a theology of what it is to be a bishop that may be somewhat different from the prevailing one. Many bishops seem to feel that Rome leaves them very little freedom in these matters of church teaching, but the theology of episcopal collegiality in Vatican II surely implies that a bishop has a duty to listen to the Spirit in his own life and in his own diocese. It is only by doing this that collegiality and a sense of what all the faithful think and believe can have any real meaning. Otherwise, collegiality simply becomes another name for a rubber-stamping conformity and the church is robbed of the richness that comes from diversity, a diversity that can include doctrinal development.

It is often said, when discussion of these topics comes up, that the church is not a democracy, as if this was the answer to all issues about power and truth. In fact, there have always been democratic aspects to the gospel and the church, at least as understood in the wider sense that is sufficient for my proposal here. What I mean by this is that neither did Jesus Christ rely solely on himself to come to truth, and nor has the church done so down through the centuries. We can be sure that Jesus learned from and was corrected by his parents, his community and others. It seems that he learned something very significant about his mission – that it might extend beyond the Jewish people – from his encounter with the Syro–Phoenician woman (Mk 7:24-30). Peter certainly learned from Paul – and indeed from his own dreams! – about the mission to the Gentiles. The bishops of the fourth century learned from the laity about what the Council of Nicea was asserting about the truth of who Jesus Christ is. Galileo has taught the church, even if he was not heard at the time. John Courtney Murray influenced the church to change a centuries-old stance on religious freedom and was only one of many at the Second Vatican Council whose positions were vindicated in a way that resulted in significant doctrinal development over against what seemed to many like unchangeable church teaching.

Ecclesiastical historian Eamon Duffy has written extensively and well about the wonderful gift to the Roman Catholic Church that is present in the *magisterium* and especially in the papal teaching office (Duffy, 2004, chapters 7-9, 16-19). They are essential to hold the diversity of the church together in a communion that allows the designation 'universal' to be applied. Many other Christian traditions, with all their strengths, have a propensity to fragmentation that makes them look with admiration to what we as Catholics enjoy. But if we should treasure this gift we should also seek to enjoy it in a way which avoids a certain tendency to claim that all teaching is equally definitive and also integrates other values, not least respect for truth and that careful listening to the faithful which I have spoken about and which bishops have a special opportunity to foster, as well as a more generous and accountable attitude and procedure in monitoring theological reflection.

One of the lessons we have all learned from the terrible scandal of child sexual abuse by priests and religious is surely that silence and denial about important truths are not good ways to proceed. In the matter of child sexual abuse, they have led to the unspeakable suffering of victims as well as to a strong anger, a sense of betrayal and almost even despair among so many others in the church. But in other areas also, including those referred to in this article, silence and denial at best bring a false peace, without sure foundations. At worst, they encourage an anti-intellectualism and mediocrity of mind and heart which shirk awkward questions and answers and which run the risk of laying intolerable burdens on the shoulders of good men and women. Pope John Paul II has quite rightly condemned the 'totalitarian ideologies' (n 112) which darkened Europe in the twentieth century: we as church need to avoid any totalitarian tendencies in our own conduct of affairs, combining firmness of decision with a serene confidence in the power of the Holy Spirit to bring truth and life out of open debate and even disagreement. It is surely not healthy to live as a church with disagreements which can only be aired at the cost of being labelled disloyal?

Conclusion
I have indicated that church teaching on Europe has an extremely important and valuable contribution to make, not least at the visionary level but also in critiquing wrong turns and lending additional moral weight to directions that are good. I have also pointed out that there is a danger that the church's voice will not be heard as widely as it deserves – both within and outside its own community – for reasons that are not directly associated with the content of its teaching on Europe. I refer to the credibility problem that the church as institution has – in particular with its teaching in the sexual area and its tendency to exercise power in a way which stifles dialogue with opposing voices. This credibility problem extends, of course, to non-Catholics as well as Catholics: references to the universal moral law and natural law do not convince non-Catholics when they issue in the kind of sexual teaching that I have referred to and when they are commended to the assent of the faithful by what are perceived as excessive reliance on appeals to the power of authority in contrast to judgements emerging from a more reasoned and inclusive dialogue in search of the truth.

There are signs of hope that this situation may change. Many bishops now encourage more lay involvement in church affairs, not least by the establishment of parish councils. Lay people themselves are more theologically literate and pastorally competent, and many want to claim their baptismal mission by playing a more active role in the church. Some bishops have shown a willingness to listen carefully to what people are saying, to face the awkward questions, to show a collegial independence of mind in the answers they give and to bring their concern to higher bodies in ways that are encouraging. And Pope Benedict XVI (2005) in his beautiful encyclical letter, *Deus Caritas Est*, has shown that when the church speaks out wisely in matter of love and sex, fair-minded people are appreciative. However, there is still a long way to go, resistance is deep, a big cultural shift is required.

There is an 'elephant in the room' of the Catholic polity. It is its teaching on certain aspects of sexuality and related areas, and its exercise of power in seeking to impose this teaching. There is a delicate discernment to be made – are Catholics who disagree with this teaching more in tune with the 'signs of the times' or are they simply disobedient, perhaps selfish, selling out to the pre-vailing values of the culture? And given that many do agree with the teaching and have made considerable sacrifices to follow it, given that despite its more general unpopularity in this important area of human living, the church does still retain a great deal of credibility in other areas, perhaps it is better to go on ignoring the elephant rather than putting the church through the turmoil of a review of teaching with all the likely concomitant turmoil and conflict.

But there was turmoil in the early church when the mission to the Gentiles was being discussed, and many times later when sig-nificant changes happened. Surely we need to be more confident, if not in ourselves, then in the power of God's Spirit to lead us into the deep and into truth? I am arguing that the non-reception of church teaching in a central aspect of people's lives damages the credibility of the church and that it would be a good thing to exam-ine the reasons for this non-reception and emerge from the uneasy silence which now obtains. Cardinal Martini has several times called for a new council of the church, in the context of discussing some of the issues I have referred to. And in Ireland there have been intermittent calls for a synod or some such gathering. I be-lieve these kinds of fora, organised with good consultation and participation, may well be what is needed at this time to release the imagination and renew the energy of our church so as to allow the good news of Jesus Christ be heard more clearly.

References

Duffy, Eamon (2004) *Faith of our Fathers: Reflections on Catholic Tradition*, New York and London: Continuum.

O'Donnell, Christopher O Carm (1996) *Ecclesia, A Theological Encyclopedia of the Church*, Collegeville, Minnesota, The Liturgical Press.

Pope Benedict XI (2005) *Deus Caritas Est* (God is Love), Encyclical Letter, 25 December 2005, London: Catholic Truth Society.

Pope John Paul II (2003) *Ecclesia in Europa* (The Church in Europe), Post-Synodial Apostolic Exhortation, 28 June 2003.

Pope Paul VI (1968) *Humanae Vitae* (Human Life) Encyclical Letter, 25 July 1968, London: Catholic Truth Society.

Thornhill, John (2000) *Modernity: Christianity's Estranged Child Reconstructed*, Grand Rapids, Michigan: Eerdmans.

Vallely, Paul (2005) 'What Europe Now Needs is Faith', *The Tablet*, 12 November 2005, pp 6-7

Vatican II (1965) *Gaudium et Spes* (Pastoral Constitution on the Church in the Modern World), 7 December 1965 in Austin Flannery OP (General Editor) *Vatican II: The Conciliar and Post Conciliar Documents*, revised edition 1988, Dublin: Dominican Publications.

PART TWO

Islam and the Public Square

CHAPTER SIX

Asking the Right Questions:
Christians, Muslims, Citizens in Ireland

Our neighbour, eight-year old Muhammad, arrived at the front door on Hallowe'en night in the guise of Darth Vader; he was flanked by two other children from the road, disguised as a pirate and the devil. Later, his eleven-year old sister, Selma, arrived on her own, gorgeously dressed as a witch. As they departed with their trick or treat goodies, I recalled the words of President McAleese, addressed to Muslims in Ireland at the tenth anniversary celebrations of the Islamic Cultural Centre in Clonskeagh, Dublin: 'Your being here helps us and keeps challenging us to find ways to be joyfully curious about each other ... we, I hope, will try our best to make Ireland a country of real welcome and a country of celebration of difference ...'[1] Are the President's words realistic or are they naïve? I want to explore the kinds of questions we need to put to one another as Irish citizens so that obstacles to the realisation of the President's hopes can be overcome.

Muslims in Ireland
The 2002 Census of Population recorded that there were 19,147 Muslims in Ireland, of whom 17,979 were 'normally resident' in the country. Over 5,000 gave their nationality as Irish.[2] When the full results of the 2006 Census become available it is likely they will show the Muslim population of Ireland to be between 25,000 and 30,000.[3]

Ireland's Muslim population is estimated to include more than 42 different nationalities from many different parts of the

1. *The Irish Times*, 27 October 2006
2. Central Statistics Office, *Census 2002*, Volume 12, Religion, Dublin: Stationery Office, Table 4a, p 17
3. Email from Census Enquiries Section, Central Statistics Office, 31 October 2006

world – the Middle East, Africa, Asia, and elsewhere, including countries such as Egypt, Malaysia, Pakistan, Indonesia, Somalia, China, South Africa, Nigeria, Algeria, Libya, Bosnia and Turkey.[4] It is generally reckoned that the majority of Muslims in Ireland have a solid educational background and so, not surprisingly, are listed among the top five socio-economic and social class groups in a break-down of the 2002 Census figures by the Central Statistics Office.[5] It is estimated also that there may be in excess of 3,500 asylum seekers among them.

Religiously, the Muslim population is mainly Sunni, with up to 2,000 Shi'a; there is also a number of sects and sub-sects within these groups, including Sufis (who focus on the more mystical side of Islam), Barelvis (who are popular in South Asia), Deobandis (most common in Pakistan and India), and Salafis (similar to Wahhabism in Saudi Arabia). The two biggest Sunni mosques in Dublin are at Clonskeagh and the South Circular Road, while the Shi'a community's mosque is in Milltown. Outside Dublin the only purpose-built mosque is in Ballyhaunis, Co Mayo. Many Muslims outside Dublin and Ballyhaunis (there are vibrant communities in Cork, Galway, Limerick, Cavan, Ennis, Tralee, Meath and Waterford) gather to pray in converted warehouses, rented houses or private homes. There are up to 4,000 Muslims in Northern Ireland, the majority coming from Pakistan.

Diversity and Unity
There is, then, considerable diversity among Muslims in Ireland deriving from different nationalities, languages, the distinction

4. For these figures and for what follows, see Kieran Flynn, 'Understanding Islam in Ireland', *Islam and Christian–Muslim Relations*, Vol 17, No 2, April 2006, pp 223-238; Stephen Skuce, *The Faiths of Ireland*, Dublin: Columba Press, 2006, Ch 4; Mary Fitzgerald, *The Irish Times*, 13 October 2006.
5. Even if, somewhat curiously, around 7,900 (out of 19,147 Muslims in Ireland) are recorded as being in the category, 'socio-economic status' and 'social class' categories, 'All others gainfully occupied and un-known'. Central Statistics Office, *Census 2002*, Volume 12, Religion, Tables 20 and 21, pp 114-115.

between Sunni, Shi'a and others, liberal and secular, as well as more mainstream and even stricter interpretations. Given this diversity, it is more accurate to speak of 'Muslim communities' rather than the shorthand 'Muslim community'.

In this context, it has been difficult to establish an overall governing body and umbrella group organisation for all mosques and Muslim organisations in Ireland. The Supreme Council of Muslims was formed 'with the general though uncommitted confidence of Muslim leaders' in 2005.[6] More recently, the Irish Council of Imams was launched in Dublin on 19 September 2006, representing all 14 imams in Ireland of both the Sunni and Shi'a tradition and wishing to speak with authority on relevant issues on behalf of the Muslims of Ireland.[7] Chaired by Imam Hussein Halawa of the Islamic Cultural Centre of Ireland at Clonskeagh, its Deputy Chairman is Imam Yaha Al-Hussein of the Islamic Foundation of Ireland on Dublin's South Circular Road, while its General Secretary is Ali Selim. It lists among its aims the encouragement of the positive integration of Muslims into Irish society; the provision of social and educational programmes for imams; the formation of a specialised official Muslim body to give the Islamic view on topical issues in Ireland; dialogue with people of other faiths and the spread of the spirit of Islamic tolerance. Unlike other religious bodies in Ireland, its remit does not seem to extend to Northern Ireland.

Obstacles to Dialogue
What then are the obstacles to the kind of mutual enrichment and tolerant dialogue which President McAleese and the Irish Council of Imams hope for as Muslims in Ireland – many of them already Irish by birth and most of them well educated – negotiate a space for themselves in Irish society?

Shortly after the President's address at Clonskeagh an *Irish Times* columnist wondered: 'How is our legal system to deal with the Islamic claim that Muslim men have a right to physically chastise their wives?'[8] In the same edition of the newspaper, a corre-

6. Kieran Flynn, op cit, p. 229.
7. *The Irish Times*, 19 September 2006.
8. John Waters, *The Irish Times*, 30 October 2006.

spondent to the Letters Page who had worked in Saudi Arabia for five years queried the wisdom of a school in Tallaght arranging a special parent-teacher meeting for Muslim women who were uncomfortable being in the same room as men who were not their husbands: 'In their ignorance they believed they were integrating these people, but I feel this is a very dangerous step to take. What next? Separate waiting rooms in hospitals, doctors' clinics, dental clinics, etc?'[9]

These are but two instances of a more general fear which many Irish people have that somehow our values and our way of life may be threatened by the presence of Muslims among us. Sometimes this fear finds its focus on the seemingly small questions of dress. The wearing of the head-scarf or hijab has not become a contentious issue in Irish society, but the furore over Jack Straw's remark in October 2006 about the face veil or niqab provoked much public interest and debate in this country. It may be asked: Is the niqab a sign of difference so extreme as to indicate alienation, perhaps even radicalisation, and so not to be welcomed?

Lurking under the surface of these questions is the even deeper fear and bigger question of physical violence and terrorism. The claims of Sheikh Shaheed Satardien, who is associated with the Supreme Muslim Council of Ireland, that Muslim clerics here were 'in denial' about rising extremism within certain elements of the community in Ireland were rejected by clerics and many ordinary Muslims.[10] Similarly, the Taoiseach was reassuring in the Dáil about the report from declassified official US papers that up to six Islamist terrorist groups had units in the Republic three years ago to deliver financial and logistical support to other cells abroad.[11]

Influences on the Debate
This deeper fear is, of course, shaped by recent events outside Ireland, such as the murder of film-maker Theo van Gogh in

9. Joan Barry, *The Irish Times*, 30 October 2006.
10. Mary Fitzgerald, *The Irish Times*, 13 October 2006; see also Patsy McGarry, *The Irish Times*, 19 September 2006.
11. *The Irish Times*, 24 October 2006.

Holland, the controversy over the Danish cartoons and the Pope's Regensburg address. It is influenced too by the terrible unrest in the Middle East: the pivotal and ongoing Israeli-Palestine conflict, the suspended war in Lebanon and the ongoing violence in Iraq. It reflects the disquiet in some places regarding the possibility of Turkish accession to the EU with, among others, some prominent political and church leaders expressing extreme caution, if not outright disapproval. One can add to all this the ongoing tensions in other European countries such as England and France about issues of integration, assimilation and multi-culturalism.

It is clear, then, that dialogue in Ireland is inevitably influenced by the wider European and world situation as it unfolds. What may seem, at first, like a relatively quiet and containable conversation among ourselves is, in fact, joined by the many clamouring voices of our contemporary world.

And the conversation is joined by not just the voices of today, but also those from history. Think of the folk-memory of the Crusades, the long period of Islamic greatness and imperialism, which ended with the fall of the Ottoman Empire in the early twentieth century. But, in reality, Islamic imperialism was overtaken centuries before that by Western modernity with its enlightenment and industrial revolution, its science and technology, its capitalism and democracy, its separation of church and state, its rule of law and declaration of universal human rights.

The Partners in the Dialogue
One can readily understand that many Muslims worldwide might have a love-hate relationship with this Western world as they try to make their own attempts at coming to terms with modernity. They can be envious perhaps of the obvious successes, resentful at the arrogance that goes with it, angry at what is perceived as the imperial and partial stance of the world's only surviving superpower (the USA), frustrated at their own slowness in adapting to the modern era, and deeply critical of what they see as Western moral bankruptcy on so many fronts.

And in this context they have as dialogue partner a Western world in which the project of secularism increasingly reveals its own narrow base and lack of moral capital.[12] In significant ways, Ireland exemplifies this: with all the welcome successes of our Celtic Tiger, this is a country still failing to match social with economic progress, to provide for the have-nots of our society, and where values are often compromised so that, for example, our culture is excessively sexualised in ways that damage both physical and emotional health and puts enormous pressure on young people in particular.

And we have a Christian faith which is less sure of itself. Sometimes, it is so tolerant in its inclusive pluralism that one wonders why in the end it is important at all to want to be a Christian; sometimes (as in the Religious Right in the USA) it is so intolerant as to rival anything that so-called Islamic fundamentalism can produce. And all the time, Christian faith in the Western world is faced with the challenge of trying to renegotiate its own space in the public square as well as its relationship to other religions.

Questions for the Way Forward
Given this heady cocktail of diverse factors, how can the different partners in our Irish conversation – Muslims, Christians, members of other religions, citizens of the state and of our island – engage in the kind of conversation that overcomes simple denial on the one hand and cultural panic on the other? It may help to identify some of the deeper questions and issues behind the obstacles that I have already mentioned.

Let us take as a starting point the seemingly small question of the veil. Is this, in whatever form, a strict requirement of the Qur'an? Muslims themselves seem to differ on this, so that, for example, in admittedly secular Turkey, women attending university are forbidden to wear it and many devout Muslim women in Europe and elsewhere, now and more so in the past, have not worn it. Culturally, one can well understand that in certain situations women themselves want to wear the veil for many different reasons – for example, as a mark of their identity, in particular when feeling under threat from their socio-political environment.

---

12. For a development of this theme, see Gerry O'Hanlon, 'Religion and Society', *Studies*, Vol 95, No 378, 2006, pp 141-152 – chapter 9 here.

Many say they experience wearing the veil as empowerment, not oppression.

However, one also notes the kind of underlying issue that is involved here and that some Muslim women themselves articulate. As one Muslim commentator has pointed out: female modesty in most religions tends to make women 'the bearers of honour and shame, the repository of sexual ethics and family values ... the problem with this is that it also camouflages a lot of the abuse and subjugation that goes under the guise of honour.'[13]

Clearly, the disputed question of the religious normativity of veil wearing within Islam is vital both to the issue of the equality of women and men and to the issue that Jack Straw raised as to how Muslim women negotiate a space for themselves in public life.

Religious Authority within Islam

Several more major questions can be seen to follow. If the religious normativity of the veil within Islam is disputed, who has the authority to settle the dispute? In fact, while there are subtle differences within the different branches of Islam itself on this matter of religious authority, in particular between Sunnis and Shi'as, the bottom line seems to be that it is one of the glories of Islam that each Muslim decides for him/herself before Allah. Of course, imams, representative bodies, the fatwahs (or legal pronouncements) of respected clerics and scholars, are all taken into account: but there is certainly nothing like the normative role played by the *magisterium* within the Roman Catholic Church. In practice, of course, it can be hoped that a body like the Irish Council of Imams will speak effectively for the Muslims of Ireland.

Nonetheless, this structural reality of Islam in respect to authority is important to bear in mind when one listens to the different interpretations of the Qur'an worldwide, not just on a matter such as veiling, but on issues of life and death like suicide bombers. Islam has good claims, both historically and within its own self-

---

13. Professor Mona Siddiqui, Director of the Centre for the Study of Islam at Glasgow University: 'To me, as a devout Muslim woman, the veil has become a totem issue.' *The Tablet*, 14 October 2006, p 9

understanding, to be a religion of peace and tolerance.[14] But it be-
muses many how respected and often charismatic Islamic leaders
can justify the killing of innocent women and children by means of
suicide bombers.[15] During our own terrible conflict, the churches in
Ireland on all sides were often, with some justification, accused of
not doing enough to bring about peace. But it would have been
truly shocking had any church leader tried to justify republican or
loyalist violence.

The Authority of the Qur'an

Another question which follows from the issue of the veil is the
much more delicate one of the authority of the Qur'an itself.
Christians need to understand that within Islam the text of the
Qur'an is viewed with the kind of reverence which Christians
themselves might show not just to their own scriptures but almost
to Jesus Christ himself. The Qur'an, with the hadith (the documented traditions of the teachings and actions of the Prophet
Muhammad which were not in the Qur'an but which were recorded
for posterity by his close companions and family members) and
the Sunnah (the habits and religious practices of the Prophet,
similarly recorded) are what Muslims base their faith on. These
are the foundations of Shariah, the body of Islamic sacred law,

---

14. For example, see Seyyed Hossein Nasr, 'Islam and the Question of
Violence' and Khaled Abou El Fadl, 'Islam and the Theology of Power', in
Aftab Ahmad Malik (ed), *With God on Our Side, Politics and Theology of the
War on Terrorism*, Bristol: Amal Press, 2005, pp 273-276 and pp 299-311.
15. In a series of articles on Islam in Ireland (*The Irish Times*, October 2006)
Mary Fitzgerald, refers to views expressed by Sheikh Yusuf al-Qaradawi,
chair of the European Council for Fatwa and Research (ECFR). (The
Council has its headquarters at Dublin's Clonskeagh Mosque, its serving
Secretary General being Sheikh Hussein Halawa, himself Chair of the
Irish Council of Imams.) Sheik al-Qaradawi is, apparently, seen by many
Muslims as a charismatic and moderate reformer who helps seam Islam
with modern life and who has enormous influence. Yet he is reported as
supporting Palestinian suicide bombings, justifying civilian casualties on
the basis that Israeli society is 'militarised'. And in respect of the verses of
the Qur'an which seem to allow physical chastisement of wives by husbands, he has stated that such chastisement is not obligatory or desirable
but is acceptable if done 'lightly' as a last resort.

which has lead to Fiqh (Islamic jurisprudence – the study and application of the body of sacred Muslim law).

In practice, the interpretation of both the Qur'an and Shariah
has differed considerably down through the centuries, even if
Sunni Muslims declared in the fourteenth century that the 'gates
of ijtihad' (ijtihad is the 'independent reasoning' used by a jurist to
apply the Shariah to contemporary circumstances) were closed
and that scholars must rely on the legal decisions of past authorities instead of upon their own reasoned insights.

Much of this will recall for Christians the old, now essentially
resolved, Roman Catholic-Protestant dispute between the authority
of scripture itself and that of tradition, as well as our on-going
Christian concern to read, through the Holy Spirit and the church,
the signs of the times of our day in the light of sacred scripture. But
this resolution of the intra-Christian dispute drew on all the critical thinking of the enlightenment, the application of historical-
critical studies to the scriptures and patristic studies, and resulted
in a very real appreciation of the inherently human form of divine
revelation. There is an understandable nervousness even among
otherwise progressive Muslims about submitting their sacred
text to this kind of investigative scrutiny, and yet there are signs
that it is happening.[16]

Shariah Law

A final major question arises from this seemingly small issue of the
veil: are Muslims intent on creating a Shariah-law society wherever
they are in the majority? This is a major question because it lies behind many of the fears which non-Muslim Westerners (including
Irish) have when they view the kind of restrictions imposed on
citizens and other religions in some countries with Muslim
majorities. They wonder is this the kind of future which Muslims
in the West are obliged by their religion to strive for?

Again, only Muslims in the end can answer this question,[17] but

16. Toby Lester, 'What is the Koran?', *The Atlantic Monthly*, Vol 383, No 1,
January 1999, pp 43-56
17. I note in this respect the Islamic Charter drawn up by the Central
Council of Muslims in Germany (ZMD), which says, *inter alia*: 'There is

a few observations may be helpful. First, it is clear that several major countries with Muslim majorities do not understand Islam in this way – Turkey, for example, can have serious aspirations to EU membership only because its state is constitutionally secular in a way that can pass the test of EU membership, and Indonesia is a similar example.

Furthermore, both historically and at present, the interpretation of what is meant by Shariah law is very different and all kinds of modifications are being made today to marry Shariah with various forms of democracy: the Taliban of Afghanistan are not the only model of what Muslims have tried to do in terms of a government that is inspired by the Qur'an. Interestingly, in this context, the former Pakistan cricket captain, now politician, Imran Khan is reported to have said that the closest example he has ever seen of an ideal Islamic society in the world today is Sweden![18]

Religion and State

This is interesting, because well worth examining is the notion that a really worthwhile debate can be held between the Islamic concern with justice and its self-understanding as a 'total religion' (i.e. as applying to all aspects of life, including politics) and the Christian experience in the West of the different forms of church-state separation which have become normative. Khan can hold up Sweden as an example of a good Islamic society because of its concern with justice. Christians hold up the necessity of church-state separation because of their own experience of religious wars and the need to create space for the accommodation of difference. But it took Christians a long, and often bloody, time to come to this understanding. (In the case of the Roman Catholic Church, it took until the 1965 *Decree on Religious Liberty* in the Second Vatican Council, even if in reality the situation on the ground for Catholics was already changing in that direction in most countries of the West.)

no contradiction between the divine rights of the individual, anchored in the Qur'an, and the core rights as embodied in Western human rights declarations.' Michael L. Fitzgerald and John Borelli, *Interfaith Dialogue: A Catholic View*, Maryknoll, NY: Orbis Books, 2006, pp 130-131
18. Mary Fitzgerald, *The Irish Times*, 27 October 2006.

Maybe as we develop a better climate for dialogue, Muslims can learn a bit from the Western Christian experience in this area. But perhaps we Christians and citizens in the West can also learn from the Muslim insistence on the relevance of religion for public life. Christianity too is a 'total religion': it has a passion for justice at its core; it claims to have important things to say about all areas of life. While the current separation of church and state serves well as a governmental structure,[19] its actual implementation too often relegates religion to a private sphere which impoverishes society and the common good as well as domesticating religion.

These, then, are some of the questions to Muslims that might be part of our ongoing conversation. I have noted *en route* questions that need to be addressed to Christians – for example, the relevance of religion for public life, the limits of pluralism. I have noted, too, questions to be addressed to citizens of all beliefs or none – for example, how do we learn in a liberal democracy to treat religion less illiberally, how to draw on the resources of religion and secular humanism to correct the moral blemishes in our society. Muslims in Ireland can sharpen these and other questions to us in our ongoing dialogue.

---

19. This, by now common, church teaching is expressed in a striking way in a statement from a joint meeting of African and German Bishops: 'Experience shows that relations between Christians and Muslims can be guaranteed and enhanced by a legal framework that includes the rule of law, equal citizenship, human rights in the political, economic and cultural fields, religious freedom, good governance and the promotion of justice and peace ... That is why the church, in line with the teaching of Vatican II, advocates a secular state order ... Any legal provisions which are derived from religious traditions and teachings of only one religion, as for instance the prescriptions of the sharia, understood as a religio-politico law, are incompatible with this understanding of civic order. ... There is nothing wrong in expecting Muslims to accept that religious demands derived from Islamic law can only be enforced within the legal framework of a democratic secular state.' (*Christians and Muslims – Partners in Dialogue*, Sixth joint meeting of African and German Bishops, Akosombo, Ghana, 10–15 October 2004, Bonn: Secretariat to the German Bishops' Conference, pp 32-33)

Ways Forward

Good dialogue is not a bland exercise in being nice but is precisely a robust exchange with those who are different and yet whom one respects. It is an exercise in overcoming obstacles as one engages in a common project. We have seen the difficulties with the assimilation model of integration in places like France and the multi-culturalism model in England. Assimilation does not allow sufficient legitimacy to difference, while multi-culturalism does not lead to sufficient integration. Some people in Ireland now, including Minister for Justice Michael McDowell,[20] are talking in terms of inter-culturalism: a seeming third way which would respect difference but without sacrificing integration.

For this to happen, we need to be more pro-active in setting up fora in Ireland at many different levels to encourage a sharing of information, dialogue, and working together of the different communities involved.[21] The government should give the lead here: already, it has committed itself to a formal dialogue with faith communities and other non-confessional organisations. This is to include Muslim leaders, and, according to the Taoiseach, is scheduled to begin 'within months'.[22] And beyond the issue of struct-

20. Text of address given on behalf of Michael McDowell TD, Minister for Justice, Equality and Law Reform, to a conference, 'Changing Shades of Green: Pluralism and the Changing Face of Ireland', organised by The Milltown Institute, in association with SPIRASI and the Irish Missionary Union, in The Milltown Institute, 13 October 2006.
21. I note the by-now conventional four-fold distinction in inter-religious dialogue between different forms of dialogue – of life, action, religious experience and theological exchange. This distinction alerts us to the reality that while conceptual and even dogmatic clarity have their importance, still there are other ways to engage humanly, and there are can even be surprising compatibilities arising from life experience and action which might not seem likely viewed from a formal intellectual analysis. See also Sadik J. Al-Azm, 'Islam and Secular Humanism', in Islam and Secularism, Antwerpen: Universitair Centrum Sint-Ignatius Antwerpen, 2005, The Dialogue Series 2, pp 41-51
22. An Taoiseach, Bertie Ahern TD, as reported in *The Irish Times*, 16 November 2006. This dialogue (to be 'open, inclusive and transparent') was announced by Dermot Ahern TD, Minster for Foreign Affairs, in a speech at the Irish College in Rome on 13 November 2004 (Department of Foreign Affairs, Press Release, 15 November 2004).

ures for formal dialogue, there is the question of the social policies across a range of areas – for example, education, housing, support for community initiatives – that can encourage integration.

But apart altogether from action at governmental level, we need as citizens and religious people in civil society to find ways to encourage this kind of interaction as well. Can church parishes find ways to find common ground with Muslims in their neighbourhood? Are there common concerns regarding the environment and other issues of justice in our society which can bring together people of diverse backgrounds, including Muslims?

We need in particular to be better informed about one another. Muslims need to learn more about the self-understanding of Christians: our view of the death of Jesus Christ, for example; what we like and dislike about Western values; our attitudes to the so-called War on Terror.

Christians need to learn more about the self-understanding of Muslims. Despite the strong identification worldwide of Muslims with one another through the *ummah* – the Muslim community globally – there are nonetheless many significant differences. Predominantly Muslim countries have gone to war with one another, and the majority of Muslims worldwide are not Islamist jihadists intent on worldwide domination through violence.

Isolation or Participation?
The danger is that, if we are not pro-active, the Muslim community in Ireland will develop separately. In his study of Islam in Ireland, Kieran Flynn notes a typology of integration, from the British context, that included a 'spectrum of types', consisting of, among others, collective isolation and limited participation.

It would seem that there is a growing tendency among some groups of young Muslims in Ireland to seek new cultural ways of being Muslim and at the same time to look for constructive participation in wider society. However, the picture of the Irish Muslim community in general as it moves into its second generation still seems to reflect a trend towards isolationism and the existence of parallel cultures.

It is perhaps not difficult to see why this may be so. For newcomers in a strange country trying to make their way, there is comfort in remaining within one's own community. Moreover, air travel, satellite television and internet access mean that contact with home families and communities is greatly facilitated – 'It is possible to live in Ireland and relate globally for many individuals and families.'[23]

In addition, it is not so easy for young Muslims to socialise in the same way as other Irish young people do in the pub and drinking culture that predominates. Ali Selim, General Secretary of the Irish Council of Imams, says, 'On Friday and Saturday night in town you often feel alienated, like a stranger in this city which is your home.'[24] And in the more general atmosphere of what is perceived by many Muslims as rampant Islamophobia in the West, it is understandable that even in the smaller and quieter context that is Ireland many Muslims would feel they have enough on their hands without adding the demands of dialogue and collaboration with people they don't really know and are not sure they want to get to know them.

As France, Britain and other countries have shown, this kind of isolationism only stores up trouble for the future, for all communities. The number of Muslims in Ireland is relatively small, we have the experiences of other countries to draw on, we have our own recent history of difference and conflict in Northern Ireland to provide models of unity in diversity – there is now an opportunity for us to work together at fashioning a way of living with one another in harmony and to our mutual benefit. This will include, *inter alia*, developing good practices and habits around controversial issues to do with cultural and religious differences (for example, wearing of the veil, parent-teacher meetings in schools). Ways of dealing with these issues are better coming from a full and respectful debate rather than as *ad hoc* solutions to particular problems: this latter way of proceeding can lead too easily to raised expectations on the one hand, and the gradual erosion of cherished aspects of a way of life on the other. It will also include the gradual involvement of Muslims in key areas of Irish life such as politics, the Gardaí, sport, entertainment and so on.

23. Kieran Flynn, op cit, p 236
24. Ibid., p 235

None of this will happen by default. It needs pro-active engagement, and arguably the greater responsibility for this lies with the host community in Ireland.

Conclusion

As the Irishman is supposed to have said when asked directions by a foreign traveler: 'I wouldn't start from here.' It may seem a pity that the relationship with Islam is so fraught, even before some of us have met individual Muslims – strange starting a relationship to realise that there's already a quarrel going on!

But we are all first of all human beings, with common concerns and curiosities, getting on with life in ways both ordinary and extraordinary, as is the human destiny. And as Christians and Muslims we believe in common that we have been created by God, by Allah, to lead good lives. In addition, historically, there have been periods of great peace between our two faiths. Before the horse bolts, we now have a wonderful opportunity in Ireland to get our stable in order, and perhaps even, as aspired to in the Northern Ireland peace process, to create the kind of society that will serve as a helpful model further afield. We will be helped in doing this by focusing not just on Muslims, Christians, secularists but also on the other religions which have increasing numbers of adherents among us.

Muslims can enrich Ireland enormously with their reverence for the transcendent and their passion for justice. They can perhaps also learn something of value from their contact with Christianity and the values of liberal democracy here. This will happen only if there is constructive engagement between the communities. Only in this way can the hopes of President McAleese and the Irish Council of Imams be realised. Only in this way will little Muhammad and Selma be seen in the future as the rule and not the exceptions to the rule.

CHAPTER SEVEN

Muslims in the Free Society

John D'Arcy May refers in a recent article[1] to a book entitled *Catholics in the Free Society* which appeared in Australia in the early 1960s. The implication of the title was clear: how could Roman Catholics, beholden to the Pope and embracing a worldview at loggerheads with an otherwise Protestant and liberal society, be trusted to be loyal Australians and good democrats? The same discussion had occurred around the same time in the United States of America on the run-up to the Presidency of John Fitzgerald Kennedy. All this was before the Declaration on Religious Liberty, *Dignitatis Humanae* (1965) of the Second Vatican Council, affirming freedom of conscience in matters of religion. It is a discussion that we are familiar with in Ireland too, where the often cosy relationship between the Roman Catholic Church and the new Irish state in the first part of the twentieth century meant that the slogan 'Home Rule is Rome Rule' was no mere empty shibboleth.

It is not a little ironic then that in the West it is now Catholics – as well, of course, as other Christians, secularists and those of other religions – who express fears about the compatibility of Islam with a free society. Does the self-understanding of Islam as a total religion, embracing political as well as personal and societal reality, mean that there is a contradiction between it and a free society, the rule of civil law, the democratic system of representation in government, freedom of speech and thought, the rights of women and minorities, the administration of a modern economy? Are Muslims intent on creating a Shariah-law society wherever they are in the majority, and working towards it when they are not? In our post September 11 2001 context, with the growing visi-

1. John D'Arcy May,' Muslims in the Free Society', in *Doctrine and Life*, 56, 2006, 22-28

bility and often radicalisation of Islamic opinion in many parts of the world, these are questions of more than academic interest.

In this fraught atmosphere, many Muslims in the West feel themselves on the defensive. A recent EU report highlighted the extent of discrimination and Islamophobia experienced by Muslims in Europe.[2] It drew attention to the fact that Muslims judged as inconsistent the constant demands for integration when often they experienced exclusion at a socio-economic level. Similarly many of them perceived that 'to integrate' meant in fact a demand to lay aside their Islamic identity when they themselves believed that their Muslim values were compatible with European secular values.

Formal Positions

I want first to outline, briefly and in a general way, the formal positions on freedom in society adopted by different religions, with particular reference to Islam.[3]

For many Muslims, as Esposito notes, 'Islam is a total way of life.'[4] In this context the modern Western secular tendency to separate religion and politics or to presume that secularisation is the only option possible is not immediately obvious or acceptable. Rather, Islam concerns body and soul, social, political and religious life. The Qur'an is unambiguous in its teaching about the practice of social justice, and Muhammad's proclamation attacks a social order dominated by the interests of the rich. The Qur'anic

---

2. Tufyal Choudhury, Mohammed Aziz, Duaa Izzidien, Intissar Khreeji, Dilwar Hussain, *Perceptions of Discrimination and Islamophobia, Voices from Members of Muslim communities in the European Union*, Vienna, EUMC (European Monitoring Centre on Racism and Xenophobia), 2006
3. For what follows see Christian W. Troll SJ, *Muslims Ask, Christians Answer,(trs* David Marshall), Gujurat, 2005, especially ch 9; also available at http://www.answers-to-muslim.com See also John L. Esposito, *Islam: The Straight Path*, New York and Oxford, Oxford University Press, 2005 (especially ch 5); Aftad Ahmad Malik, ed, *With God On Our Side: Politics and Theology of the War on Terrorism*, Bristol, Amal Press, 2005; Karen Armstrong, *Islam: A Short History*, New York, Modern Library, 2002 (especially ch 5); Jaume Flaquer Garcia SJ, *Fundamentalism*, Barcelona, Cristianisme I Justicia Booklets, 2005
4. Espostio, *Islam: The Straight Path*, 159

revelation, then, is concerned not only with prescriptions for spiritual life (prayer, fasting, virtues and vices), but also with life in society (the individual, the family, marriage contracts and inheritance, the economy), the regulation of political life (instructions for the conduct of war, the duties of leaders), and also law on everyday matters (including the regulation of the status of non-Muslims). Shaped by the early political and military involvement of Muhammad, the tradition developed a theory of Islam as an all-embracing way of life: Islam as both religion and state (*din wa dawla*). In accordance with this, there developed that body of Islamic law known as the Shariah, derived from the Qur'an as well as the sunnah (the habits and religious practices of the Prophet Muhammad) and the hadith (the documented traditions of the Prophet, not recorded in the Qur'an). The Shariah is meant to govern all aspects of life. From it there arose the practice of fiqh or jurisprudence, the study or application of the body of sacred Muslim law as applied to new and different situations, undertaken by the ulama, the scholars. There has been a long struggle within Islam, which still goes on, to determine the freedom, principles and limits which should govern the interpretation and creation of laws. Could ijtihad (independent reasoning) be used by jurists to create new laws even if not based on a hadith or Quranic utterance? Even as early as the ninth century the Mutazila emerged as a formal school of theology which relied on reason and rational deduction as tools in Quranic interpretation. They regarded reason and revelation as complementary sources of guidance from a just and reasonable God.[5] But for the most part a much more conservative position was adopted and maintained, and during the fourteenth century Sunni Muslims declared that 'the gates of ijtihad' were closed.

However, while Islam rejects the separation of the spiritual and the worldly, it does recognise the distinction between them. So the classical treatises distinguish between acts of worship, which are regarded as unchanging, and social relationships, which can change. Nonetheless, already within the lifetime of

---

5. Esposito, *Islam: The Straight Path*, 70-85

Muhammad himself there took place the significant development from a movement with a moral and social vision calling into question existing social structures to the actual establishment of a state religion. In the period that immediately followed, the Caliph (the Prophet's successor) became 'God's shadow on earth' and 'the commander of the faithful'. He and his representatives were entrusted with worldly, not primarily spiritual, power – Islam knows neither a religious hierarchy nor an official teaching office. Nonetheless, the Caliphs bore religious responsibility for commanding the good and forbidding the evil. In modern times, this history of Islam as religion and state has resulted, especially in the Arab world, in an extremely close connection between religion and the state, even if there are also examples of states with large Muslim majorities which are organised on secular principles (for instance, Turkey, Senegal, Mali, Niger, Indonesia).

Interestingly since the beginning of the twentieth century some Muslim thinkers have become aware of the drawbacks of a state religion (how it limits the role of the state in various ways – for example, with respect to economic development and modernisation in general – and also how it runs the risk of damaging religion by using it as an instrument of government party officials). This has meant that for some decades in the Islamic world there has been a loud call – perhaps drowned out in the post 9/11 so-called war on terrorism context in which we live – for a separation of religion and state, and even for a secular state. However, these ideas are opposed vigorously in conservative circles which identify the idea of a secular state as 'a western and Christian heresy'. It remains the case, according to Troll, that 'countless Muslims fluctuate between these two tendencies of complete integration and total separation of religion and state'.[6]

In historical terms, Christianity and Islam have developed in similar ways. Initially, they both proclaimed a spiritual message with social implications, a message which raised questions about unjust political and social structures. In both cases, the very success of the religious message gave them dominant positions in

6. Troll, *Muslims Ask, Christians Answer*, 48

society and led to both Christianity and Islam becoming state religions.

Christianity first became a state religion in the fourth century of its history, under the Emperor Constantine. However, in the New Testament there is nowhere any basis for the idea of a 'Christian state'. Jesus did not found a state, did not establish a Christian society in competition with other political societies, did not mobilise an army to assert rights. In this sense, according to the New Testament, the Christian is a citizen among other citizens, even when the ruling elite might happen to be pagan. Worldly honour and power are rejected in favour of the kingdom of God, much to the initial disappointment of the people and eventually leading to the death on a cross of Jesus. Nonetheless, the New Testament does reject all political and social injustice – if what is of God and what is of Caesar are distinct, and if this distinction can lead in time to the separation of church and state, it still should not lead to a silencing of the voice of the church in protesting against civil injustice and in sharing its wisdom (but not any blueprint for the organisation of society or politics) about the values which should inform our civil society. In this sense, political involvement is an essential constituent of Christian mission.

However, historically, Christianity did not remain true to this New Testament teaching. Instead, for centuries, it became a state religion. In particular, the role of the Pope developed in such a way that the theory of the two swords was advanced so that the spiritual and worldly swords were united in the hands of the Pope who considered himself to be authorised to appoint kings and emperors. This uniting of both powers in one institution and person led the church to sanction and even initiate and implement policies which clearly contradicted the spirit of the gospels: crusades, imperial and colonial ventures, the inquisition.

Gradually, because of the effects of the Reformation, the reaction to the wars of religion, the enlightenment, Christians began to appreciate that they had departed from the spirit of the gospel in their understanding of the link between religion and politics, between faith and a free society. For Protestants, the *Barmen Declaration* of 1934 was of particular significance. For Catholics, the breakthrough occurred in the *Decree on Religious Freedom* of the Second Vatican Council in 1965. Christian churches now teach that a formal separation of church and state is preferable and most consonant with gospel values. This entails recognition of the rightful, if relative, autonomy of the secular, even while claiming the right of the religious voice to exercise influence on society according to standards derived from the values of the gospel. This influence will involve an attitude of engagement with the world in the eschatological tension between the 'already' and the 'not yet', an engagement which gives primacy to the Spirit of God and recognises that our co-operation will be under the sign of the cross and resurrection of Jesus Christ.

It is clear that historically the relationship between religion and politics, in Islam as in Christianity, has taken many different forms, by no means always forms of identity. Nonetheless, the struggle within Islam to get this relationship right is perhaps exacerbated by the fact that whereas formally Christianity is clearly compatible with some kind of church-state separation, this is not so clearly the case for Islam. Because a detailed blueprint for the ordering of society and politics are so much at the heart of Islamic revelation there is a natural desire to have a Muslim-majority state, an unease with how to deal with non-Muslims, a temptation to use power or even violence to enforce religious compliance, a dilemma in finding ways to be creative and modern and yet to submit to a law that emanates from a very different time. Muslims are in search for a way to be modern without being secular.

Reflections
We know that historically Christianity has had a lot of difficulty in negotiating a satisfactory understanding and living out of the relationship between revelation and faith on the one hand, and reason and politics on the other. One thinks of Roman Catholic authoritarianism and excessive emphasis on canon law, the philosophical challenges to the high scholastic compatibility of faith and reason from nominalism, occasionalism, voluntarism in all their historical forms; of the rationalism of liberal Protestantism

leading to suspicions of philosophy and of the analogy of being voiced by Karl Barth; the otherworldly focus of Orthodoxy sometimes accompanied by an extremely conservative social teaching. And yet, not without bloodshed and not without ongoing tensions on particular issues, Christianity has now, by and large, succeeded in retrieving that spirit of the gospel which enables it to live at peace in a modern democratic state, while retaining its right to engage in constructive social commentary and criticism. This is a right not always conceded by secular authorities and sometimes too easily resiled from by Christians: the peaceful coexistence of church and state in the West has too often been achieved at the expense of the excessive privatisation of religion. Nonetheless, in principle at least, and allowing for ongoing creative tensions between different schools of theological thought, there is an appropriate link between faith and reason, summarised in the classical phrase of the First Vatican Council that 'although faith is above reason, yet there can never be any real disagreement between faith and reason, because it is the same God who reveals mysteries and infuses faith and has put the light of reason into the human soul'.[7] In the moral sphere, this translates into the Catholic emphasis on that natural law which in principle all human beings share and which guides moral conduct, even if there can be differing opinions on particular moral issues. This confidence in the intrinsic but non-codified link between faith and reason allows for the eventual acceptance of the modern democratic state.

Islam, again in general (it is important to be aware that there are many different forms of Islam), has not yet reached this point of peaceful coexistence. The reasons for this are many, not all of them religious. As in Christianity, historical, cultural and political causes abound. The crusades, the loss of empire, the fear of a modernisation that would dethrone the primacy of religion, anger at the treatment of Palestinians, resentment at the perceived arrogance and partiality of the United States of America in its role as the

---

7. John F. Clarkson, John H. Edwards, William J. Kelly, and John J. Welch, *The Church Teaches: Documents of the Church in English Translation,* New York, Herder, 1955, 33

world's only surviving superpower and a concomitant suspicion of the West and its values – all these and other similar causes create a culture within Islam which is reactionary in itself and which acts as a filter for religious interpretation of an extremely conservative nature. We have seen that historically there are strands within Islam which can interpret the Qur'an in ways that are creative and up-to-date, which can distinguish between acts of worship which are unchanging and social relationships which can change. And nowadays it is said that for many in Turkey, for example, talk about Shariah is really talk about the moral life, while former Pakistan cricket captain, now politician, Imran Khan is reported to have said that the closest example he has ever seen of an ideal Islamic society in the world today is Sweden.[8] However, these are not typical positions and there may be an intrinsic difficulty with the emphasis in the Qur'an on providing a political blueprint for society and a law which governs all human conduct. Divine law is not easily subject to appeal or to human change, no matter how pressing the need. And if the focus is on law – and not also on a wider wisdom that offers reasonable grounds for change and adaptation – one is in a bit of a bind. The Christian position is different: not only is law seen as just one source of wisdom (and so takes its place in a matrix of other sources such as philosophy, politics, sociology, economics and so on) but also theologically Jesus places himself above the law, while respecting it. He is Lord of the Sabbath, his Spirit is one of freedom and not law, and Christian disciples are given this freedom of discernment of spirits which allows for a principled but creative adaptation to new circumstances as well as a real development of doctrine. This nuanced position on the compatibility between faith and reason was well expressed in Pope Benedict's 2006 address in Regensburg, infamous for other reasons.

It is, of course, for Islam itself to discover and deploy the resources within its own theological tradition which will allow it to live more participatively in a modern democratic society – not so much as rulers or as being ruled, but as active participants. For this to happen, it would seem that something like the

8. Mary Fitzgerald, *The Irish Times*,27 October 2006

Reformation, the enlightenment, Vatican II needs to happen in Islam. This would involve the painful but liberating kind of experiences which Christianity has had to undergo, including a scientific study of the Qur'an itself from the viewpoints of philology, sociology, history, literary criticism and so on, as well as an opening up of the 'gates of *ijtihad*' in a way that frees interpretation and allows greater hospitality to modern sensibilities, such as the whole area of human rights and those of women in particular. This means a mindset that is not afraid of or impervious to evidence. It can only be Muslims who can judge whether such reforms are internally consistent with Islam itself, whether, for example, in addition to allowing for a more harmonious coexistence with the gains of modernity, they might not also retrieve the original meaning of Shariah as subversive of autocracy and in favour of social justice. Such a development would allow Islam to retain its faith in the transcendent while offering a powerful critique of the excesses of modernity.

In the meantime, it might help Muslims to become more disposed to look in this direction of reform if Christians could find ways of sharing their own experiences of historical change with them. This would include the experience of failure and violence, of the time it takes for change, of recognition (*pace* Pope Benedict) of the contribution of Islam to Europe and of the intellectual richness and achievement of Islam in the past and today.[9] It would also include an appreciation of the great providential gift to Christians of the Islamic focus on God's transcendence, in particular at a time of Western secularisation which so easily elides into secularism. It would be wonderful if Muslims and Christians together could work towards a situation where the legal framework of a democratic secular state would be accepted but where civil society and indeed the whole public sphere would be subject to the influence – but not the rule – of religious as well as secular ideas.

It is also worth noting that while an intellectual reformation is important and can facilitate so many other developments, life itself is a great teacher and surprises can take place despite seem-

9. Michael L. Fitzgerald and John Borelli, *Interfaith Dialogue: A Catholic View*, New York, Orbis, 2006, ch 9

ingly intransigent ideological positions. Bernard Lonergan had great faith in what he called the 'self-corrective process of learning', believing that we all had an innate desire for truth and would not rest satisfied until we achieved our goal. In later life, he was to add the importance of 'falling in love' (ultimately with God) as the great catalyst towards truth. Who would have thought when Pope John XXIII was elected that the Catholic Church was to undergo such a profound reformation? Given his previous comments about Islam, who would have imagined that Pope Benedict would find himself praying so reverently alongside senior Muslim religious leaders in Istanbul's Blue Mosque? Similarly, Muslim commentators have pointed to the historical flexibility of Islam in adapting to different circumstances, so that there can be and have been instances of a lived compatibility between Islam and democracy when formally or dogmatically there was no such possibility.[10] In this respect it is right that the dialogue of theological ideas is aware of the often more powerful dialogues going on at the level of living together, working together for a more just world, and sharing together of religious experience.

Ireland has arrived relatively late on the stage of these dialogues and has the opportunity to learn from the successes and failures of others.[11] But in particular we have had our own long and harrowing experience of conflict in Northern Ireland in which issues of culture, identity, politics and religion came together in a seemingly intractable and violent way. In many respects the churches helped ameliorate the situation by compassionate pastoral care, by the condemnation of violence at official level, and by the behind-the-scenes highly significant work for political peace by some church representatives. And yet we saw too that the different churches often seemed to be captive to their respective communities, 'chaplains to the warring tribes', so that

---

10. Sadik J. Al-Azm, 'Islam and Secular Humanism', in *Islam and Secularism*, Antwerpen, Universitair Centrum Sint-Ignatius Antwerpen, 2005, The Dialogue Series 2, 41-51

11. Gerry O'Hanlon SJ, 'Asking the Right Questions: Christians, Muslims, Citizens in Ireland', *Working Notes*, 54, (Journal of the Jesuit Centre for Faith and Justice), February 2007, 8-14 – chapter 6 here.

the prophetic role of the scriptures in liberating us from blood ties in favour of the greater common good was often missing.[12] We need now as Christians to see dialogue with Muslims in Ireland as a graced imperative, believing that coming together with our common humanity and religious respect we can proactively help to set a peaceful and just agenda for the future. This irenic intent ought not to result in an insipid dialogue incapable of coping with anger and asking the hard questions: John D'Arcy May himself personifies the ability to be both generous and firm in his approach to dialogue.[13] We need to ask Muslims about their attitude to a free society, to violence in the Middle East and elsewhere, to the possibility of state subsidisation but also regulation of the education of imams where Muslims themselves have expressed the need for such education and where the state may be simply ignorant of the type of education being offered. Muslims will have their own questions to put to us.

I note finally that the Good Friday Agreement proposed the kind of political arrangement in which 'parity of esteem' as opposed to simple majority rule became the principle of democratic governance. In an interesting joint statement, issued in 2004, the German and African Catholic bishops note that relations between Christians and Muslims can be guaranteed and enhanced by a modern democratic state, including a civic order regulated by the rule of law. Such a civic order is incompatible with legal provisions derived from one religion only. The bishops go on to suggest that this kind of legal framework 'implies constitutional guarantees of civic rights and fundamental values that cannot be altered by majority vote'.[14] It would be interesting to explore how our dialogue in Ireland might be framed within this kind of commitment to the free society which so many citizens of Ireland, north and south, Christian, Muslim and secular, so clearly cherish.

---

12. For an attempt at self-critique by the churches along these lines, see Department of Theological Questions, Irish Inter-Church Meeting, *Freedom, Justice and Responsibility in Ireland Today*, Dublin, Veritas, 1997.
13. John D'Arcy May, 'The Dialogue of religions: source of knowledge? Means of peace?', WCC, *Current Dialogue*, 43, July 2004
14. Deutsch-Afrikanisches Bishcofstreffen, Christians and Muslims in Dialogue, *Stimmen der Weltkirche*, 38, Bonn, 2006

CHAPTER EIGHT

Western Muslims and The Future of Islam

The first report on *Islam and the West: Annual Report on the State of Dialogue* was launched in January 2008 at Davos by the World Economic Forum and Washington's Georgetown University.[1] The report found that while a majority of people in 21 Muslim and non-Muslim communities surveyed believe that violent conflict between the West and Islam can be avoided, still they are pessimistic about the present state of relations between the two sides. Even if Ireland was not one of the countries surveyed, and if we are still at a relatively early stage of our dialogue with Islam in this country, still in our globalised world we cannot expect to remain immune from the bad feeling, mutual suspicions and contentious issues that often bedevil Christian-Islamic relations worldwide.[2]

This was not how the Second Vatican Council (1963-1965) wanted things to be. In its *Decree on Non-Christians* (*Nostra Aetate*, 1965, n 3) the council professes its esteem for Muslims, notes what we have in common, and concludes by saying: 'Although in the course of the centuries many quarrels and hostilities have arisen between Christians and Muslims, this most sacred synod urges all to forget the past and to work sincerely for mutual understanding and to preserve as well as to promote together, for the benefit of all humanity, social justice and moral welfare, as well as peace and freedom.' Can these idealistic-sounding words from the optimistic 60s have any real resonance in our grimmer, post 9/11 situation?

1. Report in *The Irish Times*, Tuesday 22 January 2008, p 10
2. For a consideration of the Irish situation cf G.O'Hanlon, 'Asking the Right Questions: Christian, Muslims, Citizens in Ireland', *Working Notes*, 54, February 2007, 8-14 (chapter six here) and for a more general account of some of the issues around Islam and democracy, O'Hanlon, 'Muslims in the Free Society', in John O'Grady and Peter Scherle (eds), *Ecumenics from the Rim, Explorations in Honour of John D'Arcy May*, Lit Verlag, Berlin, 2007, 271-277 (chapter seven here)

An interesting, and even stimulating, contribution to this attempt at mutual understanding is provided by Tariq Ramadan in his book *Western Muslims and the The Future of Islam.*[3] Ramadan, a Swiss born and Oxford- based academic, whose grandfather was a founder of the Muslim Brotherhood in Egypt, is part of a reformist tradition within Islam that aims to protect Muslim identity and religious practice, to recognise the Western constitutional structure, to become involved as citizens at the social level, and to live with true loyalty to the country to which one belongs. Although refused a visa to take up a Chair at Notre Dame university in the United States, allegedly because of financial donations to organisations linked to terrorists in the Middle East, he is one of the 138 Muslim scholars who wrote *A Common Word* to the Pope and other Christian leaders, which has elicited a positive response from the Vatican to the invitation to dialogue. As a sometime advisor to the UK government and the EU, invited to speak at events by Bill Clinton, he is a substantial if somewhat controversial figure both within Islam and within the West in general.

Muslims in the West
Tariq Ramadan wants to persuade Muslims to become full participants in Western societies, without loss of their Islamic identity. He believes this is possible because Islam, properly understood, has a universality which can integrate pluralism and the belief of the other (p 6).

This is a different position from that adopted by many Muslim and indeed Western commentators. Muslims – in particular non-Western Muslims – tend to see the plight of the Muslim in the West in a bi-polar way. For them the West is *dar al-harb* (The Abode of War), in contrast to parts of the world where there is an Islamic majority which is *dar al-islam* (The Abode of Islam). In the Abode of War the Muslim feels part of an isolated minority. In this context he/she is advised to fight for rights and is allowed certain concessions, by way of exception, to strict Islamic law. Some

---

3. Tariq Ramadan, *Western Muslims and The Future of Islam*, Oxford University Press, 2004.

Muslims even interpret this 'outsider' situation in terms of opposition, outright hostility, and even aggression.

Ramadan wants to challenge this typical, bi-polar Islamic stance towards the West. He argues that this is not a stance which can claim Qur'anic grounding. Instead he proposes that five fundamental rights are guaranteed in the West that allow Muslims to feel at home in their countries of residence: the right to practise Islam, the right to knowledge, to right to establish organisations, the right to autonomous representation, and the right to appeal to law (p 70). With this background Muslims may be confident in the ability of Islam to co-exist on equal terms with the West. Western Muslims should shed their 'outsider', minority mentality, and become full and contributing citizens to the states they live in. They should regard the West as *dar al-dawa* (the abode of invitation) or *dar al-shahada* (the abode of witness or testimony).

This principle of integration, while retaining identity, will mean that Western Muslims must be intellectually, politically, and financially independent. This does not entail severing links with other Muslims worldwide (the umma), much less, with the community of scholars (ulama), given the lack, till now, of scholars born and bred in the West. But it does mean that Western Muslims need to think for themselves in their own unique situation. They need to refuse to be colonised by allowing other Muslims worldwide to speak for them, or indeed by allowing 'enlightened Westerners' to tell them how Muslims should think or behave in the West.

Tariq Ramadan is outlining a vision with which Christians will be familiar. It involves an ability to live with the secular humanism of the West, without loss of one's own religious identity and prophetic critique. Integration, in this context, cannot mean assimilation, even if it also avoids the trap of an isolationist multiculturalism. Ramadan believes that if Islam in the West can re-envisage itself along these lines, if it can live inter-culturally within a societal ethos of equality-in-diversity then, not only will Western Muslims be happier and less internally divided, but also Islamophobia will decrease.

But can Islam re-interpret itself in this way?

Re-interpreting Islam in the West

There are several co-ordinated steps in Tariq Ramadan's argument for a re-interpretation of Islam in the West. First, he wants to hold on to the universal and comprehensive nature of Islam itself. At the heart of Islam is the notion of *tawhid* (faith in the unity of God). This involves three unquestionable principles: the absolute oneness of the Creator, the impossibility of there being a representation of him, and the truth of his word revealed in the Qur'an. There is already a revelation of God in creation at large, and a desire or longing (*fitra*) put in us as part of our human nature to turn to God. This natural revelation is confirmed and, where blurred and distorted, reconciled in God's Qur'anic revelation (with its prophetic traditions or Sunnah), the culmination of the previous historic (Judaeo-Christian) revelations. In this whole process there is no contradiction between the realms of faith and reason: the Qur'an itself has to be read and interpreted by human intellect (pp 11-20).

In particular, secondly, one may and must distinguish between what is unchangeable and what is changeable in the Qur'anic revelation. It is the job of the 'Islamic sciences' (Ramadan prefers not to use the term 'theology' in this context) to make these distinctions. This refers in particular to *fiqh*, Islamic law and jurisprudence. What Ramadan wants to maintain here is that while, particularly in the specifically religious and private domain, there are certain clear revelations which are absolute and unchangeable, still there are other areas, in particular the public and social arenas, where new situations demand a re-interpretation of the Qur'an, even while remaining faithful to its own spirit and never allowing what is explicitly forbidden. According to Ramadan while certain verses of the Qur'an (actually a minority) leave little or no scope for interpretation, the great majority demand real interpretative effort (p 22).

This task of interpretation (*ijtihad*) is not arbitrary, much less some facile, liberal accommodation to modernity. Instead it must take account of objective guidelines, principles and methodologies in order to issue *fatwa* or legal rulings that apply to specific situations that may be quite novel. Of particular importance in this respect is the interpretive criterion of *al-maslaha* (the common good), always in tandem with the proviso that any new *fatwa* deriving from this principle cannot contradict obvious proofs from the Qur'an and the Sunna.

In general, while respecting the interpretative methods and often sophisticated jurisprudence of all schools, Ramadan himself seems to lean towards a reformist approach which privileges the original scriptures and the interpretations of the first generations. He believes however that Muslims need as well to give weight to the contemporary *ulama* and specialists in law and jurisprudence, and to other experts from various fields (the human as well as the natural sciences – p 163), as well as to the experience of women (pp 141-143). What he is seeking, then, is a more contextual reading of the scriptures and the world. And of course, despite the historical objections of some, this entails that 'the doors of ijtihad' always remain open (p 48).

On this basis, Ramadan can, thirdly, advance a notion of *Sharia* (The Way) that is altogether less threatening than what is usually conjured up by use of the term in the West (fear of repression of women, physical punishments, rejection of secular democracy and so on). For him *Sharia* (also known as 'the path that leads to the spring'), in so far as it is the expression of 'the way to faithfulness' deduced and constructed *a posteriori*, 'is the work of human intellect' (p 34). Again, in the area of religious practice, 'the margin for interpretation is virtually nil' (p 35): but in the wider area of human and social affairs 'the scope for the exercise of reason and creativity is huge' (p 35). There is then a distinction between 'the universal principles to which Muslim consciousness must seek to be faithful through the ages and the practice of those principles, which is necessarily relative, at a given moment in human history' (p 35). The corpus of the *Sharia* is, then, 'a human construction' (p 37) which may evolve. At the heart of this evolution is the principle of integration: Muslims must feel free to integrate the good, from wherever it may come, provided it is not against an established principle or revelation. In doing this they should feel free to make their own all that is good in the West, confident that in so doing they are being faithful to the universality of Islam and to the belief in the non-contradiction between faith and reason.

The fourth and final step in Tariq Ramadan's re-thinking of Islam in the West looks to the societal potentialities and consequences of the three previous steps. Muslims worldwide have often been accused of being pre-modern, of being backward, hindered by their religion in their approach to science and technology. Ramadan argues that this need not be so: the universal message of Islam, and the ethics that flow from it, are perfectly compatible with a set of completely autonomous scientific rules and methods (p 59).

Similarly that 'distinction of orders' in Christianity between 'the restraining authority of religion and the civic independence of the individual, between the realm of dogma and that of reason, between the private and the public' that led to the clear separation between church and state, is 'very accessible to Muslims' (p 145). In this respect Ramadan argues that Islam will prefer to speak of a distinction rather than a separation between religion and politics. In so doing he is not trying to regain political power for the religious authority, but rather to assert that Muslims 'continue to find in their scriptural sources principles that inspire their social and political commitment'(p 145). But is this not very similar to the contemporary Christian demand for the right to have the voice of religion heard in the public square, to avoid surrendering to the ideological claims of some secularists that would have citizens become 'religiously invisible' (p 146)?

Ramadan goes on to articulate how compatible Islam is with social justice and rights, citing affinities with Christian liberation theology and other secular movements in the resistance to the neo-liberal economic model which is so powerful in today's world (p 173). He notes the vibrancy of Islamic feminism in the West (spoken of in terms of an equality that recognises the natural complementarity between the sexes – pp 136-145), leading increasingly to women (whether veiled or unveiled) in leadership roles and at the cutting edge of the re-reading of scriptural sources. Against some scholarly opinion, he is in favour of political involvement by Muslims in Western societies (pp 158-165). He wishes Muslims to become socially involved at all levels, and so with all due respect to the need they will have to nourish their own identity through contact with 'their own', still he urges that they avoid any ghetto-isation and join with fellow-citizens at all levels of civil society – in a more critically-oriented and contextual experience of education and schooling; in leisure and cultural pursuits; in justice projects and so on.

There will be some differences of course – so, for example, a Muslim will not drink alcohol if s/he wishes to be faithful. But Western rights and freedoms do not require any Muslim to do anything against their faith, and in the rare instances that this might occur (for example, being obliged to fight an unjust war), there is always the right of conscientious objection, of invoking a conscience clause (pp 96-101). And these differences are not such as to require Muslims in the West to assume minority, much less victim status: instead, and this is Tariq Ramdan's constant and sustained thesis, they ought to assume full citizenship, under-standing that 'to apply the *Sharia* for Muslim citizens or residents in the West means explicitly to respect the legal and constitutional framework of the country of which they are citizens' (p 95). With this mindset they can be confident in their own identity and in their ability as Muslims to offer Western society a diversity that contributes constructively to the well-being of all.

Incidentally, true to this entire logic of the 'principle of integra-tion' and the notion of *Sharia* that accompanies it, Tariq Ramadan responded unenthusiastically to the nuanced proposal of the Archbishop of Canterbury, Dr Rowan Williams (February 2008) concerning the possibility of 'supplementary' jurisdiction, along *Sharia* lines, for Muslims in Britain in areas like marital law, the regulations of financial transactions and authorised structures of mediation and conflict resolution. He is reported as saying in re-sponse that 'these kinds of statements just feed the fears of fellow citizens. I really think we, as Muslims, need to come up with something that we abide by the common law and within these lat-itudes there are possibilities for us to be faithful to Islamic princi-ples'.

Test-case: Economics

Perhaps somewhat surprisingly it is in the sphere of economics –

not of *Sharia* in general or the rights of women in particular – that Tariq Ramadan's overall framework seems to come under some strain (Ch 8).

He notes, reasonably and helpfully, the stress in Islam on an ethical approach to money and property, illustrated not least by *zakat*, a kind of social tax on wealth and the third pillar of Islam. Likewise – akin to critiques that are common in liberation theology and even in main-stream Christian and Catholic Social Teaching – he is critical of the excesses of a globalisation that is structured according to a neo-liberal economic model. In this respect he believes that the West may indeed be called *dar al-harb* (The Abode of War), in that its policies bring about a situation of great social injustice worldwide and ought to be resisted. Western Muslims, in this context, are urged to become the voice of the voiceless, 'the conscience of the South' (p 171).

So far, so reasonable. But Ramadan makes it clear from the start that his critique is not just against the excesses of capitalism as found in the neo-liberal model, but against the lending of credit with interest (*riba*), which is intrinsic to even responsible forms of capitalism. He believes that all forms of speculation, usury and interest are clearly part of what is explicitly forbidden in the Qur'an and Sunna and so are not amenable to a more liberal, adaptive hermeneutic. The most he will allow is, given the complexity and all-pervasive nature of the Western financial system, a reluctant and Islamic legally-guided minimalist compliance with the system, pending construction of a necessary alternative and a commitment to participating in this alternative. He takes this line conscious that others, especially those inspired by the teaching of Abu Hanifa and his school, not least many individuals in Turkey and Pakistan, adopt a more liberal approach. It is a line which has gained some practical support within Western banking circles – for example, the Financial Services Authority in Britain has authorised the Islamic Bank of Britain (now with seven branches) to be set up and has enabled it and several already established banks to offer products compliant with *Sharia*, while more recently there has been a call for *Sharia*-compliant financial services to be available in Ireland.[4]

4. Report in *The Irish Times* by Mary Fitzgerald, Friday 30 May 2008

However, apart from the practical issues involved, why in principle should we go in this direction? It is one thing (and, arguably, a very good thing, given the recently manifest excesses of the system) to criticise unbridled capitalism and even usury (if defined as lending money at exorbitant rates). It seems to me quite a different matter to forbid all transactions which involve interest. Tariq Ramadan seeks to give reasonable grounds for this position, given his overall thesis that what the Qur'an commands is in harmony with reason. The grounds he advances are that 'the idea that underlies the notion of *riba* is one of profit that is not in exchange for any service rendered or work performed: it is a growth of capital through and upon capital itself' (p 185). But surely it may be counter-argued that the advancement of credit at a time of personal or business need is indeed a 'service rendered', and, given the fulfillment of all conditions of equity, a perfectly honourable service at that?

What is at stake here, beyond the important issue of economics itself, is the more fundamental matter of whether Tariq Ramadan's overall framework – with its confidence in the universality and comprehensive nature of Islam, its claim of compatibility with reason, and its ability to accept and integrate all that is good in the West – can really deliver in a way that is faithful to Islam and facilitative of Western Muslims becoming citizens in the full sense.

Parallels with Christianity
Christians, gifted with a divine revelation which includes the Old Testament, a plurality of oral and written accounts of the Christ-event, and faced with the challenge of communicating that revelation to a contemporary audience, have long experience of the complex task involved in the interpretation of core truths of revelation. There will then be many points of contact and room for mutual learning between the Christian and Islamic hermeneutical enterprises.

In particular one notes in more modern times, with the development of historic consciousness, the growing understanding within Christianity (think of Newman, Lonergan, the teaching of Vatican II on Revelation) that doctrine develops. Also in modern times one has witnessed the Catholic engagement with modernity in a way that Protestantism in many respects was already familiar with (a more scientific approach to scriptural exegesis, the acceptance of the rights of conscience and religious freedom in Vatican II, and in that same council the *Constitution on the Church in the Modern World,* articulating a much more positive stance towards modernity). All this has been accompanied in more contemporary times by a critique of the deficiencies of modernity, not least of an ideological secularism and relativism as well as an over-reliance on an excessively empirical scientific model of knowledge. However, not least because of the experience of the many wars of religion, there has been an acceptance of the benefits of church-state distinction and remorse expressed for the violence used in the past to impose religious faith (not least through events like the crusades and institutions like the inquisition).

Christians then, over time, have come to some kind of broad consensus about matters of scriptural interpretation and of relationship with (post-)modernity, even if there is constant need for ongoing discernment and all issues are far from settled (one thinks, for example, of matters like homosexuality and other issues of sexual morality, the ordination of women and many others). Islam is at a different stage in this process, and must be given time to arrive at the point which is proper to them. This is what Tariq Ramadan is about. In his attempt he is aided by his belief in the universal and comprehensive nature of Islam, and the rich and often sophisticated tradition of Islamic legal interpretation, similar in some respects to the traditional Christian notions of 'theological notes' and the 'hierarchy of truths' with their attempt to weigh the importance and certainty of proposed truths.

He does not have at his disposal (and nor would he want to: such is the nature of our different faiths) the well-defined authority structure of the Catholic Church in particular, which allows for the clear articulation of teaching (*magisterium*) and policy. And neither does he have at his disposal a belief in the presence of the Holy Spirit as the dynamic element in church truth and institution, guarantor of the ultimately faithful development of truth and policy. He is dealing with the Word of the One God which comes as a command, a prophetic revelation, and is to be obeyed by us human beings with the help of interpretations of a predominantly legal nature. Christianity, with its trinitarian structure, is focused rather on the living presence of the one God among us in the historical person of Jesus Christ, now, after his death, made present by the Holy Spirit who interprets him to us by means certainly of law, but also, and much more, by all the 'signs of the times' that are at our disposal – theology, church and life in the broadest sense.

There will then be similarities and differences in the common task involved in the dialogue between faith and our times – a good basis for the injunction 'to work sincerely for mutual understanding' articulated by *Nostra Aetate* (Vatican II) in 1965.

Conclusion
It is for Islam itself to decide if the approach of Tariq Ramadan is the right one. He himself is conscious that what is involved for Islam is nothing less than a true 'intellectual revolution', a 'Copernican revolution' (p 53), that his writings 'make humble claim to opening the way to the first steps on this road, but there is still much to be achieved and many obstacles to be overcome' (p 225). This is a road which he believes can put an end to that 'double inferiority complex' which Muslims in the West suffer from – in relation to the West, with its domination of rationality and technology on the one hand, and in relation to the rest of the Muslim world on the other hand, which alone seems to produce the great Arabic-speaking spirits of Islam, who quote the texts with such ease (p 225). He argues strongly that his approach is not an adaptive liberalisation of Islam, but is instead true to the radical meaning of the Qur'an and The Prophet.

Can Islam sustain the claim to universality and comprehensiveness, to harmony between faith and reason, which Ramadan wishes to advance? One wonders, in particular, whether in recommending critical engagement with the sacred texts, one can delimit, in the manner of the 'Islamic sciences', with their meticulous legal approach (p 95) what is 'unquestionable' and what is 'questionable', and avoid that full-blooded theological enquiry of all and sundry – including sacred sources – so familiar to Christianity. The difficulties noted around the test-case of economics are not enough, in themselves, to issue in a negative judgement on this matter: there are, after all, plenty of unresolved issues in Christianity *vis-à-vis* the claims of compatibility between faith and reason.

If Islam can prove itself robust enough to withstand the approach of Tariq Ramadan, and if this approach can win widespread acceptance among Muslims, then this 'Muslim Martin Luther', as he has been called, will have done us all a great service. The moral earnestness of Islam, its deep commitment to justice, its concern for ecology, if all these can be transposed into a modern key that respects Universal Human Rights, then all of us will benefit. In addition the deep respect for the transcendent, the belief in the reality and attainability of truth, the emphasis on the distinction but not outright separation between religion and state –all these, as advanced by Ramadan, can be powerful allies for Christians in their struggle against the prevailing secularism and relativism of our times in the West.

Of course one real test of Islam's ability to re-invent itself along the lines that Ramadan advocates would be in its response to the so-called 'reciprocity' challenge: that is, the call for those in majority Muslim countries to respect fully the rights of other religions. But Ramadan is perhaps right to limit himself to the situation in the West. He does so not in order to avoid the difficult questions which arise worldwide for Islam, but rather as an expression of his own conviction that the future of our world – including the prospect of Huntington's 'clash of civilisations' – depends more on the debate between Muslims and the West within the West, than it does between the West and Islam worldwide (p 226). One can see the logic of his position, and its compatibility with those who want to support the accession of Turkey to the EU on the grounds that it can act as a bridge between the West and Islam. If Western Muslims can demonstrate the compatibility of Islam and the West, if the West can be open to this possibility, then we are all winners.

Ramadan's proposal is stimulating. Time will tell whether it is feasible. And in the meantime he has done us all a service in contributing to this important debate in a visionary way.

PART THREE

Foundations

CHAPTER NINE

Religion and Society[1]

Introduction

We live in interesting times. In our Western world there is church-state separation and within liberalism (the dominant cultural, political and economic force) a distrust of religion, which has tended to banish the voice of faith from the public square. This tendency has been reinforced in Ireland by the loss of the moral authority of the Catholic Church, due to the scandal of child sexual abuse, its authoritarian mode of governance in the past and its difficulties in communicating a faith of mystery in the context of a culture which often denies mystery. At the same time, particularly in Ireland, there is a sense of a moral vacuum. The economy in the Republic up to 2006 had done extremely well; the political situation in Northern Ireland had improved considerably; there was new confidence and hope. And yet all this was accompanied by high suicide rates, violent crime, pressurised lives and an underlying sense of unease about how to enjoy wealth in a way that enhances the good life. Who speaks to us persuasively any more about what the good life might mean? And accompanying all this there is worldwide evidence that another, growing religion (Islam) does not understand itself as playing the kind of privatised role that Western society has assigned to Christianity. The growing presence of Islam, with its reminder that, despite secularisation, religion remains a potent force in so many people's lives, is another pressure on Westerners to re-examine their presuppositions about the role of religion in public life.

Can a way be found to understand that role positively, to flesh out the official view[2] that the 'assertion of the importance of the spiritual ... is a powerful antidote to a purely functional view of

---

1. This article was written early in 2006, in pre-recession Ireland
2. As expressed by former Taoiseach Bertie Ahern

human beings and society ... in that sense, religious belief and practice is not a purely private matter, with no place in public discourse ... on the contrary, a truly democratic and inclusive society values its faith community and respects the voice of those who offer spiritual insight and leadership ... as a source of values and meaning for our people' (*Irish Times*, 23 February 2006)?

The role of religion in public life: two conventional approaches
I have noted that there is a liberal distrust of religion in Western society. This is often reinforced by instances where religion has succeeded in bucking the trend and finding a voice in the public square with negative consequences: one thinks of the strong influence of the Christian Religious Right in the United States of America, and the disproportionate power of Islamic fundamentalism worldwide. Religion is seen by many liberals as a source of division and conflict, and historical instances are cited (for example the crusades, the religious wars in Europe over many centuries). Religion does not abide by the canons of ordinary public reason and discourse but too often appeals to authority or to sources of non-empirical revelation for its criteria of truth: thus runs the argument. How, from a Christian perspective, might one address the concerns implicit in this argument?

There are two obvious approaches. One is that, as Christians, we limit ourselves to discourse within the faith community only, a community which might be expected to share our worldview. This would entail a conversation within the faith community about the relevance of faith for life in general and public life in particular. Of course this conversation already takes place; it is part of the matter of sermons and articles in religious journals and of ecumenical dialogue; it engages our theological community; it is perhaps what An Taoiseach refers to when he says that his Catholic faith 'is both a personal matter for me as well as being an important part of my life and of my perspective on public affairs' (*Irish Times*, 23 February 2006). It is a conversation that, for many, would be greatly enriched by a better understanding of Catholic Social Teaching. This intra-church conversation will rightly be part of our approach, but it seems unduly restrictive. Can

Christians not find ways to the wider, extra-ecclesial sphere of public life?

The second obvious approach is to offer the fruits of Christian wisdom to the wider body politic, but to do so in a way that remains at the level of secular analysis. We would not bring faith into our discussion at all, certainly not at any explicit level. There is good theological justification for this approach; after all, as Irenaeus made it clear, the God of Creation is also the God of Redemption, and, as Aquinas argued, the natural law is written on all our hearts. Therefore Catholic theology, in particular, has always upheld the goodness and proper autonomy of secular disciplines and, even in areas like moral theology, it has been argued that it is best in the public arena to use the language of natural law and the common good, without recourse to explicitly Christian themes.[3] Such an approach has obvious attractions: it allows for the distillation of Christian wisdom on public affairs according to criteria of rational discourse that are shared with liberal culture and so, in principle at least, may expect to find a sympathetic hearing there. So, for example, the discourse in Catholic social teaching on solidarity, on subsidiarity, and so on may have clear and useful resonances with secular discourse on how we order society.

However, there remains a nagging sense that this reductive approach is still too restrictive: it means detaching the natural law discourse from its Christian roots, with an inevitable impoverishment of meaning. Of course the motive – to get a hearing in a culture dominated by liberal secularism – is good. But suppose for a moment that the very values liberalism wants to protect and cultivate are best promoted by a more robust articulation of the Christian faith – what then? Can we find grounds to venture into the more daring approach of coming to public debate with the 'full hand' of religious faith?

A more daring strategy
Considerations from two different academic disciplines offer

---

3. cf Patrick Hannon, 'On Using Religious Arguments in Public Policy Debates', in Treacy and Whyte, eds, *Religion, Morality and Public Policy*, Doctrine and Life Publications, Dublin, 1995, 68-70

some possibilities, at, least for a more daring approach. First, from the viewpoint of cultural anthropology, many analysts note that there is a shift occurring within the centuries-long project of modernity which, with the deconstruction of postmodernity, is opening up a space for the re-enchantment of our world.[4] Put briefly, modernity's trust in a restrictive, scientific notion of reason, its optimism with respect to the inevitability of human progress, and its denial of the spiritual and the transcendent are all coming under increasing strain. The terrible wars of the 20th century, the persistence of injustice on a global scale, the loss of meaning at a personal level (as instanced in increased number of suicides), all these and many other factors are leading people to question whether the instrumental rationality at the heart of modernity, with its focus on means rather than ends, really satisfies the soul. Even the 'tyranny of relativism' at the heart of postmodernity at least opens up a hearing for alternative, even religious, points of view.

One can sense all this happening in Ireland: the realisation that the demise of church authority has left a spiritual and moral vacuum, and the dissatisfaction with the *de facto* attempt of media commentators to fill it. Nietzsche had already identified the terror behind a notion of reality that saw 'man' as the measure of all: 'Where has God gone ... I will tell you. We have slain him – you and I ... But how did we do it? How could we drink up the sea? Who gave us the sponge to wipe out the whole horizon? What did we do when we unchained the earth from its sun? ... Do we now not wander through an endless nothingness? Does empty space not breathe upon us? Is it not colder now? Is not night coming, and even more night? Must we not light lanterns at noon? God is dead. God stays dead. And we have slain him ...'[5]

We all have our awake-late-at-night moments when we won-

---

4. cf Michael Paul Gallagher, *Clashing Symbols*, Darton, Longman and Todd: London, 1997; John Thornhill, *Modernity, Christianity's Estranged Child Reconstructed*, Eeerdmans, Michigan, 2000; Kevin J. Vanhoozer, *The Cambridge Companion to Postmodern Theology*, Cambridge University Press, 2003

5. F. Nietzsche as quoted in John Thornhill, *Modernity, Christianity's Estranged Child Reconstructed*, Eerdmans, Michigan, 2000, 31-32

der about what life is all about, how failure, suffering and death may be understood, how to live with outrage about injustice, how is it all going to end. It seems that once again, even in our Western world, which is increasingly being spoken of now as post-secular, a space is opening up for religious stories to be heard in answer to such perennial questions. Hence, for example, the positive reception in the secular press in Britain for the recent Encyclical Letter of Pope Benedict XVI, *Deus Caritas Est*. There are resources within the Christian tradition to root and nourish the liberal concern with the dignity and freedom of the individual and the belief that reason can attain to true knowledge. Might we not all benefit from a more public use of these resources?[6]

A second helpful viewpoint is that of political philosophy. Of relevance here is the distinction between the state and society: so, even if, as the church itself agrees, there should be no reversion to a confessional state, and so the separation of church and state is a good thing, still society is bigger than the state. In particular, political philosophers have noted the role played by institutions like universities, religious groups, media and so on in civil society by way of contribution to a debate that helps form opinion and values and eventually feeds into the political decisions of government.

Pushing this further, it can be argued that the freedoms, which liberalism treasures so dearly, can best be supported, not by a philosophical culture of self-interest, but more by one of the common good.[7] If self-interest dominates, then trust erodes to the detriment of all. We need a notion of freedom which combines 'freedom from' with some vision of 'freedom for', a consideration of what the good life is about, and in this respect the project of liberalism may be helped by the type of discourse about the common good found in Catholic social teaching.

This understands the common good as an analogous term, the

6. cf Cardinal Godfried Daneels, 'The Role of Ethics in an Enlarged Europe', in *Christianity in Present Day Europe*, The Dialogue Series, UCSIA, Antwerp, 2004, 11-18

7. cf Patrick Riordan SJ, *A Politics of the Common Good,* Institute of Public Administration, Dublin, 1996 for an extended treatment of this point from within the discipline of political philosophy.

full realisation of which would involve the life of all creation at the end times with the Trinity, but more limited versions of which are achievable in our life times. Some of these more limited versions are the responsibility of the state, under the rubric of public order (e.g. economics, party politics and government, law and order). Others have to do with civil society (values and norms) and the church in such a way that a conversation around the partial and full meanings of the common good may take place in civil society by all the relevant conversation partners.

In this conversation, as influential theorists like Rawls and Habermas are increasingly recognising, the religious voice has a role. It has so within a more generous interpretation of the canons of public reason, within which secularism too admits its own non-provability by the criteria of empirical reason and so does not automatically veto the contribution of that other belief system, organised religion. This more hopeful development within liberalism is due not least to its own realisation of the need for moral capital to support the incoherence of its own overly-individualistic project, and to documents like the *Declaration on Religious Freedom* in Vatican II which makes it clear that all are free to follow their own conscience and that religion does not make coercive claims, but seeks to communicate through dialogue and persuasion.

I note that the discussion so far has focused on modern liberal democracies in general: the situation of Ireland needs particular consideration within that context. Here there has been a history of undue church (clerical) influence on the state, and now the erosion of church authority due to child sexual abuse. If the former would caution against a too hasty demand for the Christian (at least Catholic) voice to be heard in the public square, the latter, paradoxically, may alleviate some of the concern about the dangers of a church takeover in the civil sphere. Everyone knows that in the Ireland of today that is just not possible – the church is too weak to gain that sort of power, and anyway does not want it.

However, it is true that in the particular case of Ireland we do not have that long post-enlightenment experience of the separation of church and state, and so there will be a contribution to be

made by theology in critiquing the kind of religious fundamentalism in public life which does nothing to advance the case being
made here that religion may have real wisdom to offer in the conduct of our public affairs.[8]

The nature of the link between theology and social reality
Proximately we inherit a model of doing this kind of theology
from liberation theology. It proposes a so-called virtuous circle
moving from the steps of experience/insertion (i.e. focus on an
issue), social analysis, theological reflection, pastoral action (for
example, advocacy) and evaluation. This model will require some
modification in our post-1989 collapse of the Berlin Wall world,
since it relied, at least to some extent, on a Marxist-inspired social
analysis that focused excessively on a structural reading of reality.

Perhaps to some extent always, but now more clearly than before, social analysis will have to include not just an understanding
of a situation from a sociological point of view but also from all
other relevant disciplines. Depending on the particular issue
being investigated these may include economics, psychology,
anthropology and gender studies, culture, aesthetics, political
philosophy, nationalism and so on. This more general approach
reflects a consensus that, while economics and social systems and
structures are important, they are not on their own sufficient to
explain reality in a way that will lead to change. So, to give one
fairly obvious example, a strictly socio-economic analysis of
Northern Ireland might overestimate the shared interests of
working-class republicans and loyalists, who are divided by loy-
alties of nationalism and culture.

This, in turn, points to another aspect of social analysis in need
of modification. In the light of the crisis around the Marxist-
socialist theoretical model, we need to become more aware of the
presuppositions behind whatever interpretative tool we might
use. This may mean in practice that we need a little more humility
and empirical analysis rather than reliance on the grand theories

---

8. cf Gabriel Daly, 'Theological Analysis and Public Policy Debate in a
Pluralist Society', in Treacy and Whyte, eds, op cit, 1995, 75-91

(the grand narratives) of left and right. A simple oppressor/op-pressed socio-economic analysis is unlikely to stand up to critical scrutiny.

This more nuanced approach should not lessen our passion and urgency to tackle injustice and bring about change, that hugely important dimension of liberation theology, with its evangelically inspired option for the poor. In our Western world a more nu-anced analysis of this kind will identify the loss of a sense of God and the transcendent as one of our great needs, resulting in a poverty and aimlessness of spirit already alluded to, a situation of injustice in its own way which perhaps other parts of our world can help us to remedy. This focus on spiritual poverty in the West should not lead us to lessen our commitment to the eradication of actual poverty everywhere. Instead we need to ask ourselves if the two are not related: has our loss of a sense of God reduced our sense of solidarity and of what is changeable, so that poverty in our world is viewed as simply inevitable?

Within this more nuanced model of liberation theology, what is the nature of the link between the great Christian themes and the search for meaning and justice in society? I am thinking of themes like God as Trinity, human beings created in the image and likeness of God, we as sisters and brothers of Jesus Christ, the love of Jesus for the marginalised, the place of the cross and resur-rection, the Eucharist, the fall and sin, Mary, the church, the king-dom of God, eschatology, the communion of saints, providence and so on. There is need of some care here lest a too hasty accom-modation of Christian themes with certain values and social policy lead to unsatisfactory conclusions: for example the Christian aphorism that it is better to give than receive might lead one to suppose that altruism is the preferred Christian political philoso-phy, a position rejected by many political philosophers, who argue that altruism would simply lead to the breakdown of social cohesion and who instead espouse the value of the common good.

Similarly, the Christian warning against riches and the abuse of power might have led to a too ready acceptance by Christian thinkers of the dependency theory used to explain the economic problems of Latin America and now rejected by most experts;[9] while the reputed over-reliance of Poland on idealistic Roman Catholic (mainly Jesuit-inspired) teaching in the 17th century[10] to the detriment of the demands of Realpolitik recalls Bismarck's remark that one cannot govern a state according to the Sermon on the Mount. There is then need for a careful mediation between faith and secular reality. Allowing for the need of this appropriate care, it does seem that the nature of the link between theology and social reality is mainly at the level of vision.

Postmodernity is comfortable with the notion of story, and the Christian narrative proposes a vision, a horizon, a perspective, a worldview, a foundation, a symbolic discourse and a content which can inspire, motivate, develop and mobilise a moral imagination and sensibility towards a more just world. The significance of vision, with the values that accompany it, is that it may dispose otherwise seemingly neutral or commonsense data towards both a new interpretation and the possibility of a consequent commitment to a transformation that is liberating. And so in many historical instances that we know of (slavery, the suffragette and civil rights movements, the fall of communism) it is clear that the Christian story was used in this mode of liberating interpretation and transformation. This liberating power is crucial: it nudges people faced with data susceptible to many interpretations in one direction rather than another, it makes possible breakthroughs at the level both of analysis and sensibility as well as galvanising appropriate action for change with respect to seemingly permanent and intractable situations of injustice ('for nothing is impossible to God').

Of course it is true that there are many other potentially liberating stories besides the Christian one and so, in the West, modernity itself has had many liberating dimensions. It is also true that the Christian story is itself a disputed one and versions of

9. cf Peadar Kirby, *Poverty Amid Plenty, World and Irish Development Reconsidered*, Trócaire / Gill and Macmillan, Dublin, 1997
10. cf Raymond Gawronski SJ, 'The Distant Country of John Paul II', in *Creed and Culture, Jesuit Studies of John Paul II*, eds Joseph W. Koterski SJ and John J. Conley SJ, St Joseph's University Press, Philadelphia, 2004, 61-74.

it have been used for the purposes of domination. All this means, as we know, that there are pluralist and conflicted sources of vision, value and meaning in our society, and we proceed by persuasion, learning and dialogue towards some kind of shared position. However, arguably, the Christian vision is not so commonly presented to people as part of this dialogue, for the reasons already adverted to, and there is a new opportunity to remedy this situation in the Ireland of today.[11]

Christians who want to avail of this opportunity will be aware that it is important to be as rigorous as possible in whatever social analysis is used, even if they will also be open to considering faith (revelation, church teaching) and not just reason as a source of truth, always preserving however a compatibility between the two. The advantage of this 'full hand' approach is that it allows the Christian to be upfront about the sources of his/her position. But there are perhaps many agnostics too who are looking for deeper foundations to root the values and meaning which shape their lives and who, in the context of a rigorous analysis, might be more open to a consideration of the plausibility of the Christian story as a reinforcing factor in advocating particular policy solutions.

It is also true, of course, that Christianity and theology in particular do not have a blueprint of how society should be ordered. In fact the more specific we get around issues of social policy (should our health service be partly privatised, should immigrants from the new EU accession states be required to have work permits?) the less dogmatic we must be, at least from the formal theological point of view. This is because in such matters we are in the realm of prudent political judgement about concrete particularities and not infallible truth about general propositions. This does not mean, however, that wisdom cannot be offered, that we are not strong and sure in our protest against injustice, that we should not speak out accordingly. It does suggest an appropriate modesty in advocating solutions, a care in going from the theological general to the secular particular, a need to draw on all the different re-

---

11. For an outstanding recent example of the wisdom capable of being provided by social theology, cf.John Marsden, *Redemption in Irish History*, Dominican Publications, Dublin, 2005

sources and skills at our disposal: theology in general, moral theology and social ethics in particular, social and political activism, social analysis, and social policy.

This 'full hand' approach has one further advantage of great significance. It allows Christians to root their engagement in public discourse in their lives of prayer and worship. This means that the Christian can enter this debate with a sense of gratitude as being loved unconditionally by God and believing that God similarly loves the others engaged in this dialogue. This opens a space up for a conversation which respects and can work with otherness and difference, without getting locked into ideological ghettos. This is also a space which believes that our world is intelligible, that evil and suffering are not the last word, that love while vulnerable is also what will endure and overcome – in short, a space which gives sustenance for the long haul in the struggle for peace and justice in our world.

I am not suggesting that every debate about matters of public concern should be organised as a theological seminar or a prayer meeting. Most often, as noted above, the Christian will engage in public debate as any other citizen, in the civic fora which are provided. What I am proposing, however, is that there are good reasons to suppose that civil society is ready to hear the explicitly religious and Christian voice in a way that was not so in the past. If this is right then there is a responsibility on the religious and theological community to explore how this might come about more effectively.

Islam

I have noted that this issue of the voice of religion in public life has been raised with new urgency by the predominant self-understanding of Islam, which does not admit so readily the Western relegation of Christianity to the private sphere.[12] Of course many

12. For what follows cf Karen Armstrong, *Islam, A Short History*, Modern Library Paperback Edition, New York, 2002; John L. Esposito, *Islam, The Straight Path*, Oxford University Press, 2005; Jaume Flaquer Garcia SJ, *Fundamentalism, Amid Bewilderment, Condemnation and the Attempt to Understand*, Cristianisme I Justicia Booklets, Barcelona, 2005; Christian W. Troll SJ, *Christian Responses to Muslim Questions*, 2005 at http://www.answers-to-muslims.com

of us in Ireland are only beginning to get to know Islam and our Muslim sisters and brothers and we are already finding out that, as among any group of people, including Christians, there are many different approaches within Islam. We do well to resist the facile tabloid caricature of Islam as simply fundamentalist, as inherently sympathetic to terrorism. We know that secular states like Indonesia and Turkey, for example, are different from Saudi Arabia and Iraq, while even within countries like Iran there are many different strands competing for dominance.

Nonetheless what does seem common to most strands of Islam is a refusal to buy into modernisation at the cost of an out-and-out secularism. Very often this is how they understand the West and Christianity: that the enlightenment has brought with it great progress, but at the price of relegating religion to a spiritual and private sphere that would be alien to the Islamic understanding of Allah as the God who is involved in every part of our lives and who has a particular regard for social justice and the civic and political order. The challenge to Islam of course is to come up with a model of modernisation that is post-agrarian, a way of living with their desire for a *Sharia*-imbued civic sphere that can be tolerant and democratic, a way of negotiating their own enlightenment experience.

While it is right that Western secularists and Christians hold firm to basic human rights and their non-negotiability, it ill behoves us to lack comprehension of the great struggle going on within Islam to modernise without losing their core values. After all, we in the West have had our long experience of religious wars, our slogans of 'error has no rights', our streets the scenes of violent sectarian demonstrations as recently as February 2006 in Dublin.

Islam and Christianity come to this debate from what seems like opposite ends of a spectrum: in many situations Islam has difficulty in allowing a proper autonomy to the secular, while Christianity has difficulty in reclaiming its voice in public discourse. For some secular liberals all this must represent a nightmare: the re-emergence of what they would no doubt regard as fanaticism, mildly annoying and irritating in the case of Christianity and deeply dangerous and worrying in the case of Islam. But,

perhaps, for many other liberals and non-believers it makes sense
to put into effect their own pluralist principles of respect for and
tolerance of different views, and to allow that religion too has the
right to have its voice heard in the public domain. In doing so they
will, arguably, win themselves staunch allies in support of many
of their own positions, as well as buttressing the progressive
forces within their religious dialogue-partners. This kind of mutual
respect and learning in dialogue and collaboration, even while
remaining true to one's own position, is urgently needed in our
dangerous and polarised world. It should involve not just Christian,
Muslims and non-believers, but where needed members of all
other world religions as well.

Conclusion
Many in Ireland would agree that even though things are so much
better for so many of us, still there is also a perceptible sense of
drift, of the lack of a moral compass. I can well understand the
scepticism that some will bring to the proposition that the church
– in its own words 'an expert on humanity"' – can help to remedy
that situation. It does seem, however, that much social commentary is characterised by an ironic kind of cleverness rather than a
wisdom that nourishes and a passion for justice that is intelligent
and lasting. Despite its grievous faults, there is in fact a long history
of sustained reflection on the meaning of life and commitment to a
better world within the Christian ecclesial community and within
other faith communities. It makes sense for all of us, believer and
non-believer alike, that this wisdom and commitment are more
publicly available. We can hope that the formal dialogue between
the government, faith communities and other non-confessional
organisations due to commence in the coming months will be a
helpful step in this direction.

CHAPTER TEN

Religion and Politics[1]

Introduction

I want to offer some theological reflections on the relationship between religion and politics. I do so with several contexts in mind – the tendency to relegate religion to the private sphere in liberal democracies; the influence of religion in conflict and post-conflict situations; and the claims of Islam concerning the intrinsically public and indeed political role of religion. I will focus mainly on what Catholic social teaching (CST) might have to contribute. I will offer a brief outline of the relevant CST, the implications of which will then be developed in respect of each of the several contexts mentioned.

As a background to these reflections I am aware of the many questions, fears, even exaggerated hopes that people have with respect to the interaction between religion and politics. For many secularists, convinced that religion in public life is divisive, it is a 'given' that religion ought to be relegated to the private sphere, the claims of political Islam are disturbing, and they are afraid of any Christian resurgence in the public domain. For many others in post-communist Europe, however, religion was a powerful bulwark against communism, a re-enforcer of national identity, and there can be unrealistic expectations of the political power of churches in the future public life of the nation. Above all, perhaps, the claims of political Islam motivate us all to remind ourselves of, and even, where necessary, to rethink our own position on the relationship between religion and politics.

My reflections in the main are directed to our situation in Europe. Throughout Europe, in different forms, there obtains some kind of separation between church and state, and yet, again

1. A revised version of an address given at a Conference in Zagreb in 2007, attended mainly by academics and politicians from Croatian, Serbia and Balkan countries

in different forms, the religious question remains relevant. Many Greek Catholics feel they are not really accepted as Greek because of the identification of Orthodoxy with national identity. This used to be the experience of Protestants in the Republic of Ireland. How are faith schools to be accommodated in secular Britain, how does the French *laicité* accommodate the Muslim veil, how are Catholics and Protestants in Northern Ireland, Catholics, Orthodox and Muslims in the Balkans, to live together in ways that promote civic peace? It seems that, willy-nilly, the religious question arises: can we devise an approach to it that is constructive, that is not divisive? Catholic social teaching claims to offer such an approach.

PART ONE CATHOLIC SOCIAL TEACHING ON THE RELATIONSHIP BETWEEN RELIGION AND POLITICS

Jesus Christ, the incarnation, the mystery of the one person in two natures known as the Hypostatic Union – this is the paradigm of all relationships between the sacred and the secular: there is distinction but not separation, a unity-in-distinction. A further, political, differentiation of this paradigm is obtained from the saying of Jesus with respect to the payment of taxes to Caesar: 'Give back to Caesar what belongs to Caesar – and to God what belongs to God' (Mk 12:17). The church has come over time to acknowledge the proper, relative autonomy of earthly affairs (Vatican II, *The Church in the Modern World*, 36,). This autonomy is relative, it is given by God: 'You would have no power over me if it had not been given you from above' (Jn 19:11) – the words of Jesus to Pilate.

Over time – and due to a history in Europe that has included the terrible wars of religion and the political developments of liberalism and democracy attendant on the enlightenment – this insight has matured into an acceptance by the church of the desirability of a distinction –referred to in secular discourse as a separation – between church and state. The two spheres, church and state, are distinct, yet always interrelated. This interrelation does

---

2. cf *Compendium of the Social Doctrine of the Church*, Veritas, Dublin , 2005 ch 8 for what follows

not involve the church having any power over the state (*Deus Caritas Est,* 28).[3] The just ordering of society and the state is a central responsibility of politics, not the church (*DCE,* 28). The state must allow the church –and other religions – their proper freedom to operate; and the church will exercise its freedom to comment constructively and critically on the moral and religious implications of political policies (*Compendium of the Social Doctrine of the Church,* n 424). But the church has no blueprint for the ordering of society or the state, nor any particular area of competence concerning the structures of the political community (*Compendium,* n 424,) nor, in a democracy, is it entitled 'to express preferences for this or that institutional or constitutional solution' (*Centesimus Annus,* n 47).[4]

However, this mutual autonomy 'does not entail a separation that excludes cooperation' (*Compendium,* n 425). On the contrary, the church has enormous resources – including those of an institutional nature – which can help the state in its responsibility towards the common good of a just society. Above all its social teaching, based at its most accessible on reason and natural law, can help to form consciences in political life and to create a culture in civil society of authentic humanism and care for the environment.

Over the centuries the church has come to appreciate the value of democratic forms of government and politics, involving the 'rule of law', usually in the form of a separation of powers between the legislature, the executive and the judiciary. This best corresponds to the canons of participation and verification (accountability) which should attend the exercise of sovereign power proper to a people or nation (*Compendium,* 394). However, even if this is so, there needs to be constant vigilance to ensure that democracy retains its authority as a moral force – so, for example, there may be political corruption in favour of vested interests, while laws or policies which are promulgated simply by majority

---

3. cf Pope Benedict XVI, *Deus Caritas Est,* 2005
4. cf Pope John-Paul II, *Centesimus Annus: On the Hundredth Anniversary of Rerum Novarum,* 1991 in David J. O'Brien and Thomas A. Shannon, eds, *Catholic Social Thought, The Documentary Heritage,* Orbis, Maryknoll, New York, 2005

vote or by some negotiated consensus are not necessarily, *ipso facto*, just.

This principle of the over-riding importance of the basic moral law means that there is a right to conscientious objection and to resistance in instances where the free decision of government or people is in violation of natural law. One notes here the potential for a conflict of rights – in particular the right of freedom and the right of truth – to which we will return. It will help, however, to note that the church in its social teaching came relatively late to recognise the right of freedom – there were many things about the French Revolution and the liberalism of the 19th and early 20th centuries which made freedom problematic for church authorities. In fact it was probably due in the main to the need to assert its own freedom in the face of communist oppression in Europe in the second half of the 20th century, as well as the North American Catholic experience of being classed as an outsider in public life, that together resulted in that breakthrough with regard to the value and right of freedom of religion, and hence other freedoms, in Vatican II's *Dignitatis Humanae*. This has since been reinforced in the more anthropologically based social teaching of recent Popes, in particular that of Pope-John Paul II and now Pope Benedict XVI.

Two further points from CST are relevant. First, the moral order, the natural law, including its unfolding in the political sphere, is not something which is already complete and that we fully know, but rather it 'must be gradually discovered and developed by humanity' (*Compendium*, n 384). There is a certain epistemological humility here which is respectful of history, without succumbing to any form of normative relativism.

Secondly, even if the right to freedom and religious freedom in particular, is not unlimited, still 'the truth cannot be imposed except by virtue of its own truth' (*Compendium*, n 421) so that all men and women should be free from every constraint in the area of religion. This is an admirable principle and yet one can see the potential for conflict: what happens, for example, if someone believes his/her religion allows them to have more than one spouse in a society which forbids this? In fact the statement above needs to be balanced by the notion that 'religious freedom is not a moral

license to adhere to error, nor is it an implicit right to error'
(*Compendium*, 421) – but again this surfaces the issue of the relationship between truth and freedom (and not just religious freedom) and how one may resolve the conflict of rights which is often
involved in this relationship.

It may be said in summary that CST is extremely positive in its
approach to the relationship between religion and politics. So
much so that John-Paul II in his Apostolic Exhortation *Ecclesia in
Europa* (2003) says to Europeans: 'Do not be afraid! The gospel is
not against you, but for you ... (n 121).

Let us turn now to our several contexts to tease out how this
positive approach stands up to the difficulties posed by particular
situations.

PART TWO: SEVERAL CONTEMPORARY CONTEXTS

a) Liberal Democracies – the tension between freedom and truth
There is real substance to the claim that Christianity can and does
make a much needed positive contribution to liberal and social
democracies. It matters if there are individual people and a civic
culture which believe in and commit to basic human values, and
which are rooted in a narrative of meaning which says that love
and goodness will prevail. In the face of so many problems and so
much evil it is easy to lose heart or to take refuge in a desperate
expediency rather than in a search for solutions rooted in values.
The Christian narrative offers its adherents – and through them all
of society – a purposeful approach to human history, attentive to
individual as well as social and political concerns and ambitions.
This approach is shot through with the kind of self-sacrificing love
which, faithful to the deed of Jesus Christ in his incarnation, life,
death and resurrection, his preaching of the kingdom with its
thirst for justice and peace and its preferential hope for the poor
and forgotten, grounds hope for our world. Christianity then, in
the words of British Province Jesuit James Hanvey, is a source of
'civic grace' for our world.[5]

5. James Hanvey SJ, *Deus Caritas Est: The God Who is Love in the World,* The
Institute Series, 5, Heythrop Institute for Religion, Ethics and Public Life,
2007, 14 (9-40)

In this context it would seem short-sighted and even churlish of secularists to remain as 'cultured despisers of religion' and not realise that it is in liberalism's own self-interest that it take advantage of the co-operation offered by religion. Many commentators now routinely diagnose the liberal project in its post-modern phase as being without direction, almost willfully self-indulgent and with a moral bankruptcy that fails to tackle the issues of social justice that arise in the context of growing inequality. Thus it is not only the Catholic Church that questions the 'tendency to claim that agnosticism and sceptical relativism are the philosophy and basic attitude which correspond to democratic forms of political life' (*Centesimus Annus*, 46). This dialogue with religion may, in the Catholic understanding, be conducted on terms of reason and the universal moral law which are acceptable, in principle at least, to secularists. There may also be space in our post-modern world, which claims to be open to alternative voices, for discreet and appropriate references to the full Christian story, the ultimate source of Christian hope and even of purification of reason and awakening of the spiritual energy which leads to justice (*Deus Caritas Est*, 28).[6] We need to continue to persuade our fellow-citizens that they do not need to be afraid of this public debate, we need to be courageous ourselves in offering our contribution in the measured way that is characteristic of CST. In Ireland, incidentally, the government, inspired by the EU Reform Treaty, has already initated a formal, structured dialogue between the state and religious leaders.

Why might secularists resist this hand of friendship from Christians? It might partly be that those in power fear the social justice agenda of the church, that vested interests would prefer that the voice of the excluded be kept silent. Certainly it is true that when the church is faithful to the preaching of its social gospel there may be elements of discomfort in its relationship with the state: but in a healthy relationship such elements of discomfort are good, can be productive. Besides, there are many respected secular

---

6. For a fuller discussion on this possibility of a Christian 'full hand' approach to dialogue with society, see Gerry O'Hanlon SJ, 'Religion and Society', *Studies*, 95, 2006, 141-152 – chapter 9 here.

voices raised in favour of social justice. Might it be that a deeper source of resistance and even of distrust is the suspicion that the church does not really value pluralism and freedom, that in her view truth is always more important, and that in her insistence on truth she is really trying to hold on to or to regain power in the secular realm? We need to take a closer look at this relationship between freedom and truth in CST as it bears on the relationship between religion and politics.

Moral theologian Charles Curran has an interesting perspective on this issue.[7] Curran notes the insistence in CST on the connection between freedom and the truth. The problem of course is that there is great disagreement about the truth, in particular about the goods and values that we hold in common. While many philosophers argue for a 'thin' concept of the good that limits the amount of substantive agreement that is possible, others –and CST is certainly of this school – argue for a very 'thick' concept. Curran is inclined to think that CST claims more certitude and agreement than is possible in a pluralist society, that its teaching is rooted in a positive understanding of nature and creation which, different from the more sin-based teaching of Lutheranism (e.g. the State seen in a minimalist and negative way as a dyke against sin, as coercive rather than as directive), fails to give sufficient weight to the reality of conflict and how one should proceed when agreement cannot be reached by shared understanding. So, for example, in approving human rights, CST gives little attention to solving the question of conflict of rights.

Curran develops his point further in the context of a discussion on law and morality. He notes that Vatican II's *Dignitatis Humanae* adopted most of the thinking of John Courtney Murray on religious freedom. In particular it adopts the distinction between the common good – which pertains to the whole of society – and public order which is the domain of the limited constitutional state. In this context the purpose of the limited constitutional state is to provide as much freedom as possible and to use the coercive

---

7. cf Charles Curran, *Catholic Social Teaching, 1891-Present, A Historical, Theological, and Ethical Analysis*, Georgetown University Press, Washington, 2002, chs 5 and 7

power of the law only when public order requires it. Public order refers to justice, public peace and public morality: but this is a limited justice which 'demands that the rights of all citizens be effectively safeguarded and that provision is made for the settlement of conflicts' (*Curran*, 228), even if it ought to be interpreted to include economic and social justice also (*Curran*, 236). This is different from the emphasis in other parts of CST which will link the role of government with the more extensive range of the common good, and with a more extensive notion of justice and law which goes back to the natural law Thomistic tradition.

In this tradition a law that contravenes natural law is an unjust law and does not oblige in conscience: in the understanding of Aquinas human law would cohere with a strong ethical and even religious role for the state in guiding and governing the life of all (*Curran*, 237). This is so, even if there is not an exact equation between natural law and civil law, or what today we would call morality and law. Not all morality needs to be legislated for, and even more, human law does not have to prohibit all evils (Aquinas, for example, did not believe that adultery should *ipso facto* be declared illegal, and he approves of Augustine's toleration of legal and public prostitution).[8]

The Thomistic approach then starts with the demands of natural law, even though these demands might not always hold. The religious freedom approach begins with the principles of a free society – as much freedom as possible and as little restraint as possible. In this latter worldview what matters is the good of public order, that law must be enforceable and equitable, and that law in a pluralistic society necessarily involves prudential, pragmatic and feasible aspects. There is, then, a distinction between the relationship of moral freedom to truth and that of civic freedom to truth, the latter relationship being more a work in process than an achieved identity. The practical implications of the two approaches may be seen in different decisions and emphases on matters like legislation on contraception, abortion, homosexuality and so on.

8. cf Vincent M Dever, 'Aquinas on the Practice of Prostitution', in Bestill and Hall, eds, *Essays in Medieval Studies*, Illinois Medieval Association, vol 13, 1996

Curran's point is that the freedom / public order approach has not been taken up in CST after *Dignitatis Humanae*, but has been replaced by the more traditional truth / common good approach. He believes that the freedom approach –which does not, of course, prevent one from seeking to persuade others that one's own notion of (true, objective) morality needs to be enshrined in law, but which willingly submits that activity of persuasion to the outcome of the democratic process – is better suited to achieve that 'overlapping consensus of public reason that can be supported by many different comprehensive doctrines' (242). This is congruent with the thinking of political philosopher John Rawls in his attempt to support a political liberalism that may integrate an understanding of political justice in a pluralist state.

It is true that neither a consensus (where this is possible) nor a majority rule approach to government and legislation are in themselves a sufficient basis for guaranteeing the truth and goodness of the policies and laws being discussed. But, at least in the shorter term, neither is government possible on the assumption that we are all engaged in a search for the truth together and that we must wait to act until we are in agreement. Irish Jesuit Edmund Grace quotes John Courtney Murray again in this context: 'We are not really a group of men (*sic*) singly engaged in the search for truth, relying solely on the means of persuasion, entering into dignified communication with each other, content politely to correct opinions with which we do not agree ... The real issues of truth that arise are complicated by secondary issues of power and prestige, which not seldom become primary.'[9] And Grace himself notes the value for the democratic process of majority rule because 'it denies entrenched factions the power to hold the process to ransom'.[10]

Is Curran correct in identifying an unresolved, oppositional tension within CST on this issue? Certainly the issue itself is important: it would seem that a more whole-hearted acceptance of the religious freedom approach would go some way to disarm fair-minded secular critics who may still be sceptical of the

---

9. cf E. Grace SJ, *Democracy and Public Happiness*, Institute of Public Administration, Dublin, 2007, 144
10. Grace, op cit, 71-72

church's *bona fides* in public debate. It is reported that the present Pope wants to revive natural law ethics and that there may be an effort to rethink the theory in an effort to present it to our world.[11] Perhaps this rethinking might be an opportunity to take on the concerns of Curran and others and see how they might be accommodated? Is this a good example of the notion already referred to that the moral order, the natural law, including its unfolding in the political sphere, is something that 'must be gradually discovered and developed by humanity' (*Compendium*, n 384)? This eschatological, 'already and not yet' note might allow church teaching to accord more value to civic freedom in the ongoing pursuit of truth in a pluralist society, without succumbing either to libertarianism or a prevaricating ethical relativism. And part of this rethinking might also involve considerations of the tension that inevitably arises when teaching addresses the two-fold audiences of church members and all people of good will – in other words, how one works towards a more integrated faith and reason approach within CST in general.[12]

b) Religion in Conflict and post-Conflict Situations
I speak from the experience of the Northern Ireland conflict, a political conflict with a strong religious dimension. I am of course aware, at least in a general sense, of your own Balkan experience of conflict. There may be some overlapping areas of interest and mutual learning.

The Northern Ireland conflict, euphemistically referred to as 'The Troubles', arguably dates back to the 12th century conquest of Ireland by Britain, but more proximately to the civil uprising against discrimination that took place in 1969. This civil uprising soon took on a violent aspect. The eventual political settlement was arrived at in the Good Friday or Belfast Agreement of 1998, which only achieved full implementation in May 2007. The churches – Catholic and Protestant – helped ameliorate the situation by compassionate pastoral care, by the condemnation of

---

11. cf *The Tablet*, 3 November 2007, 2
12. Curran, op cit, 230-231

violence at official level, and by the behind-the-scenes highly significant work for political peace by some church representatives.
And yet it was also the case that the different churches often
seemed to be captive to their respective communities, 'chaplains
to the warring tribes', so that the prophetic role of scripture in liberating us from too tight an allegiance to ties of blood and tribe in
favour of the greater common good was often missing.[13]

From this Irish experience, and from what has already been
said about CST on religion and politics, it is possible to identify
some important resources for conflict situations that involve religion. First, it is important to maintain the church-state distinction,
all the more so when there is a tendency in a mixed religion situation to identify the state with one particular religion. In addition,
whatever legitimate role religion may have in reinforcing national
identity in a positive way (one thinks, for example, of Catholicism
in communist Poland), this must be a generous, 'arms-length' reinforcement, so that the universality of Catholicism in particular
never gets limited by being complicit in the exclusion of legitimate
minority groupings. There is also an important honouring of politics, and of democracy in particular, that flows from CST and can
be a crucial contribution in conflict situations. Without abandoning all critical judgment, the church can show an appreciative
understanding of the value of democratic politics. This will extend
not just to the role of politicians themselves but also to the indispensable part played by public servants in their administration of
the bureaucracy that is essential to the running of a modern state,
as well as to the NGOs and the other voices that go to make up the
public debate of a healthy civil society. This critical appreciation
of the church is all the more important at a time in Europe when
there is widespread apathy and indeed cynicism towards the political process. It must include a healthy respect in a democratic
system for the voices of opposition. This respect will only be credible if the church is seen, albeit in a manner appropriate to its own
nature (e.g. while the *sensus fidelium* is not simply a matter of

13. cf Department of Theological Questions, Irish Inter-Church Meeting,
Freedom, Justice and Responsibility Today, Veritas, Dublin, 1997 for an attempt at a self-critique by the churches along the lines suggested.

counting heads, of deciding truth by majority vote, still it ought to be accepted as a valid source of theological truth), to honour voices of opposition within its own body.

A central part of any authentic ecclesial contribution in our times will be the thrust to solve conflicts by peaceful, democratic means – hence the need for vigilance to ensure that democracies remain strong. In any invocation of the Just War theory, churches must be clear that the *ius ad bellum* is only permissible as an absolute last resort and even then only where feasible; while the *ius in bello* forbids anything like the killing of civilians, much less anything resembling genocide or ethnic cleansing.

It may well be – and this was the case in Ireland – that some creativity is needed in resolving seeming intractable conflict situations. So, for example, while parliamentary debate and negotiated settlements are the normal ways to address political issues in a flourishing democracy, they may not be sufficient in the case of situations of seemingly intractable weakness and even humiliation. In Ireland in recent history we have had two instances of this kind of weakness which resulted in creative solutions arising from a process of dialogue, in which weakness could be admitted and addressed in a way that is not possible within the parameters of ordinary parliamentary debate or even normal multi-lateral negotiations. In 1983 the government established the New Ireland Forum to begin a process of dialogue among Nationalists in Ireland which paved the way for the Northern Ireland peace process. And about three years later, a similar process of dialogue between government, business leaders, trade unions and farmers developed into the social partnership process, which, at least for a time, played an important role in Ireland's period of economic success.[14]

Indeed one may say that in general the Northern Ireland peace settlement is posited on such notions as 'parity of esteem' and consensus, rather than simple majority rule, in a way that is also true of the constitutional arrangements of countries with historically divided communities like the Netherlands and Belgium. Religion can help to create the climate of opinion necessary for

---

14. E. Grace, op cit, 132-139

such 'out-of-the box' kind of thinking. The remarks of Edmund Grace to his Irish audience are apposite: 'The task of rethinking democracy in a manner which accommodates the voice of the humiliated is one in which we can invite our European partners to join us in the confidence that our invitation is timely. This is not just a challenge for Ireland and Europe. It is a challenge for the world.'[15]

Finally, what is one to say about a Christian contribution to the notions of a 'politics of forgiveness' or a 'politics of reconciliation' that are sometimes mooted in conflict or post-conflict situations? Well, it is true that certain important political developments have been rooted in the desire to reconcile, to ensure that there will never again be war: one thinks immediately of the founding of the European Community in this context, with inspirational roots in the Christian message. What seems to be important for the success of such ventures is the proper autonomy and reasonableness of the political approach in the given historical situation to which it is applied: there must, then, be a careful mediation, not a simple direct application, between Christian principles and political reality.[16] In particular, great care must be taken to integrate the notion of justice with that of forgiveness and reconciliation,[17] even if of course it can be most helpful to insist that justice in the Christian vision does not involve the iron logic of revenge.

What all this may mean in practice can be very different. So, for example, South African, post-apartheid society, inspired by Christian principles, judged it right to set up a Truth and Reconciliation Commission. In Spain, by contrast, after a very divisive Civil War in the 1930s, the key to success of a smooth transition from a fascist dictatorship to a parliamentary democracy some 30 years ago was the so-called *pacto de olvido*, 'the pact of forgetting', a letting go of triumph and defeat to allow the emergence of a peaceful way of settling conflict. Only now is the Spanish parliament ready to enact a 'law of historical memory', designed to address grievances,

---

15. E. Grace, op cit, 139
16. cf O'Hanlon, op cit, 145-149
17. cf G. O'Hanlon, Justice and Reconciliation, in M. Hurley SJ, ed, *Reconciliation in Religion and Society*, Institute of Irish Studies, 1994, 48-67

mainly of the left, when the Spanish church has just celebrated the mass beatification of hundreds of church members mainly associated with the right.[18] There have been similar strategies of 'forgetting' in Ireland after our own Civil War and in Germany after WW2, before addressing issues of forgiveness and reconciliation. So, just as with personal loss and injustice there is need to respect the manner and pace at which conflict is resolved, so too, analogously, groups and nations must be allowed their own time and space to come to terms with the past. An intelligent reading of the religion-politics nexus will respect this dynamic.

c) Islam and politics

We are aware that within the Islamic community worldwide there is a lively debate, even struggle around the compatibility of Islam with modernity. This debate centres on issues like the provenance and interpretation of the Qur'an, the compatibility of violence and religion, the role of women in Islam, the extent to which Muslims are committed to establishing everywhere a society ruled by the *shari'a*, the revealed Law of Islam, the question of who can speak with authority on behalf of Islam – and so on. These issues and questions are first and foremost a matter for the Islamic community worldwide to resolve and answer themselves.[19] However it behoves those of us from a Christian background to be sympathetic and helpful, not least because the outcome of this debate is vital for the peace and security of us all.

We can be sympathetic by reminding ourselves that it was only over the course of many difficult, often bloody centuries that we as Christians, thanks to the experience of the enlightenment (with all its shortcomings), have come to our own partial resolution of the difficult issues facing Islam.

How can we be helpful? I want to suggest three points. First, as Edmund Grace has indicated, it would seem that, *inter alia*, the

---

18. cf *The Tablet*, op cit, 2

19. cf G.O'Hanlon SJ, 'Asking the Right Questions: Christians, Muslims, Citizens in Ireland', *Working Notes*, Jesuit Centre for Faith and Justice, Dublin, 54, 2007, 8-14 and 'Muslims in the Free Society', in *Ecumenics from the Rim, Explorations in Honour of John D'Arcy May*, John O'Grady and Peter Scherle, eds, LIT Verlag, Berlin, 2007, 271-277 – chapters 6 and 7 here.

Islamic post-imperial experience is one of humiliation *vis-à-vis* what is perceived (often with a love-hate ambivalence) as Western prosperity and modernity. In this context it would seem important to encourage not just strategies of armed defence, parliamentary debate and multi-lateral negotiations – all of them necessary, as appropriate – but also strategies of dialogue in which mutual vulnerabilities can be admitted and shared. Europe and Ireland has had plenty of such experiences of dialogue, eminently compatible with the gospel spirit of trinitarian *kenosis*, that self-emptying love of Father, Son and Holy Spirit, personified in the crucified figure of Jesus Christ who is also the Risen One.

Secondly, we must not confuse the gospel spirit, or dialogue itself, with simply 'being nice' to the other. We cannot afford a naïve translation of gospel precepts into the political domain. Instead we must strive for a form of dialogue that allows us to speak our truth, while respecting the truth and freedom of the other. In particular this will mean sharing our conviction that the relationship between religion and politics has to be one of distinction and not confusion, that it is only thus that even religious rights (think of the 'reciprocity' denied Christians in many predominantly Muslim countries) may be safeguarded. We need to be able, kindly but firmly, to say in the words of Christian Troll that 'We will be able to accept as co-citizens whole-heartedly only those who in principle accept and are willing to defend a socio-political constellation in which equal co-citizenship and all the basic human rights, including active and passive freedom in tune with the 1948 UN Charter of Human Rights, are accepted and defended.'[20]

After the American Civil War it was determined that no state in the union had a right to secede;[21] the Good Friday Agreement in Northern Ireland is premised on the need for a majority in both conflicting communities in order for power to be exercised – a simple overall majority does not suffice. These examples point to

---

20. Christian W. Troll, 'Christians and Muslims: Dialogue in the Light of *Nostra Aetate*', Text of talk given at the Milltown Institute, Dublin, September, 2007
21. Grace, op cit, 65

the need to be creative – and indeed coercive – in ensuring that basic democratic rights are maintained. If church-state separation, the rule of law, constitutional guarantees of civil rights and fundamental values are all essential to our future well-being, then they are not, in principle, amenable to alteration by simple majority vote. But of course in practice should an Islamic majority, committed to a strict version of a *shari'a* state, come about in a European country then it would of course be more difficult to hold the line. The likelihood is remote: arguably most Muslims in Europe are happy with the freedoms they enjoy and interpret *shari'a* practically to mean natural justice as opposed to a strict interpretation of Islamic Law applied to the civil domain. Still, the remote possibility, not to mention the intrinsic merits of open debate and dialogue, remind us that to be helpful is not to be confused with 'being nice' in the sense of failing to insist on basic human values and rights.

Thirdly, and finally, it is worth recalling that life itself has a wonderful way of breaking through and down the seeming iron logic of systems. There is a universality to basic human rights that resonate with the human spirit: again we are asked to have confidence in the universality of Catholicism and human rights in general, even if, of course, in practice they need to be deepened and expanded beyond their Roman and Western sources respectively. Muslim commentators themselves have pointed to the historical flexibility of Islam in adapting to different circumstances, so that there can be and have been instances of a lived compatibility between Islam and democracy when formally or dogmatically there was no such possibility.[22]

Conclusion
I have sought to outline a constructive approach to the relationship between religion and politics, based on CST. At the heart of this approach was the notion of the distinction and yet interaction between church and state, between religion and politics. The

---

22. cf Sadik J. Al-Azm, 'Islam and Secular Humanism', in *Islam and Secularism*, Antwerpen, Universitair Centrum Sint-Ignatius Antwerpen, 2005, The Dialogue Series, 2, 41-51

shape of this interaction involves an affirmation by religion of the validity of the political process and a prophetic reminder that it must include the voice of the poor and powerless. It is tested by the unresolved issues of the respective priorities to be accorded to truth and freedom in the moral and civic spheres. The care needed to mediate the application of religious resources to conflict situations was noted, including by reference to mistaken approaches. And in relation to political Islam, the need for a critical sympathy was proposed.

I return to the underlying theological point that it makes such a huge positive difference to believe in the power of a transcendent loving Father/Mother God, at work immanently and intimately in our world through the coming of the Son and the ongoing presence of the Holy Spirit. This trinitarian unity-in-difference of love makes possible the relative autonomy of the political enterprise and yet its ultimate source and goal in that 'civilisation of love' to which CST often refers. All evil, all violence, all mundane and at times seemingly intractable negotiation and ordinary politicking and administrative bureaucracy are located within this divine matrix. Christianity may be counter-cultural in its attitude to politics: it is not anti-cultural.

CHAPTER ELEVEN

The Work for Justice and Deus Caritas Est

Campaigners for justice are often wary of the term 'love', especially when used in a religious context. It sounds too soft. It conjures up notions of emotional attachment and altruism, rather than human rights and entitlements. It threatens to disturb the wisdom of many good and enlightened people since the 60s that what is required in our world is not charity, but justice. It may even raise the old spectre of the Marxist critique of religion as opium of the people. How does Pope Benedict XVI's first Encyclical, *Deus Caritas Est*[1] (DCE), measure up to this hermeneutic of suspicion?

In what follows I engage in a conversation with *DCE* from the perspective of justice. It will be my contention that DCE, in at least one important way, is novel, inspiring and challenging; that it confirms the work of justice, even if it needs to be complemented by other aspects of Catholic Social Teaching; and that it raises extremely interesting questions for our contemporary situation, questions which require careful consideration for the future.

PART ONE: GOD IS LOVE AS FOUNDATION FOR THE WORK OF JUSTICE.

Benedict is aware that there is a problem of language – the term love is too often misused. And yet, because of its foundational importance for all of us, he takes the risk of using it himself. He wants to ponder the nature of God's love for us, its intrinsic link with human love, and how this love from and for God has to involve love of neighbour.

Traditionally the image of Jacob's ladder – the dream of Jacob in which he saw the angels of God ascending and descending on a ladder that reached from earth to heaven – has been invoked to liken *eros* to the human desire to ascend to God, and *agape* to the

---

1. Pope Benedict XVI, *Deus Caritas Est, God is Love*, Encyclical Letter, Dublin: Veritas, 2006

divine descent, even condescension, towards us. Within this tradition – expressed theologically in the 20th century by Nygren –
eros, with its connotations of passion, sex, desire, was associated
with something rather selfish and inferior, which the human
being, even in marriage, might be hoped to sublate in the more
other-regarding, self-sacrificing nature of *agapaic* love.

But – and this is novel – Benedict refuses to accept this dichotomy
between *eros* and *agape*. He admits that Christianity has often been
seen, with some justification, to oppose the body (*DCE*, 5). And of
course the passion of early love needs testing and its maturation
will involve the kind of acknowledgement of the reality of the
other, the beloved, that implies self-sacrifice and suffering. But he
wants to insist that *eros* too is good, is authentically human.

Of course love in God is unimaginably more wonderful than
love as we experience it, but analogously this love in God – also for
us – is full of *eros*, is a unity of that *eros* and *agape* to which we, in a
manner appropriate to creatures, aspire. Receiving, then, is as
intrinsic to love as giving, being loved and falling in love are
foundational to a love that can truly give, and we do not have to
renounce our humanity to be caught up in God's dream for us.

The wonderfully passionate and self-sacrificing love of God is
revealed above all in the historical person of Jesus Christ. Jesus
shows us that God is love by nature (Trinity) and in God's dealings with what is other than God (in creation and in salvation). In
Jesus passion and self-sacrifice are united on the wood of the cross
and the beautiful words of lovers – 'I love you to death' – are given
unique expression. Jesus also shows us (remember the great parables about the rich man and Lazarus, the Good Samaritan, the Last
Judgement scene in Mt 25) that while this love is extraordinarily
personal (*cor ad cor loquitur:* heart speaking to heart), it is also
social, universal, and with particular application to the poor, the
foreigner, those in need.

Benedict's novel approach to love can be a source of both
inspiration and challenge. Sometimes good people – and maybe
this is a particular temptation of some of us involved in the work
for justice – think that love is selfless in a way that suggests imper-
sonality. It's as if one has been commanded to love all, including

enemies, and one obeys with a dutiful commitment that avoids real engagement with people. This is a recipe for an ideological approach to justice and for personal 'burn-out'. Pedro Arrupe (1907-1991), deceased General of the Society of Jesus, was aware that his advocacy of the need for Christians to be 'men and women for others' carried with it the danger of a self-alienated zealotry. Arrupe himself countered this danger with the kind of insightful wisdom about love that harmonises well with what *DCE* is proposing. He is quoted as saying: 'Nothing is more practical than finding God, that is, than falling in love in a quite absolute, final way. What you are in love with, what seizes your imagination, will affect everything. It will decide what will get you out of bed in the morning, what you will do with your evenings, how you will spend your weekends, what you read, who you know, what breaks your heart, and what amazes you with joy and gratitude. Fall in love, stay in love and it will decide everything.'

In similar vein, we are told that the late Dorothy Day, co-founder of the Catholic Worker Movement in the United States, combined her wonderful work for justice with a love of literature, an eye for beauty, a capacity of joy, a spirit of adventure, always trying to remember 'the duty of delight'. We are told that in response to what was often the drudgery of life among the 'insulted and injured' she once said: 'I was thinking how, as one gets older, we are tempted to sadness, knowing life as it is here on earth, the suffering, the cross. And how we must overcome it daily, growing in love, and the joy which goes with loving.'[2]

In different ways, then, Arrupe and Day are pointing to the reality that while guilt may be a necessary motivating factor when all else has failed, it does not sustain over the long haul. Even duty, while admirable, is less likely to sustain us than desire, the Ignatian *id quod volo* (that which I want), with its contemporary echoes in the *jouissance* (delight/pleasure) of Lacan, rooted in the (com-)passionate love of God in Jesus Christ. By reminding us that *eros* and *agape* go together, that being loved humanly (by parents, spouse, friends, family) and by God in Christ are mutual and

---

2. Robert Ellsberg, 'Rebel with a Cause', *The Tablet*, 5 April 2008, pp 4-5

co-mediating realities, Benedict is deepening our work for justice in a profound way.

Of course it will not be possible to get to know personally all the people we do justice work with or for, much less like all the enemies and poor (and rich) people we meet. But there is wisdom in Aquinas when he says that we learn how to love by being in contact with our family and friends: through them we develop the humanity which allows us to love our enemies in a human and not in an impersonal way. Benedict develops this further by noting how this love is grounded and nourished by God's love for us in Christ.

This unconditional divine regard allows me to share *myself* – not just my expertise or even my noble ethical outlook – in response to the needs and suffering of others – 'if my gift is not to prove a source of humiliation, I must give to others not only something that is my own, but my very self; I must be personally present in my gift' (*DCE*, 34). In so doing I myself am conscious of being loved by someone – Christ – who took the lowest place in the world, of my need for this love, and so I help others not as one who is superior but as one who knows that he learns and receives by helping. In this context work for justice, with the poor, is not simply doing good to a statistical cohort in need, but rather, even when what is involved may be quite academic and/or structural rather than interpersonal, is grounded in a real appreciation for and meeting with the humanity of those in need.

It is better of course that we work for justice out of a sense of duty, even of guilt, than that we do nothing at all. But Benedict is always trying to persuade us that best of all is to understand this duty as a grace (*DCE*, 35). Love can only be commanded because it is first given: ethical choice and lofty ideals are best rooted in the encounter with that event and that person that is Jesus Christ (*DCE*, 1). And it is by 'putting on the mind of Christ', whose love 'urges us on' (2 Cor 5:14) that we learn to love others, even the most unlikely, with that combination of *eros* and *agape* that is at once so authentically human and transparently divine.

I note an interesting question for our contemporary situation and into the future, arising from our account thus far. For many different and often very good reasons (the need to work with non-

Christians and non-believers for a more just world; the predominant secularisation of the 'public square' in Western liberal democracies; the theology, in one form or another, of the 'anonymous Christian', which reassures Christians that God is everywhere active in Jesus Christ even when the name Jesus is rarely mentioned) Christians working for justice have, for the most part, been content to think, speak and act in a secular mode of discourse. In doing so we are true to the tradition of Catholic social teaching which holds that moral discourse is fundamentally rational, that there is no conflict between faith and reason, that the 'natural law' is inscribed on the hearts of all men and women in a way that bridges the enormous pluralism we find in our world. However, if love is so foundational, if in particular the unconditional love of God in Jesus Christ is so crucial, may we so easily continue with a discourse which brackets this out? And, if not, how does one begin to integrate the religious with the secular so as to preserve the gains of the enlightenment and, more latterly, of inter-religious dialogue, without losing the benefits accruing to proclamation of the gospel?

PART TWO: THE RELATIONSHIP BETWEEN LOVE AND JUSTICE

Deus Caritas Est: Part Two

The love that DCE speaks of is not just personal or inter-personal: it is social, to the point of being universal. The second part of DCE (19-39) treats of this wider dimension of love, of the 'ecclesial exercise of the commandment of love of neighbour' (DCE, 1) and, of particular interest to us, the relationship between justice and charity (26-29).

Benedict understands the church as expressing the love of the Trinity through word and sacrament, but also through the practical service of charity. Early on this charity became structured through the order of the diaconate (diaconia), so that in the eyes of the church 'love for widows and orphans, prisoners, and the sick and needy of every kind, is as essential to her as the ministry of the sacraments and preaching of the gospel' (22). Such is the deepest nature of the church (25). And this charity extends to all within the church but also ad extra, universally (25).

Benedict now tackles head-on the relationship between love and justice (*DCE*, 26-29). He is well aware of the Marxist critique: charity allows the rich to shirk their obligations to work for justice, it is a means of soothing their consciences and preserving the *status quo*: what is needed instead is the establishment of a just social order (26). He admits that there is some truth to this argument, but states that there is also much that is mistaken.

His admission is along the lines that the church was slow, with the rise of the industrial revolution, to realise that the just structuring of society needed to be approached in a new way. However, his claim is that with the emergence of Catholic social teaching (from *Rerum Novarum* in 1891 onwards) the church has been offering a set of guidelines to understand our new structural situation. These guidelines are valid even beyond the confines of the church itself, at a time when the Marxist vision of world revolution as a panacea for the social problem has been shown to be an illusion (27). That Marxist vision is ultimately inhuman: 'people of the present are sacrificed to the *moloch* of the future – a future whose effective realisation is at best doubtful' (31).

It is at the core of these guidelines to affirm that 'the just ordering of society and the state is a central responsibility of politics' (28). Here Benedict is re-asserting the distinction (often called separation) between church and state, based on the rightful autonomy of the secular sphere as articulated in Vatican II. However this distinction involves not separation but co-operation. In particular the church may aid the state in its responsibility towards justice. It is not easy to define what justice is, never mind work towards its implementation. The church, with reason that is purified by faith, may through its social teaching be a resource for the state in its responsibility towards justice by helping 'to form consciences in political life and to stimulate greater insight into the authentic requirements of justice as well as a greater readiness to act accordingly, even when this might involve conflict with situations of personal interest' (28).

Benedict is extremely careful, in offering this service to the state, to insist that Catholic social teaching 'has no intention of giving the church power over the state' (28): nor is it 'the church's responsibility to make this teaching prevail in political life' (28). In fact this political task 'cannot be the church's immediate responsibility' (28), 'the church cannot and must not take upon herself the political battle to bring about the most just society possible' (28) – 'She cannot and must not replace the state. Yet at the same time she cannot and must not remain on the sidelines in the fight for justice ... A just society must be the achievement of politics, not the church. Yet the promotion of justice through efforts to bring about openness of mind and will to the demands of the common good is something which concerns the church deeply' (28).

Benedict goes on to argue that love is always necessary, even in the most just society. Only a utopian and materialist notion of reality would claim that the state has the answer to all human needs: the suffering, lonely person will always need love, even within the most just of structures (28).

And so, Benedict goes on to teach that 'the formation of just structures is not directly the duty of the church, but belongs to the world of politics, the sphere of the autonomous use of reason' (29). The church does indeed, as noted, have what Benedict calls 'an indirect duty' in this respect. However, he grants that 'the direct duty to work for a just ordering of society ... is proper to the lay faithful...(whose mission it is) 'to configure social life correctly, respecting its legitimate autonomy and co-operating with other citizens according to their respective competences and fulfilling their own responsibility' (29). This mission of the lay faithful in the social and political sphere will, nonetheless, be animated by 'social charity' (29), even if it remains distinct from the church's own charitable organisations in which the church acts as a subject with direct responsibility.

Many questions emerge from the foregoing discussion.[3] Perhaps most central to these questions is the kind of distinction drawn by DCE between love and justice, and the concern by some

---

3. For a sample of such questions, cf in particular *Deus Caritas Est*, The Institute Series: 5, London: The Heythrop Institute for Religions, Ethics and Public Life, 2007 – with contributions from Archbishop Peter Smith, James Hanvey SJ, Terry Connor, Elizabeth Davies, Chris Bain and Catherine Cowley.

justice activists that perhaps Benedict gives priority to charity over justice, or even opposes them, in a way that may be problematic. Does the distinction between 'direct' and 'indirect' work of the church for justice really hold up, does not the concomitant distinction between laity and church run the risk of a return to the old, pre-Vatican II days of ecclesial stratification? Are we dealing with a substantive issue of content here, or perhaps only with a matter of different emphases or tone, a matter of more or less passion for political or spiritual change?

Peter McVerry SJ: Jesus – Social Revolutionary
It may help to understand these concerns by noting briefly a recent publication[4] on Jesus by Peter McVerry SJ, a lifelong passionate advocate for change at the socio-political level. McVerry's general position would be shared by many proponents of liberation theology and by many justice activists.

At the centre of McVerry's approach is the thesis that the answer to the question of why Jesus died by crucifixion yields the understanding that reform (11), even revolution (142) of social, economic and political structures are demanded by the preaching of the kingdom of God. Jesus, then, did not die because he urged people to be morally good in a personal/interpersonal way, nor because he claimed to be Son of God (the Christian community only understood this after Jesus' death – 12). No, he was put to death rather by 'good people, acting for good reasons, because the God that Jesus revealed had radical consequences for the ordering, behaviour and structures of society, consequences that threatened the existing order of society' (13). And so, for example, the simple act by Jesus of friendship with tax collectors and so-called sinners was 'at the same time a profoundly political act … the crucifixion was another political act, the inevitable consequence of that political act of eating with tax collectors and sinners' (23-24).

One can sense throughout Peter McVerry's reflection a passion for the work of justice. He does not explicitly reflect on the role of the church as such: but it is clear that, for him, the mission of the Christian has at its centre the work for social, economic and politi-

4. Peter McVerry SJ, *Jesus: Social Revolutionary?* Dublin: Veritas, 2008

cal reform – we are called to a 'radical personal conversion that would revolutionise our world' (142). This conversion is rooted in God's love as expressed by Jesus Christ – so once again the link between love and justice is maintained. But somehow the tone is different from *DCE*: it's as if the focus is now on love of neighbour rather than love of God, with more hope for what can be achieved in this world. Is this just a difference of tone?

Spes Salvi and Jesus of Nazareth

Since the publication of *DCE*, Benedict XVI issued a second encyclical on Christian Hope (*Spes Salvi*, 30 November 2007) and, in a personal, theological capacity, not as an exercise of the *magisterium*, a book, *Jesus of Nazareth*,[5] an expression of his personal search 'for the face of the Lord' (Ps 27:8). I propose to note these two publications briefly with a view to further clarifying our discussion.

In *Jesus of Nazareth* Joseph Ratzinger has a significantly different 'take' on the Jesus event than Peter McVerry. With all due acknowledgment to the valid contributions of the historical-critical method of scriptural exegesis, he argues strongly for a unity between the 'Jesus of history' and the 'Christ of faith'. This entails an important hermeneutical option – 'the main implication of this for my portrayal of Jesus is that I trust the gospels' (xxi). And out of this trust comes the understanding that Jesus died on the cross not for socio-political reasons, but precisely because of his claim to be God's Son.

The scandal of Jesus was not his claim to be a social revolutionary (he had distanced himself from Barabbas and the Zealots, he had avoided the title 'Messiah' – Christ – precisely because of its political connotations). He – as indeed the early church after him – had acknowledged the lawful, if relative, authority of Caesar, the civil power. Rather, as Rabbi Jacob Neusner also makes clear in his reading of the Sermon on the Mount[6] a good Jew could accept all the moral teaching here, with its socio-political implications: so

---

5. Joseph Ratzinger, Pope Benedict XVI, *Jesus of Nazareth*, London: Doubleday, 2007
6. Jacob Neusner, *A Rabbi Talks with Jesus*, Montreal: McGill-Queen's University Press, 2000 – cf J. Ratzinger, *Jesus of Nazareth*, op cit, especially ch 4

much was already present *in nuce* in the prophetic critique of the Old Testament. What was shockingly new, and therefore scandalous, was the question of identity – the claim to forgive sins, to be master of the Sabbath, to be at the centre of the teaching about the kingdom, to be in fact the Son of God. Caiphas is not shocked by the politics of Jesus: rather he himself shows political pragmatism in handing him over to Pilate, the civil authority, as a way of dealing with claims which to a pious Jew were genuinely blasphemous. The 'revolution', in this reading, would be the incarnation *per se*, not any new socio-political programme.

Ratzinger will go on to agree that the consequences of this shocking claim do indeed imply a God who sides with the poor and therefore a mission to Christians to engage in the struggle for a just society. But in Ratzinger the main emphasis is always on faith in Jesus as God. And so while in his understanding of the temptations of Jesus, the kingdom of God, the Sermon on the Mount, the 'give us this day our daily bread' of the Lord's Prayer and so on, he will always include reference to the socio-political implications, still at the centre is the insistence that what saves is relationship to God in Jesus Christ, who is both God and man.

It is the nature of the connection, articulated by Ratzinger, between the identity of Jesus as Son of God and the socio-political implications that this entails, that may give some concern to justice activists. It sometimes seems as if the primary focus on faith in Jesus as God almost relativises to insignificance the exigency to express the concomitant love of neighbour in appropriate structural forms. So, for example, in his commentary on the temptations of Jesus, in reference to the temptation to change the stones of the desert into bread, Ratzinger highlights the plausibility of what the tempter proposes – 'Is there anything more opposed to belief in the existence of a good God ... than world hunger? ... Isn't the problem of feeding the world – and, more generally, are not social problems – the primary, true yardstick by which redemption has to be measured? (31). However, as Jesus understood, at issue is the primacy of God, the correct ordering of goods, and when this primacy and ordering are not respected, Ratzinger argues, 'the result is not justice or concern for human suffering. The result is rather ruin and destruction even of material goods themselves. When God is regarded as a secondary matter that can be set aside temporarily or permanently on account of more important things, it is precisely these more important things that come to nothing' (33).

But does Ratzinger here tend excessively to one pole of the inevitable tension between what is urgent and what is important in the 'correct ordering of goods'? If a house, with people inside, is burning, does one call the fire-brigade or the priest?

We see the same tension being articulated in *Spes Salvi*. Here Pope Benedict insists that our hope is grounded in God's promise of salvation, revealed in Jesus Christ, which transforms our existential and social situation, even when many unjust structures may remain. Thus 'Christianity did not bring a message of social revolution' (4) but rather an encounter with Jesus which has the power to transform both personally and socially. This transformation, *pace* the enlightenment and Marx, does not include the promise of a full political realisation of the kingdom of God on earth (16-23). There can be incremental progress, through science and technology, at the material level, but in the field of ethical awareness and moral decision-making progress is more fragile, always dependent on human freedom and its responsible exercise.

And so structures are important and necessary, but not sufficient: they depend for their efficacy on the free conviction of citizens, they need constant revision in the light of changed circumstances, and they can never satisfy the ultimate human need for love (24ff). While 'we need the greater and lesser hopes that keep us going day by day' (the struggle for good structures, for the common good, a kind visit, the healing of internal and external wounds, a favourable resolution of a crisis, and so on – 39), we need above all the great hope which 'can only be God' (31).

In the context of this great hope and of the Last Judgement, we understand also that 'grace does not cancel out justice' (44), that, in the light of all the innocent dead, the centuries of suffering, 'there can be no justice without a resurrection of the dead' (42), that 'Evildoers, in the end, do not sit at table at the eternal banquet besides their victims without distinction, as though nothing had happened' (44), but that 'there is an "undoing" of past suffering, a reparation that sets things aright' (43). It is in this context that Benedict can say: 'I am convinced that the question of justice constitutes the essential argument, or in any case the strongest argument, in favour of faith in eternal life' (43).

There are, then, real differences in tone, emphasis and content between the approaches of Pope Benedict and that of many justice activists, as represented in our discussion by Peter McVerry. May we understand these differences in a way that can give fresh impetus to our work for justice?

PART THREE: PLOTTING THE WAY FORWARD

Religion as Foundation of Work for Justice: A Sign of the Times?
We are now in a position to explore further the interesting question and challenge identified in Part One about the possible contribution of explicit faith discourse to justice work. Many of us, knowingly or unknowingly, in our work for justice, have lived out of some form of that 'anonymous Christianity' theology expressed in classical form by Karl Rahner in his 1961 article.[7] In this article Rahner posited that many good non-Christian people somehow have a *fides implicita* (an implicit faith) in Jesus Christ. What is less remembered about this article is Rahner's contention that explicit faith maintains its importance and is in fact a higher stage of development, demanded by 'the incarnational and social structure of grace and of Christianity'.[8]

It is of course important to retain our ability as Christians to dialogue with non-Christians, particularly in the realm of work for justice, without presupposing faith commitment. Anything other would be a recipe for silence in our pluralist world of today. Similarly there always has to be a respectful acceptance by Christians of the proper autonomy of the human and natural sciences in their invaluable contribution to the discovery of truth and hence the search for justice.

---

7. Karl Rahner, 'Christianity and the Non-Christian Religions', in John Hick and Brian Hebblethwaite, eds, *Christianity and Other Religions*, Oxford: Oneworld Publications, 2001 (also in Rahner, *Theological Investigations*, vol V, 1966)
8. Rahner, op cit, p 36

But does this mean that we need to be silent about God, about Jesus Christ, in public discourse? It often seems that way in our Western world today, and we Christians generally comply with this default position. Religion somehow has lost its public, intellectual respectability: the high moral ground is with atheism, or at least agnosticism, and if more allowance is made for faith to operate in the privacy of one's own personal life, the same hospitality is not extended to it in the public domain. What is not spoken about can be easily forgotten. A 'cultural amnesia' develops, such that God becomes 'missing but not missed', and even people of faith become infected by a certain practical atheism which reduces 'faith and justice' works to justice only, because we are no longer sure why faith in Jesus as God makes all the difference.

And so one has the curious phenomenon in Ireland that in response to a wonderful, searingly honest interview with journalist and writer the late Nuala O'Faolain about her terminal illness, the questions she raised about the meaning of life and death ('what is the point of it all?') were referred for response in the public arena to psychologists (the article by Tony Bates in *The Irish Times* of 16 April 2008) and to the hospice movement. Both responses were sound, and necessary. But her agonising protest about meaning, her great cry of 'why', cried out for a religious response. And so too the answer to all those other great 'why' questions – why are human beings of such dignity that human rights accrue to them, that the work of justice is vital; why is the earth to be treated with respect?

We take it for granted that some issues may not be raised from a religious point of view in the public forum. And yet this conventional reticence towards public religious debate is the anomaly rather than the rule in human intellectual history, an anomaly furthermore which is restricted even today to parts of our Western world. Is it not strange when life and death issues cry out for religious responses that we 'don't go there'? Strange above all for those of us whose whole life is committed to a religious viewpoint and to 'finding God in all things'. And impoverishing to fellow citizens, who even if they do not share a faith perspective, are often open to and indeed needy of alternative narratives of meaning.

Because of course we are told increasingly that, despite the appearance of an increase in militant atheism, our world is growing weary with the 'dis-enchantment' of secularism characteristic of modernity. We are entering a 'post-secular' era, there is a renewed desire for an 'enchanted' world, often expressed in terms of spirituality or New Age Religion.

This new situation may be a 'sign of the times' for us Christians. We need to find ways of grounding the intelligibility of religious faith and of our Christian faith in particular. One thinks of the foundational theology articulated in the 1970s by Bernard Lonergan:[9] faith as the knowledge born of religious love, expressing itself in the words of religious belief, all seen as part of the authenticity of humankind which is achieved through self-transcendence. We need to engage in the kind of social and political apologetics of our faith, which narrates the story of Jesus Christ in a way which resonates with the constant human search for justice and recognises that atheism, at its best, is a moral protest against suffering and injustice.

This amazing story tells us (uniquely among world religions) that God came among us, became a human being – such is the dignity of what it is to be human. That God is completely a God-with-and-for-us, understanding us from the inside, 'like us in all things but sin', loving us with a suffering unto death, and with a love which through resurrection pledges ultimate justice and happiness. This is a God who wants justice for all, especially the poor, and whose search for justice is suffused by love, which implies not just retribution but also forgiveness, and which gives meaning to suffering. That Jesus is not just a prophet, a messenger of God, but he has seen God face to face, is in truth 'the Son of God'.

Is it time – a 'sign of the times'- to use our 'baptised imagin_ ations' to find ways of getting this story out into the public domain again? Can we find a narrative mode that will invite listeners to ponder the implications (some of which will be socio-political) of a plot-line which reveals that the truly human Jesus Christ is also the Son of God?

9. Bernard Lonergan SJ, *Method in Theology*, London: Darton, Longman and Todd, 1972, chs 4 and 11

It will not be easy: to break through the ideology of secularism while retaining respect for the proper autonomy of the secular, and to proclaim the salvation promised by Jesus Christ while remaining in respectful dialogue with other religions. But if God is love, if love is expressed uniquely in Jesus Christ, if love is the foundation for our work of justice, do we really have any choice except to try, relying on God's spirit who will teach us what to say, and make our witness more persuasive by what we do? And do we not owe this narrative and witness to atheists who protest the existence of injustice, to human rights activists who, inspired often by now long-forgotten religious roots, may not easily sustain their activity onto succeeding generations without the foundations and roots which nourished it?

The Link between Love and Justice

It's clear from all that has been said that love does not do away with the necessity for justice. If it's going too far to say that justice is 'the sacrament of love', nonetheless one can see a certain truth to this phrase because 'thanks to its incarnated expression in action for justice, love becomes a reality, it acquires a real presence.'[10] Nonetheless justice is itself humanised by love. Love allows justice to flow not just according to rules and duty, but according to the innate dignity of every human being, which is rooted in the grace of being created and loved by God.

It seems to me that in terms of content, justice activists need not fear a 'rowing back' in the formal position articulated by DCE, in particular in the delineation of spheres more properly the direct concern of church and state. Few would want a return to the Constantinian era where the relationship between church and state was so close as to verge on identity. It is better that the church exercises its political function more indirectly, in terms of sharing its wisdom and inspiring good living in the sphere of civil society so that this may have real results for justice and the common good in the political arena proper to the state.

---

10. Peter-Hans Kolvenback, *The Service of Faith and the Promotion of Justice,* Promotio Justitia, 96, 2007/3, p 15 (pp 9-18): he, now retired Fr General of the Society of Jesus, is quoting his deceased predecessor Fr Pedro Arrupe.

In this sense too I can see a certain sense in maintaining a working distinction between the church (understood as the teaching and leadership functions of church represented above all by the bishops and the Pope) and the laity whose proper function it is to become more directly involved in the civil and, for some of them, the political process. After all, rightly, not all Christians will agree on social policy much less party political details: better that this creative freedom is maintained than that the church, *qua* church, attach herself to particular partisan positions.

And this creative freedom usefully extends to Catholic agencies that are often staffed primarily by lay people, and sometimes too by unbelievers: there is a certain freedom to engage in the political process –and sometimes even to be less than dogmatic on strict church positions – that extends to such organisations when they are not identified so strictly with the church as such. One thinks of the political advocacy of agencies like Trócaire, the work of many Catholic organisations affiliated to the UN.

This working distinction between laity and ordained (sometimes referred to as hierarchical) church may cause unease in seeming to conjure up a pre-Vatican II model of church. This need not be so. Equality of status is perfectly compatible with some differentiation of role. We are, as Vatican II made it so clear, first of all equal members of the People of God, sisters and brothers of Jesus Christ, after which all talk of lay / priest / bishop / pope is secondary. This useful working distinction should never be developed along lines which imply inequality, nor even along lines which would delineate function so sharply as to deny the role of the laity in contributing to internal church life and teaching (the *sensus fidelium*) or indeed the occasional direct intervention of the hierarchy in situations of extreme political injustice and even anarchy (one thinks of places like Zimbabwe and Sudan).

It seems to me, however, that there remains some learning to be done between official church teaching on justice as articulated in *DCE* (and also *Spes Salvi*) and by the approach which inspires justice activists articulated here by Peter McVerry. On the side of *DCE* I wonder is there still not a somewhat dichotomous position being advocated *vis-à-vis* hope for a better 'this-world'? I think the teaching is quite right to stress the provisionality of human progress in the political realm, but it almost seems that this 'Christian realism' tends in practice to deflect attention and effort away from necessary political engagement on behalf of justice.

Catholic social teaching needs to inspire people towards secular 'miracles' like the founding of the EU after a time of terrible war, the Good Friday Agreement in Northern Ireland with its legacy of peace after decades of violence, and the albeit flawed economic achievements in the Republic of Ireland since the 1990s which, for a considerable period, have seen such a reduction in the scourge of unemployment. And of course such achievements, and others like them worldwide, are precarious and imperfect – the EU needs to win more democratic credibility, the Good Friday Agreement could potentially institutionalise difference in a sectarian way, the Irish Celtic Tiger has yet to realise the kind of social dividend which would reduce inequality. But do we not need to hear more unambiguously that these achievements are intrinsic to what Christian faith is about?

Similarly, I wonder do we justice activists who operate from a faith perspective too readily assume that the solution to the plight of the poor is to be had at the level of economic, social or political realities, but not at the level of religious faith? After all, if Pope Benedict is correct and if every human being has a deep longing that can only be satisfied by God, if in fact 'often the deepest cause of suffering is the very absence of God' (DCE, 31), then why would we bracket out this dimension of our work for justice? This is not the case in the developing world where the poor are still nourished by faith: have we too easily settled for the predominant –but mistaken – common sense of our liberal Western world which reduces justice to what can be empirically measured? Maybe we are suffering from a failure of imagination or courage in not proclaiming a faith which can be an important source of both energy and comfort to those in great need?

Finally, it would seem important that to have credibility in the area of justice, the church would need to attend to 'blind spots' in its own organisation. One thinks of the child sexual abuse issue (Pope Benedict gave such a good lead on this in his April 2008 visit to the United States), or those ongoing neuralgic points of doctrine (often related to sexual issues) and ways of maintaining discipline that are proposed in ways detrimental to more open debate.[11]

Conclusion

Usually reliable sources indicate that before too long Pope Benedict XVI will publish an encyclical in more direct line with Catholic social teaching.[12] It will be interesting to see if this putative text can inspire more passion for the work of social justice in this life, as is so apparent in the writings and life of Peter McVerry. Nonetheless, as I hope to have shown, already the Pope with *Deus Caritas Est*, glossed by *Spes Salvi* and his *Jesus of Nazareth*, has significantly confirmed and also challenged our work for justice.

11. G. O'Hanlon SJ, Europe and the Roman Catholic Church', in *The Future of Europe*, Jesuit Centre for Faith and Justice, Dublin: Veritas, 2006, pp 57-72 (chapter five here); Cathy Molloy, 'Families in Exile', *The Furrow*, 59, April 2008 pp 206-213

12. cf Pope Benedict XVI, Encyclical Letter, *Caritas in Veritate*, 2009

CHAPTER TWELVE

Hope[1]

Introduction:

On Good Friday, 6 April 2007, the Irish Jesuit Provincialate was set on fire for reasons which remain unclear. No one was injured, much less killed, so this was not a tragedy. Nonetheless a building which was home to some and workplace for others, symbolising hope for many, was extensively damaged and put beyond use, causing enormous inconvenience and considerable stress. As the flames licked skywards, it felt to the Provincial and others that all our dreams and projects were going up in smoke.

This got me thinking and remembering, particularly in the context of what we are trying to do here in Piest'any. My thoughts and memories are personal, but they extend to the wider stage upon which our theological reflection on hope needs to be presented.

PART ONE: OUR CONTEXT

Europe

I remember well the so-called student revolution of the late 1960s. We dreamt of a radically changed world, one of justice and equality. We were still living out of the myth of inexorable progress so rooted in modernity, with Darwin but especially Marx in the background, and for us Christians and Jesuits we were inspired by the *rapprochement* between church and world articulated in Vatican II. It was exciting to be alive, and we were full of optimism.

That era didn't last too long and we quickly learned that there was no inevitability about progress, no quick fix to the problems of the world. The oil embargo of the 70s led to economically more austere and then selfish times. The neo-liberalism of the 80s began to flourish and the terrible injustices and sterility of communism became evident, even to many fellow-travellers in the West, with

---

1. An address at a Jesuit Conference in Slovakia

the fall of the Berlin Wall in 1989 and the liberation of Central and Eastern Europe that was shortly to follow. You here in Slovakia know well the hard work that is involved in consolidating this liberation, in building up a constitutional democracy and in trying to develop your 'Tatra Tiger' economy in such a way that economic growth is not achieved at the cost of high unemployment. Now we all have another chance to build a more prosperous and just Europe, with an enlarged European Union.

The Jesuits and companions
I remember the excitement and struggle within the Society of Jesus, and among our religious and lay companions, as we tried to come to terms with the challenge of General Congregation (GC) 32 (1974-5) to understand our mission in terms of 'the service of faith, of which the promotion of justice is an absolute requirement' (D 4, n 2). It seems to me that we have responded to this challenge in terms more of wisdom than of prophecy. I mean that it is certainly true that justice has become much more to the forefront of the consciousness of the Society, it is truly a dimension of all our works. And yet we hear from Fr General, and we know from our own experience, that often the Social Sector of Jesuit Provinces is weak, fewer want to experience the life of the poor, our institutional thrust has not been as radical as we might have hoped.

I was privileged to be part of the reception and confirmation of GC 32 in GC 34. There one had a sense of a closer lived integration of faith and justice, as well as the welcome additions of culture (think of post-modernity in Europe), inter-religious dialogue (think of our post 9/11 need to engage with Islam) and co-operation with laity. But if we are clear-eyed we know that we have a long way to go: we have been divided ideologically in the past, perhaps now we too easily settle for peaceful coexistence rather than real engagement with ideas and difficult choices. There are obvious lay-Jesuit tensions to be negotiated. Some of us have experienced the terrible reality of intra-institutional conflict, when good people differ destructively and we all feel the weight of social sin.

The Local: Cherry Orchard

I remember too the excitement of moving into Cherry Orchard, a poor area of Dublin, in the 1980s, inspired by this new understanding of our mission, and hoping to do academic theology from this perspective. I will always be grateful for this move, and yet it did not turn out quite as I had expected. The move certainly helped us to theologise, to think and write differently. And we made a modest contribution to the betterment of our area. But the major change that occurred in the lives of people had nothing to do with us – the emergence of the so-called Celtic Tiger economy of Ireland in the 1990s resulted in a reduction of unemployment from around 19% to 4.5%, with huge benefits for our neighbours.

Northern Ireland

I remember the excitement of doing doctoral studies in Belfast at the height of the Northern Ireland Troubles in the 1980s, an excitement quickly tempered by the feelings of hopelessness and intractability which were then pervasive. One is almost tempted to say that if things can change so radically for the better in Northern Ireland, then anything is possible, anywhere ... and remember Berlin in 1989, the end of apartheid, the Civil Rights movement in the USA.

But, of course, it's not as simple as that. We live in a post-Holocaust, so-called war on terrorism world, with globalisation that is characterised by massive poverty and inequality. We must face the new challenge of sustainable development owing to the threat to our environment. There are many other challenges: the widespread movement of peoples, AIDS, cultural issues like gender inequalities, religious issues like the loss of our sense of God in many parts of Europe.

The Personal

Then there are the personal realities of ageing, of poor health, of death: easy to speak of these in terms of statistics, impossible to preserve such detached coolness at the graveside of a loved one or with regard to one's own weariness and failing powers.

Temptations around hope
Disappointed hopes, the daunting nature of the task, the pervasive banality and radicality of evil – you will have your own memories and experiences of all this. And in any case it is enough to open up the newspaper any day to have all this confirmed: accidents, crimes, structural injustice, terrorism, neo-imperialism ... and, almost, it seems, to tease and deceive us into continuing to hope, the occasional success or good-news story.

One of the protagonists in von Donnersmarck's *Das Leben Der Anderen (The Lives of Others)* says cynically 'Hope is the last thing that dies.' He was referring to the repressive regime of the ironically named Democratic Republic of Germany (DDR), where that ultimate signifier of loss of hope, suicide, occurred at such high rates. It is indeed ironic that now in parts of Europe, seemingly far from repressed but with a liberal surfeit of 'freedom from' and sunk in what Metz refers to as a postmodern 'cultural amnesia'[2] with regard to what 'freedom is for', rates of suicide have again soared. And for some, like Dostoyevsky's Ivan Karamazov, life is simply not worth the price if salvation involves the suffering and tears of even one innocent child.

And so we are tempted: maybe not to despair, for most of us, but perhaps to a kind of weary resignation, to see life in terms of a Sisyphus-like project where problems recur eternally and all effort seems in the end to be in vain. The temptation for an older generation is to pour cold water on the idealism of the generation that follows, to warn that all this has been tried before, that your hopes for a better life are bound to deceive, new problems will always arise, while the same dynamics of evil are everywhere at work. One can easily enough clothe this lack of hope in the kind of respectability referred to as 'realism' or, more easily available for older people, a kind of 'nesting' that is in effect a semi-retirement from the struggle, a Nicodemus-like restriction of activity to the night, away from the heat and light of the daily strife. The ultimate expression of this temptation is, vindicating Marx's critique of re-

2. J.B. Metz, 'God: Against the Myth of the Eternity and Time', in *The End of Time*, eds Tiemo Rainer Peters and Claus Urban, English translation, Paulist Press, New York, 2004, 30-31

ligion, to take refuge in a Christian hope which restricts itself to the next life.

On the other side, often more typically the attitude of young people, we can be tempted to try too hard – Prometheus and Pelagius now the role-models and Paradise on this earth the goal – to abuse power as a tactic, and to be reactively ideological in ways that are naïve (for example, to so stress the value of wealth distribution that wealth creation gets overlooked; or to believe uncritically in the inevitability of progress).

Burn-out and demoralisation have been occupational hazards of the social sector. Poet Seamus Heaney notes that 'Even if the hopes you started out with are dashed, hope has to be maintained.' But how? Can a theology of hope help? Let us try to 'give an account of the hope that is in us' (1 Pet 3:15-16). It must be a theology which takes account of disappointment and failure, of the need for the Long March through institutions and systems, and which gives nourishment for the long haul.

PART TWO: A THEOLOGY OF HOPE

Theology and hope
Theology has been traditionally spoken of as faith seeking understanding. However, our faith is in a God who loves us and encourages us to hope that this love will save us, set us free, raise us up to be a 'new creation'. Theology, then, is also hope seeking understanding. I offer some reflections on the complex nature of Christian hope.

Hope in the Hebrew Scriptures
The Jewish people, with all their reverence for the transcendence of God, believed that God was involved in their history: in the exodus Yahweh had brought them out from slavery. There was a relationship then with the people – a Covenant – and with it a Law, and in time kingly governance, to see that this relationship was well lived. There were many lapses into idolatry and injustice, as the Prophets constantly reminded them. Gradually they came to understand that Yahweh was not just Lord of history but was also creator, Lord of heaven and earth, and wanted to extend

this covenant more deeply to the hearts of each Jewish person but also more widely to all humankind. But the lapses continued, the poor continued to suffer and from outside there was the reality of imperial domination. And so there developed in the time before Christ both a messianic expectation and also an Apocalyptic sense in which many Jews hoped for the radical overthrow of the evil they endured.

Hope in the New Testament
What was hinted at in the Hebrew scriptures is radicalised in the New Testament in a way that both fulfils and subverts. We are put before the wonderful and shocking claim that God's involvement with us is so immanent and so intimate that the Son becomes man. We are given a glimpse into the inner love-live of God's own self, Father, Son and Holy Spirit, with the deeply significant gloss that this is a love which 'empties itself' (*kenosis*: Phil 2:7) so that creation, incarnation, and the cross are shown to be the free and overflowing love of a God who chooses to become vulnerable to us and to our ability to say yes or no to that love. And so the principle and foundation of the life of Jesus, his *Ur-Erlebnis*, is his ability to address God as 'Abba': and what he has by nature we are called to by adoption, by participation. This changes everything: we live now not according to the law of achievement or legal contract, but according to the gratuity of a love that is both passionate (erotic) and selfless (agapaic). The language of love – *ti amo da morire*, I love you to death – is entirely appropriate here, without exaggeration. It is a love which we catch mere glimpses of even in and through our most wonderful experiences of relationships with spouses, partners, friends, even as parents of children. And that anyone – much less God – can love us like this is what we find hard to accept, and yet it is precisely this which makes all the difference.

Jesus tells us about this love and its consequences for our personal and social lives in his preaching about the kingdom of God. This kingdom, often hidden like the seed in the ground, is very near, in fact is already among us, but its full coming is not yet – that 'new creation', that 'new heaven and earth', the 'heavenly Jerusalem' which will occur at the end of history when the 'form of this world has passed away'. It involves the forgiveness of sins, table fellowship with all and sundry, the overcoming of death, but also the establishment of peace and justice among peoples. In particular, consistent with that kenotic characteristic of God's trinitarian love, it involves a solidarity with the least of us in the eyes of this world – the hungry, the thirsty, the stranger, the naked, the sick and the prisoner referred to in Mt 25 (31-46) in that text which is such a breathtaking and seemingly impossible radicalisation of the gospel revelation that love of God is expressed through love of neighbour. And not impossible only because through his incarnation, life, death and resurrection we have the assurance that this kingdom has been definitively established and will ultimately come to fulfilment: and so if at times, like Abraham, we seem to be 'hoping against hope' (Rom 4:18), still this hope is certain, it will not disappoint (Rom 5:5). The personal 'yes' to this hope in the kingdom, with all its radical socio-political implications, is expressed joyfully in Mary's *Magnificat*: 'He has put down the mighty from their thrones, and exalted the lowly. The hungry he has filled with good things, the rich sent empty away' (Lk 1:52-3). We see anticipations of this kingdom in the sharing of goods with those in need of the early disciples (Acts 2: 42-47; 4:32-37).

May we hope for a better world?
For our present purposes we need to look more closely at the socio-economic-political implications of this good news about the kingdom of God. May we hope for a better world? Can love, even a 'civilisation of love', be translated into socio-political reality?

As you will know, we enter theological territory here that has been hotly contested in recent years and decades, not least in the tensions between liberation theologians and the Vatican, still evident in the recent *Notification* concerning Jon Sobrino. Nonetheless there has been a great deal of convergence too, particularly evident in that rich and often unknown corpus of Catholic social teaching, and my approach here will be to build positively on what is a shared understanding.

Faith and politics to be distinguished

It is evident from even a cursory glance at the history of Christianity that there have been many different forms of the relationship between faith, politics and social reality. Jesus himself confounded many of those, reared on the memory of the exodus and the expectation of a politically-minded Messiah, who wanted him to engage directly against Roman imperial rule. He was not a revolutionary Zealot, and even if his Sermon on the Mount and his preaching on the kingdom have deep social and political implications, still his own practice and teaching ('render unto Caesar ...') did not focus explicitly on what we might now call 'party politics'. The contrast with Islam is striking and, in today's world, instructive. Unlike the focus on a society governed by *Sharia* law, there is no Christian blueprint for the ordering of society, much less politics. After that long Constantinian experiment, in different forms in the East and West, of a close alliance between church and state, we have come to realise the benefits of separation, the blessings of the relative autonomy of the secular.

But not separated

However, this is not the full story. Church-state formal separation need not involve the separation of faith and politics. If it did, and if – as is the form of the current imbalance in church-state relations in many parts of Europe – in the spirit of a modernity that is dying away, we were to banish the voice of the church and of Christians from the public square and limit it only to private life, then indeed we would be guilty of the Marxist critique that religion is the opium of the people. And we would have little to say to the Islamic focus on a just society and polity.

It is true that there has always been a dangerous tendency within Christian thought and praxis to over-emphasise the personal, the 'spiritual' (narrowly defined to exclude the social and material), the next life. It is a tendency reflected in John Courtney Murray's citing of the example of the early Christian monks and ascetics, part of that flight from the cities to the desert, who are supposed to have spent their days weaving baskets while thinking of God and then their nights unraveling what they had done and starting again.[3] The clear message was that nothing that we do in this life is of any importance in itself. Of course there is a place for the purely contemplative in the life of the church. But the 'daily bread' of the Our Father, not to mention love of neighbour, are central to the gospel message and we – in particular lay people – are urged to find political and social forms and expression of that common good and preferential option for the poor which are an integral part of the agreed contemporary translations of the preaching of the kingdom by Jesus. In his address to the general conference of Latin American bishops in San Paulo last May, Pope Benedict XVI is reported to have said: '… we inevitably speak of the problem of structures, especially those which create injustice … just structures are, as I have said, an indispensable condition for a just society.'[4]

Society is wider than the state, the socio-cultural is distinct from the political. At the root of the many injustices of our world is that disputed question of the meaning of life which culture, morality and religion address. The voice of faith can have a particular resonance in this realm of civil society. We are all born with a conscience, with a sense of where truth and goodness lie, and we are drawn in this direction despite the counter-tendencies of evil. The Christian faith puts a face on this 'drawing' in the person of Jesus Christ. It offers a vision of life based on justice and forgiveness, leadership as service and not just power, trust in divine providence and in one another, a realistic appreciation of the power of evil and yet a confidence that it may be overcome – all these, and the other elements of the good news, offer a powerful force for good in our world. At the root of all evil is a lack of intellectual, moral and religious conversion, with concomitant structural forms. The ultimately irresistible power of Jesus Christ – often working through others, indeed through other religions – to lure us to a conversion of mind, heart and social reality is the ground of our hope in a more just society and politics. We believe that this power, operating through the human desire for truth and

---

3. cf J. Courtney Murray, *We Hold These Truths*, Sheed and Ward, London, 1960, ch 8 'Is it Basket Weaving?'
4. *The Tablet*, 19 May 2007, 15-16

goodness, is what has brought about peace between previously warring communities in Northern Ireland.

Faith seeking political form

It is always arguable that, pushed to its logical conclusion, the thought of a certain theologian or theological movement (be it liberation theologians on the one side, or the likes of Ratzinger or von Balthasar on the other) can err in its explication of the socio-political implications of the gospel message. What is not questionable, however, is that there are such implications, and that it is our duty and mission to discover, in the concrete circumstances of our own particular lives, what these implications are and to strive to bring them about. Politics and the structural dimension of reality have become part of the differentiation of modern consciousness in a way that simply would not have been explicitly available to Jesus himself (no more than explicit knowledge of the theory of relativity would have been available to him). It seems to be a strange and egregious form of theological dualism to deny that the good news extends to how we live our lives together now, in this life, and thus to deny that we may hope for a better world.[5] The *corpus* of Catholic social teaching in particular, with its emphasis on notions like the common good, subsidiarity and solidarity are a powerful resource in the search for the construction of a just society, as the founding fathers of the European Union showed. There is no simple blueprint available from the gospel then: but there is a vision, a set of principles and values, which are of enormous importance.

Our temptations are to look for solutions which bypass the ordinary messiness of human life (and, to console us, this is how Jesus too was tempted, in his time in the desert), and to give up when this is not possible. We want some kind of 'silver bullet', some kind of magic, which will absolve us from the responsible use of freedom. So, for example, when faced with the seeming impotence of constitutional democracies in face of the terrible injustices of our world, even good people have been know to at least secretly sigh for the coming of some benevolent dictator!

---

5. cf G. O'Hanlon, 'May Christians Hope for a Better World?', *Irish Theological Quarterly*, 54, 1988, 175-189

In God's providence our temptations become the kind of testing spoken of in scripture whereby, through the endurance born of hope, we become intrinsically the kind of person who is fit for God's company, the sort who freely says yes to God's love with all the consequences that this involves. And these consequences inevitably involve the socio-economic-political shape of our lives: our dream for a better, more just world is also, and first, God's dream. And this was already the teaching of *Gaudium et Spes*: '... hope related to the end of time does not diminish the importance of intervening duties, but rather undergirds the acquittal of them with fresh incentives' (*GS* 21). The poor and suffering of our world deserve no less.

The often hidden manifestations of the kingdom
A somewhat similar text from *Gaudium et Spes* alerts us to the dimension of mystery about the socio-political aspect of the gospel: 'Earthly progress must be carefully distinguished from the growth of Christ's kingdom. Nevertheless, to the extent that the former can contribute to the better ordering of human society, it is of vital concern to the kingdom of God' (*GS* 39). There is a Christian realism about this statement. There is no earthly paradise, no promise of a necessary confluence between a Teilhardian evolutionary history and the kingdom of God.[6] The interaction of freedom, sin and grace are more dramatic than that. The classical expression of Christian thought on time and history does not speak of inevitable linear growth or a development that is cyclical, but rather a free going out (*exitus*) and return (*reditus*) to God, the hinge of this journey being the decisive coming of Jesus Christ. Within this journey there are processes of growth, decline and rebirth, deeply influenced by our use of freedom.[7] The wheat and the tares grow together; progress is often hidden so that what can seem like disaster turns out to be success. We live under the pattern of the paschal mystery.

Sometimes this results in visible anticipations of the resurrec-

---

6. cf Larry S. Chapp, 'Deus Caritas Est And The Retrieval Of A Christian Cosmology', *Communio*, 33, 2006, note 30 p 65
7. cf J. Ratzinger, 'The End of Time', in *The End of Time*, op cit, pp 18-19

tion after long experiences of the cross: for decades in Northern Ireland it seemed apt to speak in terms of desolation, but now 'You shall no more be called forsaken … you are my chosen one, in you I delight' (Is 62:4) seems more apt. We know too that good can come from evil, we have experience of how the wonderfully surprising plan of God can be shot through with that element of the *felix culpa*, God the artist and potter who can remodel the twisted shapes of our lives into something beautiful.

But what about the countless dead and innocent victims of violence, and indeed those who continue to suffer unimaginably today? What of the perpetrators, often caught in a rationalised social and cultural evil? The protests of Job and Ivan Karamazov have validity and cannot be dismissed by any easy recourse to some theological formula or aesthetic theodicy. One thinks as well of the righteous anger of Jesus when confronted with injustice, his cry of abandonment in the face of death. And yet Job at least was content at the last to be still before the mystery of God's plan, and we, with the revelation of Christ's death and resurrection pointing to the intimate sharing and yet overcoming by God of our suffering, may continue to dare to hope, even if it is true that for many this hope is vindicated fully only on the other side of the grave. Very often, of course, it is the poor and suffering themselves who, through God's goodness, are authors of the hope that is in us. Indeed it is they who through their genuine, if sometimes black, humour remind us of the Christian message that life is ultimately not tragic.

The notion of Christian realism
It may seem that by speaking of Christian realism, of the unresolved issues that must await the next life, of the impossibility of an earthly paradise, of the classical Christian thinking on history, of the lack of a blueprint to order society, we are putting unnecessarily strict limits to the scope of Christian hope. Invoking the rubric of Christian realism does alert one to certain important truths: there is no perfect society possible here on earth, 'just structures will never be complete in a definitive way',[8] one needs to

8. Pope Benedict XVI, *The Tablet*, op cit, 15-16

work hard with practical reason and prudential judgement to come up with political approximations to ideals articulated in the Sermon on the Mount. All this is important: sometimes Christian rhetoric about a 'civilisation of love' and even 'preferential option for the poor' gets carried away into supposing that a politics of altruism or some other easily available and simplistically radical solution can be applied to solve all the woes of the world. We need to remember that we live in a world shot through with the limitations imposed by nature (creation) and sin, as well as the wonderful possibilities offered by grace.

However, recourse to the rubric of Christian realism should emphatically not be used as putting any limits to what God may do in working in the world (Ignatius of Loyola) with our co-operation – 'whoever believes in me will perform the same works as I do myself, he will perform even greater works ... if you ask for anything in my name, I will do it' (Jn 14:12-14).

The founding fathers of the European Union, inspired by their Christian principles and through skillful diplomatic and political negotiation, found a way to bring peace to previously warring countries in Europe and now, hopefully, to all of Europe. The warring tribes in Northern Ireland, again after bitter conflict and through a painstaking peace process, have secured a remarkable peace. We should not allow the 'not yet' of the 'eschatological proviso' spoken about by theologians put limits to the 'already' that is achievable, when we freely co-operate with God's dream and work for our world.

We are good as Christians about being 'as gentle as doves' (Mt 10:16), advocating justice and love, and even protesting angrily and prophetically about injustice: and we need to go on doing this. But we also need to learn to be 'as cunning as serpents', to do the hard thinking, advocacy and negotiation which are involved in bringing about change. This social action will be guided by the 'dangerous memory of Jesus' (Metz), which means, *inter alia*, that it will not resort to the use of power as a tactic which unjustifiably abuses the rights of others.[9] When we act in this committed and respectful way, we know that real, if fragile, achievement is possible. And with this

9. cf J. M. Faux, *La Democratie, pourquoi?*, Couleur livres, Centre Avec, Bruxelles, 2006, 41-43

in mind why should 'the preferential option for the poor' not be capable of translation into political and structural currency, as was the desire for peace in Europe and Northern Ireland? And as we work soberly and with practical intelligence for a more just world, we need as well to realise that a theology of hope is shot through with the logic of imagination as much as the logic of inference.[10] We need baptised imaginations and desires. Given all this, given the need to search for and decide on specific solutions from a wide range of possible ones, the importance of discernment becomes obvious.

Back to the personal

This leads us, finally in this sketch of a theology of hope, back to the personal dimensions of hope. I will simply state, without developing it, that hope in the Christian scheme of things does extend to the famous four last things (death, judgement, heaven and hell). And as one gets older, this aspect becomes increasingly important! It also assumes a more social form: the hope for continuing relationship with others (the Communion of Saints), the desire that even if the 'form of this world is passing away', nonetheless the Father's plan to 'bring everything together under Christ as head' (Eph 1:9) at the end will mean that all our human effort and work, and our beautiful if blighted cosmos, will attain an unimaginable fulfilment. But in the meantime we work, and God works in us, to bring about anticipations of this reality now.

Our hope sustains us in this work: and even in dreadful and seemingly intractable situations we can 'hope against hope' and this hope is sure because it is rooted in the love which God is and pours out on us. All is gratuitous and 'all will be well' (Julian of Norwich). Not in any naïve sense such that, as with many of us in the 1960s and 70s, we think that sanctity is the same as psychological wholeness and is achievable by ourselves, or again that societally we can achieve some kind of Utopia by our own efforts. But rather out of gratitude to God's love, which has definitively overcome evil through Jesus Christ, we want others to be treated fairly

10. cf D. Lane, 'Eschatology', in *The New Dictionary of Theology*, eds Joseph A. Komonchak, Mary Collins, Dermot A. Lane, Gill and Macmillan, Dublin, 1990, 342

and we want our own lives to be formed by this mission of justice.

We need to nourish ourselves personally with this kind of perspective: the main work is not ours, we are not Sisyphus, much less Prometheus or Pelagius. And of course we are not worthy, the people we serve are often better than us, and yet God desires us:

> Love bade me welcome; yet my soul drew back, Guilty of dust and sin … You must sit down, says Love, and taste my meat. So I did sit and eat. (George Herbert, *Love*)

And we need to learn to do all this with others: infamously and ironically the social sector of the Society of Jesus was often known to be decidedly anti-social, at least in so far as many of its prophetic figures practised a rugged individualism, which made it difficult for their good works to assume institutional form and thus more permanent effect. I suppose that has all changed now?!

PART THREE: CHALLENGES AND OPPORTUNITIES

I want to list briefly some challenges and opportunities which arise out of this discussion of our context and the theology of hope which addresses it.

Communities of solidarity

GC 34 spoke about 'communities of solidarity' and one still hears talk in Jesuit circles about 'apostolic discernment in common'. I think we still underuse the potential we have for mobilising communities of solidarity. As an international organisation with lay partners at all levels of society, we need to find ways to tackle problems in a more cohesive, multi-disciplinary and focused way. Perhaps to aid this, since many problems are transnational and cohesion will involve international collaboration, we need in the Society stronger interprovincial structures. And perhaps GC 35 will help us with this. This ties in well with the conventional secular analysis of the need in our globalised world for more robust international and global institutions.[11]

---

11. cf John Palmer, 'European Integration, A Vital Step on the Road to a New World Order', in *The Future of Europe, Uniting Vision, Values and Citizens?*, Jesuit Centre for Faith and Justice, Veritas, Dublin, 2006, 130-139

Apostolic discernment in common

And we need to be able to carry out our social mission in a spirit of prayerful discernment together. I don't underestimate the difficulty of this. Prayer can be used to dull the brain and to soften the edges of necessary conflict in ways that are unhelpful. Above all we need always to keep in mind our friendship with the poor, the anger coming from the injustice they suffer which can be a powerful catalyst for personal and structural transformation. Nonetheless we lose perspective if our work together for justice is not permeated and nourished by its roots in faith. Pieris spoke about the danger that social activists who could not collaborate become 'pathological Messiahs' and Gutierrez speaks of the lack of joy which can accompany a social programme without reference to God. Prayer and liturgical celebration can open us up to the liberating perspectives offered by the presence of God in our work with and for the poor, and open us up to each other in new respect and acceptance. Reading the published account of the September 2006 meeting of the Social Sector of the Society in Santa Severa under Fernando Franco leads me to believe that this was such an occasion.[12] I think we all need to learn how to do this, not just on occasions like Santa Severa or here in Piest'any, but back home in our ordinary workaday situations.

Other important issues

I note, even more briefly, that it is increasingly clear that our social spirituality, theology and work for justice need to take account of the environmental issue. We are still at an early stage of inter-religious dialogue and the impact it may have on social issues: many have pointed out, in reference to Islam in particular, that the 'dialogue of action' (co-operation on shared social concerns) may be more feasible than the 'dialogue of theological exchange', even if one can easily see that the one inevitably leads to the other. And we have more to do on the gender issue: it is easy for a predominantly male organisation, with the best will in the world, to have a blind spot here.

---

12. cf *PJ*, 92, 2006/3, 5-10

Conclusion

We started with that Good Friday fire in the Provincialate in Dublin. There was a different Good Friday in Ireland in 1998: it was the day the Belfast Agreement (also called the Good Friday agreement) was signed. This year, nine years later, the world saw the photographs of traditional and bitter enemies, Ian Paisley and Gerry Adams, posing together at a meeting which announced their joint acceptance of the terms of that agreement. The London Independent newspaper put as the sub-title to their piece: *The Miracle of Belfast*.

> History says, Don't hope
> On this side of the grave.
> But then, once in a lifetime
> The longed for tidal wave
> Of justice can rise up,
> And hope and history rhyme.
> (Seamus Heaney, *The Cure of Troy*, a version of the Philoctetes of Sophocles, 1990).

Of course no fine words, whether of poetry or theology, can feed the starving poor or dry the eyes of a child who has lost her parents through the ravages of HIV-AIDS, much less compensate the deceased victims of injustice. But our hope in God can inspire us to make a difference, to fight for justice with ice in our brains, fire in our bellies and warmth in our hearts. It can inspire us to endure the terrible sufferings of this world with a hope that, outrageously, allows us to celebrate life and even to experience its joy: 'Ask and you will receive, and so your joy will be complete' (Jn 16:24).

PART FOUR

Popular Piety and the Public Square

CHAPTER THIRTEEN

A Miracle?

I was in Naples, visiting friends. It happened to be 19 September, feast of San Gennaro, martyred in 305 and patron saint of the city. My friends suggested I attend the ceremonies in the cathedral marking the occasion.

I had often heard about the legend of this saint: how, it was claimed, after his violent death some of his blood had been gathered by a pious lady called Eusebia, how it was held now in a sacred container in a side altar of the Duomo (the cathedral), and how on his feast day it was supposed to liquefy – a sign of grace not just for the Catholics, but for the whole city of Naples, so that believers and unbelievers alike (even the communists of yester-year) looked to this sign each year. To be truthful, I had often chuckled about all this, pulling the legs of my friends: surely no educated person believed in this kind of superstition any more?

And yet here I was, at 7.30 on that Friday morning, making my way down through a street narrower than Henry Street in Dublin, but with stall holders selling wares on either side, towards the Duomo. A big crowd, growing. An air of anticipation. A dodgy enough part of the city, home, among other, to the Camorra, the ruthlessly violent Neapolitan version of the Mafia.

Inside the vast cathedral, several times the size of Gardiner Street Church but with the same Baroque decoration, the atmosphere was reverent and recollected. A concelebrated Mass began. Afterwards a rosary, with seemingly endless trimmings, was recited. By now, one and a half hours in, the cathedral was full, and the atmosphere became more intense. There was a burst of applause as a procession of dignitaries, civil and ecclesiastical, assembled, flanked by colourfully dressed soldiers and police: the Governor, the Mayor, civic officials, priests, bishops, and, in the middle of them all, Cardinal Sepe, the Archbishop of Naples.

They processed to the side-altar: the container with the blood was retrieved from the safe and held aloft in procession towards the main altar. Behind, on a kind of stretcher, was a gold effigy of Gennaro. The crowd clapped loudly.

The Cardinal addressed us from the main altar: '*Fratelli, sorelle* (brothers and sisters), I have good news: the blood has liquefied!' Thunderous applause, some shouts, tears, white bandannas waved. Then, after two readings from scripture, the Cardinal began to speak ...

And this was the truly marvelous, miraculous thing – what he said, in that heightened context. He said how wonderful it was that once again our city has been given a sign of God's love ... but this kind of sign is less important than being a good Christian, a good citizen ... facing up to the violence of the Camorra ('those poisonous serpents', he called them) ... putting the poor in the first place, doing away with the privileges of the rich ... looking after the homeless ... giving hope to young people, who are often confused ... looking after those elderly who are isolated ... engaging in interreligious dialogue in order to bring peace and understanding among religions ... in short, putting social justice and good citizenship at the heart of the Christian response to the enormous love of God shown to the people of Naples by, among other things, this sign of the liquefied blood.

It is a great gift, a real miracle, to be able to link our prayers, our religious ceremonies, our holy thoughts with real action in real life. Love, as St Ignatius famously said, is shown in deeds rather than words. There may well be a natural explanation for the liquefaction of blood in Naples, but that is not the point. What matters is what the Cardinal so vividly expressed: God shows us love in so many ways in our lives – not, perhaps, through signs of melting blood, but through family, friends, nature, prayer and scripture, moments of peace and joy – and moved by this love we are asked to care for others.

At a time of global recession, when the era of the Celtic Tiger can seem but a distant memory, maybe we in Ireland have an opportunity to take stock. What really matters to us, what really lasts? Of course we need money to live, of course jobs are important. But maybe we got things out of balance, maybe a fast, stress-ful lifestyle made us a bit giddy, maybe our leaders too have to re-think a model of constant economic growth regardless of the harm done to the resources of our planet. Maybe now is a chance to redress matters, to settle for less in a material sense but to spread it around more equitably, and to put more focus on our re-lationships, our families and friends, and to learn to give food to our souls too?

There are all kinds of extraordinary signs that can happen, but the important miracles are those that happen in ordinary life when, like Jesus, we manage to get it right about being human. This is what Cardinal Sepe understood in his preaching about the sign of San Gennaro. This is the challenge for us in Ireland today – to allow our nostalgia for that rampant, often ruthless Celtic Tiger to be converted into a more sustainable model of human well-being, marked by social justice and by that love of God symbol-ised in scripture by the notion of 'the blood of the Lamb'.

EPILOGUE

A Response to the Murphy Report

(After this book had already gone to production, the Murphy Report was published: hence this Epilogue)

'This is, without doubt, a period of deep crisis in this arch-diocese' – *Statement of Archbishop Diarmuid Martin,*
Friday, 18 December 2009.

Archbishop Martin's observation was in response to the resignation of Bishop Donal Murray in Limerick, on foot of negative findings in the *Report into the Catholic Archdiocese of Dublin*, commonly referred to as the Murphy Report. I want to propose in this article that the crisis extends far beyond Dublin to the heart of the Catholic Church, and that this crisis offers us an opportunity for the 'radical change' also referred to in the Archbishop's statement.

The Report
The Report finds that the preoccupations of the Dublin Archdiocese in dealing with cases of child sexual abuse, at least until the mid 1990s, were 'the maintenance of secrecy, the avoidance of scandal, the protection of the reputation of the church, and the preservation of its assets. All other considerations, including the welfare of children and justice for victims, were subordinated to these priorities' (1.15).

The Irish Bishops, at the Winter General Meeting of the Episcopal Conference, accepted that 'the avoidance of scandal, the preservation of the reputation of individuals and of the church, took precedence over the safety and welfare of children' (*Statement*, 10 December 2009). The Report finds that there are now effective structures and procedures in operation in the Archdiocese of Dublin to ensure the safety of children, but questions whether these mechanisms are not too dependent on the commitment and effectiveness of two people – the Archbishop and the Director of the Child Protection Service (1.16). Perhaps in response to this cautionary query, the bishops stated that 'we agreed today to request the National Board for Safeguarding Children in the Catholic Church to explore with relevant government departments and statutory authorities, North and South, a mechanism by which to ensure that the church's current policies and practices in relation to the safeguarding of children represent best practice and that allegations of abuse are properly handled' (*Statement, 10 December 2009*).

In the meantime, we do well to acknowledge, with continuing support and gratitude, the courage of survivors in speaking out, the service the media had done in investigating this issue, and the determination of all concerned to ensure that the Catholic Church will be a safe place for children. With time there will be an opportunity to reflect more deeply on the Report itself and some of the other issues which it raises, for example how to assess the powerful influence of a dominant culture on human freedom, the notion of collective responsibility and the learning curve that, *pace* the Commission's own findings (1.14), was clearly involved in this whole sorry situation.

However, since, as Fr Donald Cozzens points out, 'the Dublin report details a pattern of church response to clergy sexual abuse that mirrors that of countless other archdioceses and dioceses throughout the Catholic world', we need urgently to enquire into the deeper causes of the 'secrecy and denial that have abetted and compounded unspeakable evils' (*The Tablet*, 5 December 2009, 6-7). Cozzens even dares to hope that 'the Catholics of Ireland will show the rest of the Catholic world how to face up to one of the saddest chapters in the history of the church – for the good of the people of God, for the good of children' (Cozzens, 7).

Deeper causes: sexuality and power
- 'But tidying up corporate governance and instituting a more transparent culture is not going to resolve the scandal of clerical sexual abuse. That will require the church to face up to a much more profound problem – the church's own teaching on sexuality' (Maureen Gaffney, *Irish Times*, 2 December 2009)
- Young people need to be presented with 'a more persuasive

sexual ethic than the no longer relevant traditional teaching, to which for the time being the church remains committed' (Garret FitzGerald, Irish Times, 19 December 2009).

- Fianna Fáil backbencher Mary O'Rourke on the 'sheer discourtesy of a body called the Congregation of the Doctrine of the Faith, or something with an equally convoluted title … this wonderful doctrine body, whatever it is, does not reply to letters … consider the discourtesy of it and the discourtesy of the head of the Vatican (sic), parading around Ireland in his wonderful glitzy clothes, but not replying to letters and not seeing fit to talk to his counterpart … It is just not good enough' (Irish Times, 4 December 2009).

No one with knowledge of Irish public life would accuse distinguished figures like Maureen Gaffney, Garret FitzGerald or Mary O'Rourke of being rabidly anti-Catholic. On the contrary, I believe most people would acknowledge both their fairness and their constructive attitude towards the Catholic Church. Taken together I believe they are pointing to a problematic nexus of issues around sexuality, power and the relationship between them, which are deeply corrosive of Catholic Church moral authority and credibility.

The roots of this crisis lie buried back in the 1960s. First, in the Second Vatican Council, there was a clear emphasis on the church as the people of God – we are all, as the great Dominican theologian Yves Congar once put it, first and foremost brothers and sisters: it is only secondarily, and in service of mission, not in exercise of power, that we are laity, priests, religious, bishops, Pope. Baptism comes first and remains primary, and all baptised people are called to exercise that Priesthood of the Faithful which is part of our service to the wider world, a kind of sacramental sign intended to give hope to all men and women that our relationship with God is both our source, our constant nourishment and our final home. To that end, with Baptism and Confirmation, with Eucharist, we are given the presence of the Holy Spirit, those who are tasked with leadership roles in the church will need to consult with the lay faithful in order to discern the sensus fidelium, the

'sense of the faithful', which is intrinsic to sound church governance and teaching. All this of course is entirely consistent with the
well-known principle of subsidiarity, so prominent in Catholic
Social Teaching.

Sadly, for a multitude of reasons, this dream of Vatican II of a
more collegial church, with active lay participation, and a balancing of the power of the papacy with the influence of local churches
(episcopal conferences, informed by lay input), has for the most
part not been realised.[1] The dominant culture of our church remains that of a dysfunctional, autocratic clericalism, as Cozzens
makes so clear. So many women religious, not just laity, know this
only too well. We have had in Ireland some small steps forward
with, for example, the development of Parish Councils, but there
has been little sense of urgency about this whole movement.
Perhaps this has been due in no small part to what theologian
Nicholas Lash has identified as the conflicting interpretations of
Vatican II, the success of the Roman Curia in resisting reform and
effectively ensuring that collegiality has yielded to a more entrenched centralisation.[2]

But if there was one event which crystallised this crisis of
power and linked it with the crisis of sexuality it was the promulgation of *Humanae Vitae* in 1968.[3] The Papal Commission leading
up to this promulgation included lay men and women, married
couples, medical and other experts. It found – much to its own
surprise, since this was originally a commission to advise the
Pope on issues of population control in response to developments
in the UN and initially simply accepted without question the traditional church teaching on contraception – that it could not establish the intrinsic evil of contraception on the basis of natural law or
reasoning. Four theologians (from a Commission variously
estimated as comprising between 58 and 70 persons) dissented

1. See the perceptive article on this issue by Fainche Ryan, 'A Theology of
Ministry', *The Furrow*, 60, November 2009, pp 588-595, in which, *inter
alia*, her argument leads her 'to wonder if baptism is not an empowerment into both Christian service and authority' (583).
2. Nicholas Lash, *Theology for Pilgrims*, London: Darton, Longman and
Todd, 2008, chs 15-18.
3. cf Lash, op cit, 233-234.

from this finding. Paul VI in his encyclical took the side of the four dissenting voices and effectively decided the issue by papal authority and power.

However, a large majority of practising Catholics have not 'received' this teaching as true, they do not find it persuasive. Theologians have pointed to an overly physicalist notion of natural law underlying the teaching, as well as an overly static notion of what tradition entails, tendencies which continue to be the case with regard to the many other neuralgic areas of sexual teaching which Maureen Gaffney identifies (such as premarital sex, remarriage, homosexuality, the role of women in ministry and mandatory clerical celibacy). It is also worth noting, in particular in the context of the novel introduction of teaching on sexuality into Catholic Social Teaching in the recent encyclical *Caritas in Veritate*, how absolute this teaching is in contrast to the more tentative stance on disputed economic and political matters. Is it not curious that the church can claim such certainty on a matter as complex as human sexuality, while being more modest about truth claims in other spheres and even admitting that the natural law is not something that we know fully but rather something about which we grow in knowledge?[4]

What has happened in our church as a result of this problematic relationship between sex and power is that there has developed a culture of 'don't ask, don't tell' (*Murphy*, 1.31), a culture which is at its most lethal of course in relation to clerical child sexual abuse, but is much more pervasive than this one issue. Catholics who have questioned this relationship have been ignored – sometimes silenced, more often simply regarded by the establishment as disloyal and even as 'cranks'. This has resulted in an intellectual mediocrity and a culture in which often very good people (lay, religious and clerical) keep quiet, even become unaware of why they believe what they believe, instead of submitting beliefs to intelligent scrutiny. And it is out of this mistaken culture of loyalty that the pool of bishops is replenished, thus perpetuating the institutional blind-spot.

---

4. cf *Compendium of the Social Doctrine of the Church*, 2005, n 384

By way of exception in Ireland, a bishop like Willie Walsh has over and again voiced his concern about a raft of church sexual and gender teaching, echoing the questioning he has heard from good, committed Catholics of his diocese. This, you would imagine, is what a bishop ought to do. But, at best, there has been a deafening silence from his fellow bishops, who in this respect seem to view their role more as vicars of the Pope than, as Vatican II would have it, vicars of Christ.[5]

Polarisation may be a bad thing, but conflict need not be, and in fact in human affairs it is often vital for growth in truth: have we forgotten that the very opening of the good news to us, the Gentiles, depended in no small measure on the conflict between Paul and Peter in the early church? And one recalls the wise counsel of the Jew Gamaliel, member of the Sanhedrin, addressing his fellow Jews in relation to the disturbances caused by this new way of looking at truth promulgated by the followers of Jesus: 'What I suggest, therefore, is that you leave these men alone and let them go. If this enterprise, this movement of theirs, is of human origin it will break up of its own accord; but if it does in fact come from God you will not only be unable to destroy them, but you might find yourself fighting against God' (Acts 5:38-39). This 'Gamaliel principle', an application of the evangelical 'by their fruits you will know them', is too often bypassed by our church in heavy-handed attempts to impose truth, not by means of the authority of persuasion and reason, but rather by the authority of power. It often seems in our church that we attempt not just to inform conscience but to coerce it.

In fact Pope Benedict XVI rightly again and again stresses the compatibility of faith and reason, and there is a lovely phrase in the *Declaration of Religious Freedom* in Vatican II which says that 'truth cannot be imposed except by virtue of its own truth, as it makes its entry into the mind at once quietly and with power' (*Dig Hum* 1). What has happened instead with regard to many controverted issues of sexual morality in our church is the development of a culture of taboo and fear, with matters being settled by appeal to authority and power rather than by means of open and reason-

5. cf Lash, op cit, 235, referring to Vatican II, *Lumen Gentium*, n 27.

able discussion. This is simply incredible to the modern democratic mindset, and it pays scant respect to the notion of that 'sense of the faithful' which is intrinsic to the church's own teaching. It lends substance to the trenchant critique of Maureen Gaffney: '… the Catholic Church is a powerful homo-social institution, where men are submissive to a hierarchical authority and women are incidental and dispensable … it has all the characteristics of the worst kind of such an institution: rigid in social structure; preoccupied by power; ruthless in suppressing internal dissent; in thrall to status, titles and insignia, with an accompanying culture of narcissism and entitlement; and at great psychological distance from human intimacy and suffering' (*Irish Times*, 2 December 2009).

This culture is now having political ramifications. In Ireland our Minister for Foreign Affairs has called the Papal Nuncio, and hence the Vatican, to account for effectively hiding behind a diplomatic smokescreen instead of co-operating fully with an enquiry into serious moral and criminal failure. The Murphy Report itself (7.13), based on the evidence of Monsignor Stenson of the Dublin Archdiocese, notes that the Vatican Congregation for the Clergy had reservations about the policy of the 1996 *Framework Document* of the Irish Bishops of reporting to civil authorities. Apparently the basis of the reservation was 'that the making of a report put the reputation and good name of a priest at risk' (7.13). This has understandably led to some unease about the role of the Catholic Church in public life in Ireland, in particular in the field of education. It is also widely reported that the Vatican has pleaded sovereign immunity with respect to being sued in courts in the USA (Patrick Smyth, *Irish Times*, 19 December), an issue which brings up both the relationship between the Vatican and local churches, but also the distinction between the Vatican as church and the Holy See as a sovereign state.

All this recalls the sardonic impatience, almost contempt, of Mary O'Rourke in the Dáil. It also alerts us to how far we have come from the notion of power and authority personified by Jesus in the washing of feet. It seems at times we are closer to the notion of power as exercised by the Scribes and Pharisees in this devastating critique of Jesus, according to a modern paraphrase:

Instead of giving you God's law as food and drink by which you can banquet on God, they package it in bundles of rules, loading you down like pack animals. They seem to take pleasure in watching you stagger under these loads, and wouldn't think of lifting a finger to help. Their lives are perpetual fashion shows, embroidered prayer shawls one day and flowery prayers the next. They love to sit at the head table at church dinners, basking in the most promi- nent positions, preening in the radiance of public flattery, receiving honorary degrees and getting called 'Doctor' and 'Reverend' (Mt 23:4-7, according to the *Message Bible*, by Eugene E. Peterson, 2003).

Of course institutions are important, and of course office should be honoured, but really do we need all this fine dress (which dates back to the paraphernalia of the Roman senate, re- inforced by the 4th century Constantinian settlement between church and state), these honorific titles like Your Grace, Your Excellency, The Holy Father? Have we not set ourselves up for the kind of autocratic abuse of power which Jesus warned against?

A Way Forward

One gets the sense that we are at a watershed moment in Irish Catholicism, with repercussions for Catholicism worldwide. There is an institutional dysfunctionality at the heart of our church which goes beyond any simple notion of governance or management reform and which needs to be tackled.

There are many good reasons, not least the emergence of a more globalised world, for a centralised papacy and, as church historian Eamonn Duffy has so well articulated, the papacy, albeit in need of reform, is a great blessing for the Catholic church.[6] It would be ironic at a time when secular commentators are point- ing to the need for global governance to tackle economic, environ- mental and political problems if we as a church turned our backs on the service to universality that the papacy can provide.

---

6. Eamon Duffy, *Faith of Our Fathers*, London/New York: Continuum, 2004, chs 7-9; 16-19.

However, already in 1995 John Paul II was aware that, particularly to non Catholics, the papacy was seen as an obstacle rather than as a sign of unity, and he asked for help to change the papacy in ways which would better fulfill its great potential.[7]

It would seem appropriate that we in Ireland might respond to this request. Again, theologian Nicholas Lash has many suggestions along the lines of greater consultation of local bishops and laity, including a standing commission of bishops and lay people from all over the world who would effectively take over the functions of the Roman Curia.[8] Cardinal Martini often called for a Third Vatican Council precisely to address the kind of neuralgic issues like collegiality, sexuality, inter-religious dialogue that did not seem to him were being well handled: again, down the road, this is surely worth considering. There will be many other suggestions also worth considering.

But first it would seem that we need in Ireland to renew our own understanding of church, along the more participative lines envisaged by Vatican II and, in particular, with a greater role for women and without any veto on the kinds of issues that might emerge in the consultative process that will be required (1 Thess 5:19: don't stifle the Holy Spirit!). Why not, then, envisage going down the road of the oft-proposed National Synod or Assembly, well prepared in each diocese, touching into the experience of believers and disaffected alike?[9]

Archbishop Martin, for one, seems reluctant to go down this route, suggesting (*Irish Times*, 2 January 2010) that perhaps 'an ongoing talk-shop may not be the answer either. I think we do require leadership, and some of us are called to do that.' But in the same interview the Archbishop admits that 'occasionally you have these seismic moments when you have a real change ... a qualitative leap to a different view of church'. I would suggest that the decisive leadership that is required is precisely the facilitation

---

7. Lash, op cit, 238ff.
8. Lash, op cit, 239.
9. This was a suggestion commonly made in the early 1990s – cf G. O'Hanlon, 'The Christian Vision of Solidarity', *Studies*, 82, 1993, 435-6 and O'Hanlon, 'A National Synod?', *Studies*, 83, 1994, 431-435.

of a much wider consultative process, like that which would cul-
minate in a National Synod or Assembly. It will not do any more
for priests, bishops, cardinals, the Pope to simply tell us what to
think, what to do. People rightly want to have a say. And of course
all this would have to be carefully thought through so that any
such Assembly would result in genuine consultation, and would
build in the possibility at least of that kind of respectful and constructive disagreement with Rome, modeled on the dialogue between Peter and Paul in the early church.

Now would also seem to be a good time to call into question
the reality that certain narrow grounds of orthodoxy are a *sine qua
non* of episcopal appointments at present, and to call for more
transparent, representative and accountable local, including lay,
participation in the appointment of bishops. It's instructive to
note that as recently as 1829, of 646 diocesan bishops in the Latin
church, only 24 had been appointed by the Pope: often we forget
how new many of our 'traditions' are![10]

The danger it seems to me is that we remain at the level of a
reform of management and communications structures in each
diocese, with effective child safety guidelines (all good in themselves), but don't tackle the deeper issues noted here. Archbishop
Martin, in an earlier statement, promised that 'there will be wider
consultations' (18 December statement): are we as a church ready
to grasp nettles, are we prepared to move beyond anger to a more
active and constructive participation?

Conclusion

Karl Rahner once said, in relation to Christmas, 'Light the candles.
They have more right to exist than all the darkness. It is the
Christmas that lasts for ever' (*The Tablet*, 19/26 December 2009).
The integration of God's justice into God's mercy and love is the
good news of Jesus, sealed in his death and resurrection. Faced
with the dominance of a clerical culture, who knows how any of
us might have coped had we been in positions of leadership?
Perhaps, as with bankers and politicians in other areas of life, we
need as well as exigent calls for justice a little dose also of 'there go

10.Lash, op cit, 230.

I but for the grace of God'. There is so much goodness among laity, priests, religious, bishops, the Pope – with God's help we will emerge from this present period of crisis, humbled but also stronger. We will do so by honouring the sufferings of the abused, and by demanding accountability from, but also showing mercy to, those who have abused.

But we will only do so if we have the courage to look at the deeper roots of what has brought us to this place, the institutional dysfunctionality which lies within our church. And to do that we will need to find solidarity with other parts of the world that have undergone a similar crisis, in order to call our universal church to account and to a more hopeful, less fearful future. We will need to do all this with a wisdom that can discern between what needs reform and what remains as truly good and life-giving in our church. The exercise of authority, however democratically structured, is never that easy for us human beings, and our fellow Christians of a non-Roman Catholic persuasion, with their more consultative processes, know this well. We need some deep, strategic reflection on what might constitute beneficial change, a reflection which will understand widespread consultation and shared decision making as a necessary, even if not sufficient, element of the process.

A daunting task? Yes, but one remembers Luther's 'I can do no other', and one remembers, above all, 'that all creation from the beginning has been groaning in one great act of giving birth ... and we too with it', and that the Holy Spirit accompanies us in this great act so that '... we know that by turning everything to their good God co-operates with all those who love him ... with God on our side, who can be against us?' (Rom 8:18-31).